PERSUASIVE SELLING

PERSONALITY/TECHNIQUES
Fieldbook of Practical Tools and Exercises

5TH EDITION

Written and Designed by

Charles Daniel Litchford, Jr.
Weber State University
and
David Orion Litchford
Utah Valley State College

Printed in the United States of America

17 16 15

ISBN 0-536-74733-4

BA 998271

AP

Please visit our web site at *www.pearsoncustom.com*

PEARSON CUSTOM PUBLISHING
501 Boylston Street, Suite 900, Boston, MA 02116
A Pearson Education Company

PREFACE AND ACKNOWLEDGMENTS

The purpose of this text is to introduce the learner to the exciting and dynamic field of selling. The concepts discussed in this text are alive and well in the real world. Most books on selling are founded on the assumption that the experience and insight of a few individuals mirrors a newly discovered truth. This text, however, is based on interviews, observations, and conversations with hundreds of sales managers and salespeople in the United States. The advice and information contained in this text is based on their combined experience and nearly sixty years of selling, training, and consulting experience of the two authors.

The text is divided into two main parts. Part one concentrates on developing a persuasive personality. Sales managers indicate that the basis for a successful career in sales is basic human relations skills and certain desirable personality traits. Part two addresses important persuasive techniques by going through eight steps of the selling process. The main emphasis, however, remains on the fact that success in personal selling depends on the total personality and not just a knowledge of standard selling techniques.

The authors wish to give special recognition to several people who were supportive and encouraging and especially important to the conceptualization of this text. The many sales managers and salespeople of the business community who shared valuable suggestions. And finally, our families for their overwhelming support, patience, love, and dedication to excellence.

Although many individuals were immeasurably helpful to us, we alone take responsibility for any errors or omissions in this text.

Charles Daniel Litchford, Jr.
January 2004

David O. Litchford
January 2004

TABLE OF CONTENTS

ONE

WHY STUDY PERSONAL SELLING?

Learning Objectives

When you finish studying the material in this chapter, you should be able to:

1. **Discuss how you will spend your entire life selling yourself.**
2. **Explain what is meant by "nothing happens until someone sells something."**
3. **Discuss why every organization needs selling.**
4. **Identify the career opportunities available in selling.**
5. **Discuss the three categories of selling jobs.**
6. **Define selling power and discuss its benefits.**

Be Sold on Yourself!

Before you can sell yourself successfully to others, and thus sell your ideas, your wishes, your needs, your ambitions, your skills, your experiences, your products and services–you must be absolutely sold on yourself: 100 percent. You must believe in yourself. In short, you must be totally aware of your own self-worth.

–Joe Girard, *How to Sell Yourself*

WHY STUDY PERSONAL SELLING?

It is very appropriate to discuss in this first chapter the reasons why you should be studying personal selling. It will be a challenging undertaking but will result in your understanding the basic principles and techniques of selling–a very demanding and exciting profession. Whether you plan to go into the area of selling or not, you will always be a consumer engaged in purchasing goods and services from salespeople, so this book will make you a wiser consumer. In addition, you will learn how selling affects your daily life. We will spend time in this first chapter looking at five main reasons why you should study personal selling.

1. You will spend your entire life selling yourself.
2. Nothing happens until someone sells something.
3. Every organization needs selling.
4. Career opportunities are available.
5. You can increase your personal selling power.

OUR ENTIRE LIFE IS SPENT SELLING OURSELVES

Probably the best word to describe selling is **persuasion**. Sit back and think about your life and look at all the opportunities that allow you to persuade others. Persuading is a universal activity–everyone does it, and persuasion plays an important role in our individual life. You started selling yourself or persuading others immediately after birth. You would cry for attention when you were hungry, if you needed a diaper change, or if you were not feeling well. You would let out a howl or cry to influence other people to do something for you. If you have been around babies, you have learned how persuasive they can be. While you were growing up, you learned how to persuade parents to take you to the park or circus. You started to acquire friends and began exchanging ideas with them.

You really developed your selling skills when you became a teenager. How many times did you talk your mom or dad out of the car for a night on the town? How many times did you persuade teachers to skip an assignment or to raise your grade? You learned how to tell your story in order to influence the behavior and thinking of other people. You really applied selling techniques when you began to date and found someone to marry through the process of courtship.

You are learning right now that you must continue to sell yourself. You will have to sell yourself when you apply for a job, seek a loan from a bank, sell your ideas to others, and advance in your career. Whatever career you choose, you will be involved in selling. Selling takes place in literally every aspect of life where people have to live or work together–with subordinates, peers, bosses, customers, spouses, or anyone else with whom you are personally working.

Let's face it! Whether you like it or not, you will spend your entire life selling yourself to other people. You might just as well learn how to sell yourself in a positive manner. Hopefully, by the end of this text you will see the benefits that come from successfully selling yourself to others.

NOTHING HAPPENS UNTIL SOMEONE SELLS SOMETHING

Personal selling is the heart of the free enterprise system of this great country. Everything that you are personally wearing today was placed in a retailing facility through the work and efforts of a salesperson. As you sit down to dinner each evening, all the food that you will consume is daily distributed to a food market because of the efforts of a salesperson. The car you drive, the furniture you sit on, the CDs, videos, DVDs, and tapes you listen to, all have found their way into your life because of the distribution process that involved some type of salesperson on a retail, wholesale, or manufacturing level.

Whenever a salesperson closes a sale and provides the customer with a copy of the purchase order or contract, the seller is continuing the process of keeping thousands of people employed. The order form that was used to close the sale was provided to the company by a printing organization. The printing organization purchases paper from a paper company. The paper company purchases the lumber to use in making paper from a lumber company. The lumber company obtains the timber logs for lumber from a logging company. The logging company obtains the right to cut down trees from some landowner. The landowner purchases the small trees for the land from a nursery owner. The nursery owner purchases seeds from a seed company. The seed company purchases the packages it uses for the seeds from a company that produces paper products and packages. The cycle goes on and on and is the continuing result of hardworking salespeople who work every day in this great land of America. Indeed, nothing happens in the economy without the exchange process between sellers and buyers. Nothing happens until someone sells something.

EVERY ORGANIZATION NEEDS SELLING

The end result of any business venture, personal or corporate, is to profitably sell its products or services. Organizations have to sell their ideas if they want public acceptance. The politician trying to win an election has to sell his public on the idea that he or she is the best person to represent them. A minister or preacher has to sell his religion and sell his flock on the need for continued financial support. Teachers and professional motivational speakers must sell ideas and concepts to their audience. Even physicians, accountants, contractors, and managers must sell their ideas and services. No matter what profession or career you personally pursue, you will have to use selling skills and have the ability to persuade.

Think of your involvement in social and civic organizations. Think of all the meetings you must attend for various reasons. Think of the lawyer going before a judge to present a case. Again, no matter what profession you will be involved in, selling will play a vital role in determining the outcome of what takes place.

CAREER OPPORTUNITIES

Some of you will consider a career in selling. Studies have shown that between 15-20 percent of college graduates will find themselves in a selling occupation. One of the reasons why so many individuals go into the selling profession is because so many jobs are available. If you look through any want ad section of a newspaper, between 40-60 percent of the jobs available are selling related jobs. The U.S. Bureau of Labor Statistics reports that between 300,000 and 400,000 jobs will exist each year in the profession of sales. The selling industry provides numerous openings in the manufacturing, retail and wholesale levels.

High Earnings

The amount of money that can be earned in sales depends on the type of job you have and the kind of product or service you are selling. In 2002, college graduates selling consumer goods had an average income of about $45,000. The average salary for a person selling industrial goods is about $60,000. Although college training is helpful, it is not necessary for a majority of the selling jobs in the industry. However, more companies are looking for professional sales people who have college degrees and related experience that enhance success in the selling environment. Degrees in business, communication, and marketing are helpful in entering the profession. Most sales jobs can be divided into three categories.

The Three Categories of Selling Jobs

⇨**Manufacturing Representatives**
 –**Sells to wholesalers and retailers.**
⇨**Wholesalers**
 –**Sells to retailers.**
⇨**Retail Salespeople**
 –**Sells to the ultimate consumer.**

- **Manufacturing Representatives**: This first group of salespeople sell primarily to wholesalers, distributors, retailers, and dealers. Manufacturing representatives spend a lot of time selling to industrial users–buyers who will resale the products to other people. Income for this group of salespeople can range from $40,000 to over $100,000 a year. This selling group is the most prestigious, as manufacturing representatives are usually recruited from the lower selling levels.

- **Wholesalers**: This second group of salespeople perform the role of a middle person by operating between manufacturers and retailers. Wholesalers will sell to every type of buyer except the ultimate consumer. This selling group serves several useful functions, from financing to storing thousands of items in a warehouse that can be quickly distributed to dealers. Wholesalers usually make between $50,000 to $75,000 a year. A wholesaling salesperson seldom involves himself with high pressure tactics–they are very punctual and service oriented.

- **Retail Salespeople**: This last group of salespeople work with the ultimate consumer. They probably do the most work and receive the least amount of money, respect, and recognition. This salesperson can either work in the store or outside by going door-to-door. Usually retail sales is a stepping stone to more lucrative and interesting work. This level of sales has the highest turnover of any selling group. Retail sales workers usually earn between $20,000 and $50,000 a year.

Stepping Stone to Top Management

Surveys have indicated that many presidents of large corporations have very extensive sales backgrounds. Most top managers began their careers at the bottom of the corporate ladder and worked their way up within the company. Top management's job is largely persuading other people to do things. For this reason a basic element that is desired in top managers is the ability to persuade other people and get along with others–basically, strong human relations skills.

Mobility

Sales is one of the few professions in which you can leave a job on one day and pick up a new job within the week. If your company goes out of business, downsizes, or is being bought out, you can usually make a connection with another firm more readily than many types of other workers. If you can sell, you will have a job.

Working Conditions

Many people have misconceptions of a salesperson's working environment. They think a salesperson travels extensively and has an unlimited expense account. Today, most salespeople travel very little because of advances in the telecommunications industry. One of the best things about selling is that in many cases there is very little supervision. Salespeople have a lot of freedom. Because there is so much freedom, people who are not disciplined have a hard time becoming successful. Remember, sales is one profession in which one is paid based on performance.

Challenge and Personal Growth

Selling is a very challenging job. Every customer is different. Competition is fierce. Also, conditions are constantly changing and products are always improving. Personal growth is gained as you learn that hard work is directly related to high earnings. You learn good human relation skills as you constantly work with people. There is not a better feeling than receiving a big commission as a result of hard, honest work.

Rapid Advancement

Selling is the one industry in which your ability is quickly recognized. If you would look through any want ad section of the daily newspaper and locate one of those selling jobs, chances are that you can move up into a level of management within six months. It is not uncommon for a retail sales worker to be moved up to a management position within the first year of employment.

SELLING POWER

We have already discussed that each of you can be considered as a salesperson. You have been selling yourself since the day you were born. You also realize that you sell something every day–if not yourself, then your ideas. The important question to ask is, "Are you good at selling yourself?" The purpose of this book is to improve your ability to sell yourself and increase your selling power.

What is **selling power**? How do you develop it? Well, you first must understand what the word **selling** means. Selling has been a garbage-can word for years to describe many ideas. The best word to define selling is **persuasion.** Selling is an art of persuading or influencing another person's thinking, feeling, or behavior. Persuasion is done with no direct power or force. Selling is simply persuasion.

Selling Power is a combination of two things:

- **Persuasive Techniques**
- **Persuasive Personality**

Referring once again to the previous questions, the way you obtain and increase this selling power is through the development of two areas: (1) **Persuasive Techniques**, and a (2) **Persuasive Personality**. We know that some people seem to be born with a natural persuasive personality. They are outgoing, motivated, and very goal oriented. But people who are weak in these characteristics can learn specific personality traits that can assist them in building a persuasive personality. We will spend the latter part of this book learning how to develop and apply persuasive techniques. You will learn these techniques through developing good, sound, human relations skills. The first part of the book will concentrate on developing a persuasive personality.

Persuasion: The Heart of Personal Selling

Persuasion is the ability to influence the thinking, feeling, or behavior of others.

Once again, selling is simply a matter of persuasion. Also, selling power is yours to obtain if you learn persuasive techniques and develop a persuasive personality. As you increase your ability to persuade, you naturally increase your personal selling power. What can selling power do for you? Just look at some of the many suggestions given by former students who are now successful professional salespeople. Place a check in the box of the suggestion that you would like to have in your life.

Assess Yourself–Ten Benefits of Personal Selling Power

1. **Sell products and services.** ❑
2. **Win elections, offices, and positions.** ❑
3. **Successfully date and marry sweethearts.** ❑
4. **Help gain family and world peace.** ❑
5. **Improve your ability to get ideas and messages across to others.** ❑
6. **Improve grades in school.** ❑
7. **Help you get promoted or obtain a better job.** ❑
8. **Develop relationships with new people.** ❑
9. **Convert people to religion.** ❑
10. **Defend and free the accused.** ❑

As you can see, selling power can increase your chances of success in the world. As you apply the techniques discussed in this book, you will be able to see the immediate benefits of selling power in all aspects of your daily life.

Self-Discovery Experience–Do You Have Sales Potential?

Go through each of the 25 statements below. If you answer "yes" then check the box. If you answer "no" then leave the box blank. It is important to be as fair and as honest as possible and go with our first initial response.

1. **I'd rather deal with things than people.** ❑
2. **I think chemistry is a very interesting subject.** ❑
3. **I like talking to strangers.** ❑
4. **I would like to be a college teacher.** ❑
5. **People find it easy to approach me.** ❑
6. **I would like to do research in science.** ❑
7. **I enjoy raising money for a charity.** ❑
8. **I would like to teach in a school.** ❑
9. **I like fashionably dressed people.** ❑
10. **I would like to be a watchmaker.** ❑
11. **I like to attend conventions.** ❑
12. **I've more than average mechanical ingenuity.** ❑
13. **I dislike people who borrow things.** ❑
14. **I would like to be a mechanical engineer.** ❑
15. **I like physically challenged people.** ❑
16. **I like to have regular work hours.** ❑
17. **I would enjoy making speeches.** ❑
18. **I would like to develop scientific theories.** ❑
19. **I like to keep meeting new people.** ❑
20. **I enjoy bargaining when I'm buying something.** ❑
21. **I would like to head a research department.** ❑
22. **I like to have a definite salary.** ❑
23. **I'd rather have only a few intimate friends.** ❑
24. **I'm better than average at judging values.** ❑
25. **I like to play cards.** ❑

The answers which are found at the bottom of this page will indicate interests and characteristics favorable to success in sales work. Add up the number of your "yes" answers to obtain your total score.

16 or above: Your chances of success in the selling field are favorable.
15 or below: You probably will have a better chance of success in some other field.
Answers: **No = 1, 2, 4, 6, 8, 10, 12, 14, 16, 18, 21, 22.**
Yes = 3, 5, 7, 9, 11, 13, 15, 17, 19, 20, 23, 24, 25.

Practical Application Exercise–Evaluation of a Selling Professional

This assignment gives you an opportunity to observe a salesperson in action and evaluate his or her performance. You will go in as a customer to a place of business of your choice and evaluate the experience. You will need to be aware of the following guidelines:

1. Choose a business that sells shopping goods. Shopping goods are items like furniture, clothing, automobiles, and appliances. Also, choose a product that you are interested in purchasing during the next year.

2. If a salesperson doesn't approach you, go and find one.

3. Allow yourself 10-20 minutes with the salesperson so that you can go through his or her entire presentation.

4. You will submit to the instructor a **one page report** about your experience and include the following information:

   a. Day and time of experience.
   b. Name of business.
   c. Name of salesperson.
   d. Product that you were looking at.
   e. Evaluation of the salesperson's opening approach, presentation, method of handling objections, visual aids, closing, and appearance, poise, and confidence.

5. Provide a summary report of the salesperson evaluation sheet found on the next page of this book.

6. Include a one to two paragraph summary in which you give the general strengths and weaknesses of the salesperson. Also, include some suggestions that will improve the salesperson's performance for future sales.

NAME ______________________
DATE __________ ____________
PRODUCT ___________________

SALES PRESENTATION EVALUATION SHEET

		POOR	FAIR	GOOD	EXCELLENT
1.	APPROACH: Opening statement; positive first impression; developed proper selling atmosphere.	0-1-2	3-4-5	6-7-8	9-10
2.	PRESENTATION: Benefits shown; showmanship; product knowledge; organization; customer involvement.	0-1-2-3	4-6-8	10-12-14	16-18-20
3.	VISUAL AIDS: Product and other visual/audio tools; logical order; appealing to five senses.	0-1-2	3-4-5	6-7-8	9-10
4.	APPEARANCE/POISE/ CONFIDENCE:	0-1-2	3-4-5	6-7-8	9-10
5.	VOICE: Tone, volume, enthusiasm, modulation.	0-1	2-3	4	5
6.	HANDLING OBJECTIONS: Understood and answered all questions and objections; responded calmly under pressure.	0-2-4	6-7-8	10-11-12	13-14-15
7.	CLOSE: Summary, recognized closing signals, asked for the order with an appropriate technique.	0-2-4	6-7-8	10-11-12	13-14-15
8.	CUSTOMER RELATIONS: Sincere interest and caring attitude towards customer.	0-2-4	6-7-8	10-11-12	13-14-15

Total Points _____ /100 Pts.

GENERAL COMMENTS:

TWO

THE MODERN DAY SALESPERSON

Learning Objectives

When you finish studying the material in this chapter, you should be able to:

1. **Discuss the five eras of selling.**
2. **Explain the roles of early traders and yankee peddlers.**
3. **Explain "caveat emptor" and the "marketing concept."**
4. **Identify several names used to describe the modern day salesperson.**
5. **Discuss the five roles performed by today's salespeople.**
6. **Explain the ten misconceptions of selling.**
7. **Explain the differences between the traditional and the modern day selling models.**
8. **Explain the change of emphasis in today's selling environment.**

It has been said that salesmen are a big problem to their bosses, their customers and their wives, to conservative credit managers, to hotels, and sometimes to each other. Individually and collectively they are cussed and discussed in sales meeting, conventions, behind closed doors, in bathrooms, bar rooms, and under one's breath from as many angles and with about the same fervor as the daily headlines. They make more noise and mistakes, create more cheer, correct more errors, adjust more differences, cause more divorces, spread more gossip, explain more discrepancies, hear more grievances, pacify more belligerents, and waste more time under pressure without losing their temper than any other class we know, including ministers. They live in hotels, and tents, on trains, buses, and park benches; they eat all kinds of food, drink all kinds of liquids, good and bad, they sleep before, during, and after business with no more schedule than the weather bureau and little, if any, effect on the public health. And yet salesmen are a power in society and in the public economy. In many ways they are undoubtedly a tribute unto themselves. They draw and spend more money with less effort and with less return than any other group in business. They come at the most inopportune times, under the slightest pretext, stay longer under more opposition, ask more personal questions, make more comment, put up with more inconveniences, and take more for granted than the U.S. Army. The introduce more new goods, dispose of more old goods, load more freight cars, unload more ships, build more factories, start more new businesses, and write more debits and credits in our ledgers than all other people in America. Yes, brother, you said it. With all their faults, they keep the wheels of commerce turning and the currents of human emotions running. More cannot be said of any man. Be careful of whom you call SALESMAN, lest you flatter him.

—Author unknown

THE MODERN DAY SALESPERSON

As we discussed in the first chapter, **persuasion** is the core of selling. **Selling** has been around since man began to trade and exchange products and services with one another. We can't attach a specific date to the birth of selling, but we can identify **five eras of selling**. This chapter will introduce you to the five eras of selling that have led us up to today's modern salesperson–the seller of the new millennium. Also, we will look at some of the misconceptions that still exist in the minds of people concerning the selling profession.

THE FIVE ERAS OF SELLING

The Early Traders

Early traders have been around since the Middle Ages in the Middle East and in Western Europe. Early salespeople of the Middle East were skilled craftsmen who sold the goods they made, usually worked on a barter basis, exchanging their fine, crafted products for something else that they needed. These early craftsmen were among the most respected people of their day. They had the reputation of producing the highest quality merchandise and spent all the time necessary in creating a product that was worthy to carry the creator's name.

The early salespeople of Western Europe were sellers who were not always held in high esteem by other people. They would use unethical techniques to dump merchandise off on other people and usually sold merchandise that was inferior or of low quality. A term that originated because of these unethical selling practices is **caveat emptor**, which means, **"let the buyer beware."** Because of many problems in the selling profession, the profession became attractive not only to the weak and uneducated but, also to the dishonest.

The Early Traders

The first salespeople were early craftsmen who worked on a barter and exchange basis.

The Industrial Revolution

The second era of selling is the Industrial Revolution. This era revolutionized production and had a profound affect upon distribution. In order to move the many goods produced by new industries, people had to be hired to transport and deliver these goods. In our country, these people were known as **Yankee Peddlers**. Yankee Peddlers would carry merchandise on their backs, on horses, or on wagons and travel throughout the country to the various settlements in the eastern wilderness. The Yankee Peddler developed a warm atmosphere through a low-pressure approach and usually sold everything he had. The distribution of goods created a major problem because it would take months to get goods from the manufacturer to a specific group of people. Goods were lost on the way to delivery and often goods were stolen because of all the obstacles the Yankee Peddler had to face. Many Yankee Peddlers never delivered the goods because they were killed by robbers and thieves. This era occurred during the late 1700s and is illustrated below.

The Yankee Peddler

Yankee Peddlers provided a valuable distribution function for manufacturers in the 1700s.

The American Peddler

In the late 1800s and early 1900s a salesperson emerged that created the majority of the myths that are found today about selling. The **American Peddler**, as he was called, was everything you hear today about the traveling salesman. He would exaggerate claims, speak fast and loud, and had the habit of being a back slapper. He would often tell inappropriate jokes and stories, and at times even attempt to chase the farmer's daughter. This salesperson did more damage for the reputation of the selling industry than any other salesperson in history. Even though the majority of salespeople were trying to make an honest living, a couple of "bad apples" produced misconceptions of selling that are still hurting the image of selling today.

The Professional Salesperson

In the 1950s, a gradual change took place in the selling world. Unlike the early high-pressure salesperson, most people involved in sales started the move toward becoming professionals. Salespeople became aware that the customer's welfare and happiness must come first. Salespeople started to look at themselves as experts in their fields and attempted to keep up on all the new knowledge of their products. This group of salespeople started the movement toward responsible sales practices and techniques. During the 1960s, a popular weekly television show named ***Father Knows Best***, starring Robert Young, gave the selling industry a big boost in image. Robert Young was the ideal family man, father, husband, community citizen, and his profession was in insurance sales. On a weekly basis, we watched this ideal family man practice honesty and integrity in all his relationships at home and at work. Salespeople were still around practicing the deceptive techniques of the 1930s, but a new breed of sellers wanted to make an image change from peddlers to professionals.

The Marketing Concept

An organizational movement toward consumer satisfaction with a concern for long-term profits.

One of the most important business concepts emerged during the 1950s–the **Marketing Concept**. The marketing concept is a movement toward consumer satisfaction with a concern of making long-term profits. Businesses became aware that you must find out what the customer wants or needs and then find a product that will satisfy that want or need. Today, many salespeople strive to give a high level of good customer service. Salespeople go out of their way to help customers. We can thank the **professional salesperson** for this new emphasis. Salespeople learned that a happy and satisfied customer can mean thousands of dollars in the future through repeat and referred business. The marketing concept is still strong today, and most companies have set up a department that concentrates specifically on working with customer complaints and issues.

The Modern Day Salesperson

The marketing concept that emerged in the 1950s is still a part of selling today. Today, salespeople realize that they are not just selling products anymore, they are selling services and benefits to the customer. Besides this concern about the customer, salespeople are now moving away from being called "professionals" and toward calling themselves **consultants, executives, associates, specialists, and advisors** because they not only sell products and services, but also educate customers. Instead of a furniture salesperson, you are a furniture consultant. Instead of an advertising salesperson, you are an account executive. Instead of an insurance salesperson, you are a financial advisor. Salespeople in our day attempt to go the extra mile in maintaining happy customers. Salespeople want to be good information sources and offer advice to buyers. Because of the abundance of products on the market and the fierce competition that exists, a salesperson must be several additional things today.

As time goes by, people are becoming individualists by developing personal tastes and wants. For example, many years ago only a few magazines were on the market geared towards the sports enthusiast. Today, because of the many target markets in the sporting industry, magazines are found not only for basketball, baseball, and football, but also for people who enjoy golf, skiing, hiking, tennis, racquetball, guns, boats, archery, soccer, horses, wrestling, track and field, swimming, and many other sports. Instead of a few major markets, our country consists of hundreds of smaller markets–a market of segmentation. This individualization makes the selling job more challenging as salespeople must package and customize their services to satisfy the customer's individual needs.

A few years ago, you could only find a few different types of jogging shoes. At the last count, over 200 different types of shoes can be found for people who are into jogging, running, and walking. Because of the abundance of products and competition, a salesperson must do more today to be successful–thus, the emergence of the **Modern Day Salesperson** of the new millennium. To be successful in today's world, a salesperson must be five things in addition to having a good product at a fair price.

Characteristics of the Modern Day Salesperson

- **Effective Communicators**
- **Problem-solvers**
- **Educators**
- **Persuasive Talkers**
- **Creative Thinkers**

- **An Effective Communicator**: The dictionary defines communication as the process of "giving and receiving information, signals, or messages by talk, gestures, or writing." We can see that communication is a two-way street, involving not only giving information, but also receiving information. Today's salespeople must be able to explain the product in a way that can be understood by the buyer. They cannot assume that the product or information will be received effectively, so they must be able to know ways of determining if the buyer is understanding and agreeing. They must do this through careful listening and skillful questioning. In addition, they must be able to read the nonverbal communication, or body language, that is given off by the buyer. Today's salespeople must not do all the talking, but should attempt to involve the customer during the presentation.

- **A Problem-Solver**: Today's salespeople must strive to become an expert concerning their own products and the problems that people encounter in searching for goods and services that satisfy needs and wants. They must realize that the buyer has needs and desires to fulfill. It is the seller's job to help the buyer solve problems in buying products. In order to do this, the salesperson must learn to see the buyer's point-of-view and see things through the buyer's eyes. The salesperson introduces products to the buyer and attempts to provide the best financing available. Salespeople show products that will make life easier and more enjoyable. The modern day salesperson knows how to work with the buyer and how to identify needs and give alternatives to fill those needs. The problem-solving salesperson is well aware of the prospect's doubts and fears and feels that it is his/her duty to help assist the buyer in overcoming them. With tactful guidance, logic, and emotional appeals, the modern day salesperson moves the buyer toward making a decision that will bring happiness and satisfaction.

- **An Educator**: Today's salespeople realize that it is their duty to sell products and to teach customers how to use and care for these products. If the customer does not understand the warranty or guarantee, the educating salesperson spends the necessary time and explains these items to the customer. If the salesperson doesn't have the product the customer needs, the customer is given ideas of where to go and what to look for. Educated salespeople realize that by educating the customer, they will make a friend and develop customer loyalty. These salespeople are concerned about the customer down the road, years in the future, and not just in selling a product and receiving the initial commission.

- **A Persuasive Talker**: Today's salespeople must know the tools of their trade–effective tools of persuasion. They must know how to ask questions, when to close the sale, and when to seek additional information and assistance in selling the customer. Persuasive talkers know what words to use–words that carry persuasive power. They don't ask a customer, "May I help you?" This gives the customer an easy out by simply saying "no." Persuasive talkers ask the customer, "What can I help you with?" By doing this, salespeople can steer the customer toward giving the seller a chance to give additional information. Persuasive talkers know when to put excitement and enthusiasm in their voice and in the words they use. They also learn how to identify those times in which additional information is to be provided to the buyer and when to back off.

- **A Creative Thinker**: Modern day salespeople have imagination and creativity. They present products in new ways. They learn how to give a presentation so that the buyer's attention and interest will be maintained. Creative thinkers know how to appeal to buying motives, stress benefits, and use stories and experiences to their fullest. They know how to turn wants into needs and features into benefits. In a world of many products and strong competition, creative thinkers must make a lasting impression in the mind of the customer.

SELLING MISCONCEPTIONS

As was mentioned earlier, many and misconceptions exist today in the selling industry. Look over the following ten common misconceptions and check the box on those you believe are false.

Assess Yourself–Am I a Selling Misconception?

1. Selling is a profession for the weak and uneducated. No talent and intelligence are needed for success. ❑
2. Salespeople must lie and be deceitful in order to succeed. A salesperson can't make a good living without being dishonest. ❑
3. A salesperson must be arrogant and overbearing to succeed in selling. ❑
4. Good salespeople are born, not made. ❑
5. A good salesperson can sell anything to anyone. Because of one's persuasive ability, no customer can resist the sales pitch. ❑
6. Most selling takes place at ball games and on golf courses. ❑
7. Selling is all showmanship and a bag of tricks. A salesperson must use "razzle dazzle" to persuade the buyer. ❑
8. Selling only benefits the seller. ❑
9. Salespeople spend a disgusting life traveling all the time. ❑
10. Selling is the profession in which you can "get rich quick." ❑

Everyone of the previous ten statements are false and are modern misconceptions so all of the boxes should have had a check mark. We all have had positive and negative experiences with salespeople and have perceptions of salespeople. Most of the misconceptions people have about the selling profession can be proven false. Many people turn away from a selling career because they believe these misconceptions that surround sales jobs. We will examine throughout this course the profession of selling and help you develop a better attitude about what a selling career can offer an individual and how selling helps the economy in which we live.

MODERN DAY SELLING STRATEGIES

Today's selling strategies are changing. The old traditional approach of the 50s, 60s, and 70s, emphasized closing techniques and giving persuasive presentations. The traditional model is, by design, technique driven and only allows about ten percent of your time to build rapport. Twenty percent of the time is spent qualifying the prospect and thirty percent presenting the product. When you have reached this point, you spend the balance of your time closing. Most of the sales training seminars during this traditional approach era emphasized hard core techniques, specifically, closing techniques. The most popular seminars throughout the country were teaching strategies that used pressure, aggression, and a little manipulation. Very little concern was on establishing a long-term relationship with the customer. This selling approach was effective for low ticket items where a mistake is not that big of deal. It also required less time in asking questions and developing a conversation on the part of the salesperson. Notice the emphasis in the traditional sales model found in the next illustration.

The Traditional Selling Model

10%	**Rapport**
20%	**Qualifying**
30%	**Presenting the Product**
40%	**Closing**

As selling organizations became more customer oriented and developed concern on satisfying needs and wants over the long run, a change in approach developed. In essence, a reverse and 180 degree shift took place. Today, selling strategies are moving from a pressure and technique approach to a rapport building and relationship emphasis. The more popular selling training seminars today deal with listening and communication skills and customer service. As illustrated in this chapter, the model of selling success in the new millennium concentrates on building trust, identifying needs, and making your product or service offerings more customized, individualized, and personalized. With customers becoming more educated and demanding than ever before, salespeople need to build a relationship that is long-term and prove their concern and care to their customers through reliable and dependable service. Specifically, forty percent of the time is spent developing a relationship with the prospect in building trust. This is accomplished by asking well thought out questions, and listening carefully to the customer's responses. The next thirty percent is identifying the needs, concerns, and objectives of the customers. As you can see, little emphasis is placed on the closing process if the relationship and trust have been developed.

Today's emphasis on relationships

40%	**Building Trust**
30%	**Identifying Needs**
20%	**Presenting the Product**
10%	**Closing**

The customer has benefitted from this change of emphasis. More time is spent listening to the customer's needs. Salespeople are realizing that there is a difference between a one-time sale and a long-term relationship. The seller's perception has improved as customers are viewed as an investment that will provide repeat business, referred business, and a potential value that can be measured in terms of thousands of dollars in the future. In fact, customers are looked at today as assets who will constantly grow in worth and value if they are nurtured. When all things are considered, the customer is the one who signs the company check. Without customers, no sales will exist. Without sales, no organizational profit will ever be obtained. Companies are instructing their salespeople to treat customers as if they are the "Chief Executive Officers" of the company. As you see in the next illustration, today's emphasis is on relationships instead of hard core selling techniques.

A Change of Emphasis

Today's selling strategies are moving from a technique and pressure approach to a rapport building and relationship emphasis.

Practical Application Exercise–Selling Field Project

You are to complete a small field project by interviewing a person you feel is an outstanding salesperson. It is suggested that you interview someone in the surrounding area and in a selling field that interests you. Please complete the following survey and submit your findings.

SALESPERSON'S NAME: ____________________

COMPANY: ________________________________

1. What exactly is your position, title, and responsibility?

2. What is your background in relationship to work experience and education?

3. How did you get started in sales?

4. What do you like best about your current selling job?

5. What do you like least about your current selling job?

6. What do you think are the three most important qualities to have to be a successful salesperson?

7. What do you believe is the main reason why salespeople fail?

8. What kind of prospecting tools do you use to find new potential customers?

9. What strategies do you use to retain customers and keep them coming back?

10. What process do you use to handle a customer who is unhappy?

11. What is the starting salary for a salesperson in your industry? How much can a successful salesperson make after five years of experience?

12. What is the basic difference between the top salespeople and the bottom salespeople in your company?

13. What is the biggest challenge facing salespeople today?

14. If I wanted to become a successful salesperson, what are some things I could start doing right now to prepare for my first sales job?

15. What are the characteristics found in today's customers?

THREE

DEVELOPING A WINNING ATTITUDE

Learning Objectives

When you finish studying the material in this chapter, you should be able to:

1. **Describe how attitudes are formed.**
2. **Explain how attitudes can change.**
3. **Identify and give examples of the four attitudes of the world.**
4. **Identify the five warning signs of FADES.**
5. **Discuss the characteristics found in a swan-like attitude.**

"The longer I live, the more I realize the impact of attitude on life. Attitude, to me, is more important than facts. It is more important than the past, than education, than money, than failures, than successes. It is more important than appearance, giftedness or skill. It will make or break a company, a church, a home. The remarkable thing is we have a choice every day regarding the attitude we will embrace for that day. We cannot change our past... we cannot change the fact that people will act a certain way. We cannot change the inevitable. The only thing we can do is play on the one string we have, and that is attitude...I am convinced that life is 10% what happens to me and 90% how I react to it."

-Charles Swindoll, Sales Trainer

DEVELOPING A WINNING ATTITUDE

Hundreds of books have been written on the subject of attitude. It is hard to go through a week without hearing some type of expression that deals with attitude. Some common expressions are "Your attitude is showing" and "You need to have some PMA (Positive Mental Attitude)." This chapter will emphasize that our attitudes are formed from the values we develop in life and that our values and attitudes determine our behavior. First, let us look at some popular definitions of attitude.

"A mental position."

"Opinions, views, beliefs, or convictions a person holds about some object."

"A feeling of emotion towards some person, object , or idea."

"That which determines a person's behavior."

I would like to sum up the previous four definitions and say that attitude is **a person's emotional feeling toward an object, idea, or person that determines behavior**.

ATTITUDES ARE FORMED

Attitudes are not inborn, they are formed over a period of time and are created from our individual experiences and interactions with other people. In essence, attitudes stem out of our personal value system. Values are simply our individual opinions, beliefs, standards, and ethics. For every value that we accumulate over the years, an individual attitude is attached to it. Attitudes are highly resistant to immediate change. Attitudes cause us to respond favorably or unfavorably to life's situations and experiences.

ATTITUDES CAN CHANGE

In order to change a person's behavior for a long period of time, a change must take place in the person's attitude. This behavioral change results from a **value clarification** experience. Value clarification occurs when an individual is confronted face-to-face with an opinion, belief, standard, or ethic that is suddenly evaluated. Generally, a past value becomes changed, altered, replaced, or solidified. A significant value clarification experience will influence a person's present attitude and affect behavior. A person might feel that automobile seat belts are not very important and seldom buckles up. This feeling is simply a belief, or value, that has been with the person for years. Let us assume that this person has a serious automobile accident and is severely injured. This person is told that seat belts would have substantially lessened the extent of his or her injuries. The attitude of this person may change towards seat belts to the extent that buckling up becomes a daily habit in the future. The person's attitude about seat belts changed because of the value clarification experience of a change in belief relating to seat belts.

I have also learned from personal experience that a person's wants and desires can change one's attitude. I had extremely long hair while in high school and during my first quarter of college. I found out that I could not get the job I wanted unless I was willing to get my hair cut, and that short hair was a precondition to getting a particular job. My attitude about hair length changed, even though I said earlier in life that I would never cut my hair for anyone. Since my first year in college, I have always had short hair. If we really desire or want something, we may have to change our attitude towards something to get it.

Another factor that can change a person's attitude is a change in how a person feels about him/herself. A friend of mine was in the process of getting a divorce from her husband. During her marriage she was very conservative in the car she drove and the clothes she wore. After her separation, something happened to her self-concept. She started to change. She became an eligible woman who wanted to favorably impress potential companions of the opposite sex. She has recently purchased a sports car and some very high-fashion clothing to match what she now believes to be her new self-image.

The previous three examples have a common thread–for a person to change his or her behavior, he or she must first experience a change in attitude. In order to change one's attitude, a change must first take place in relationship to values, or a value clarification experience must occur. As you become aware of a person's values and attitudes, you begin to understand why people act and behave the way they do. Look at the relationship between values, attitudes, and behavior and notice how one stems out of the other.

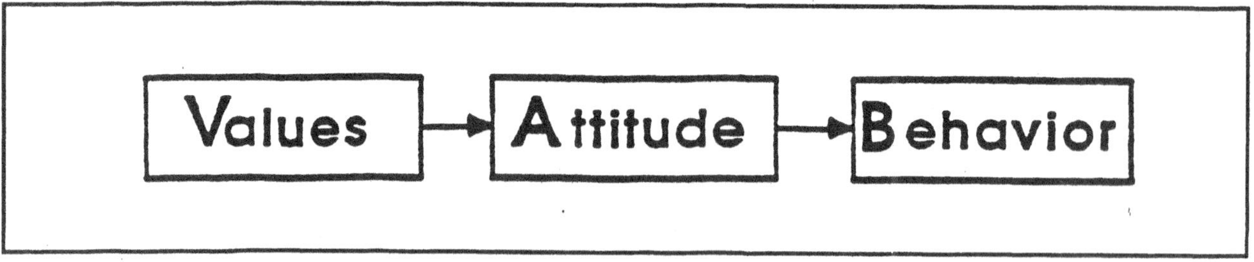

ATTITUDES OF THE WORLD

Four basic attitudes can be found in the working world today. All four attitudes reflect certain personal opinions, beliefs, and values. As mentioned earlier, these attitudes will determine the behavior of people. By identifying the type of attitude an individual has, you then can determine the behavior that will be displayed and develop a strategy to deal with the observed behavior. We will identify the four common attitudes that determine how one acts, interacts, and reacts with other people at home, work, and in socialized activities.

Win/Lose Attitude

When a person develops a **Win/Lose** attitude, one tends to develop a mental condition that states **I will win in life at the expense of others**. This type of attitude is harmful, as the individual will become successful in life at the expense of others. The person becomes very selfish, self-centered, and very insensitive to the feelings of other people. In all his activities, he made sure that he came out ahead, the true winner, even if it meant losing a long-term relationship. This attitude will eventually create a self-destructing situation because the person will lose the trust and friendships of associates and family members.

Lose/Win Attitude

When a person develops a **Lose/Win** attitude, one suffers from what I like to call the **"fire hydrant syndrome."** A person feels as if the whole world is benefitting at his expense. The person feels as if others will always take advantage and this individual treats most people as people with the win/lose attitude. This attitude makes the person feel like a martyr; that he/she is sacrificing personal happiness and possessions for the success of other people. This individual becomes a loner, fails to recognize the opportunities of life that will present themselves, and begins to accept the false idea that the other person will always get all the breaks. Eventually, this person will stop trying new or challenging things and he will say, "Why should I even try? I will fail anyway." With this type of attitude, this person, like the win/lose attitude person, will lose important friendships and respect. The behavior of this person is symbolized by a lack of effort and constant failure.

Lose/Lose Attitude

A person with a **Lose/Lose** type of attitude becomes very prideful and revenge oriented. The basic code of life tends to be **I may lose in life, but so will you because I will do what I have to, to make you lose**. This attitude creates in the person a behavior of finding faults in other people and criticizing people instead of building them up and looking for positive things. It is easier for this person to bring other people down to a low level than it is to lift oneself up to a higher level. These people become your back stabbers and are those who love to start vicious rumors and lies at work and in the neighborhood. Instead of using energy in a positive way, the lose/lose person uses all efforts in attempting to get even or by destroying other people.

Win/Win Attitude

Of course, the **Win/Win** attitude is the ideal one to develop, especially for salespeople. People who develop this type of attitude are very sensitive to the needs of others. They learn to trust other people and are willing to sacrifice for another person's happiness. This attitude has the ability to create situations in which both parties benefit and come out ahead. It creates a situation of **synergy** that improves the cooperation, cohesiveness, and outcome of two people when working together.. Synergy being the effect that takes place when two caring people work together. Two people can accomplish more together than by working apart from each other. In essence, 1 + 1 = 3, 4, or 5 instead of 2.

The behavior is easy to identify and recognize. This attitude creates the behavior of leadership and respect, and results in becoming service oriented. A customer can recognize in a matter of minutes this attitude in a salesperson. The customer senses that the salesperson is truly more concerned about the customer than the commission of the sale.

Love and care are two natural fruits that stem from this attitude. The win/win attitude builds teamwork, pride, and recognition in organizations. One of the greatest synergists, or win/win people of the past century, is the past college football coach Paul Bear Bryant of Alabama. Here are Coach Bryant's words that identify the key to a winning situation:

I'm just a plowhand from Arkansas, but I have learned how to hold a team together. How to lift some men up, how to calm down others, until finally they've got one heartbeat together, a team. There's just three things I'd ever say: If anything goes bad, I did it. If anything goes semi-good, then we did it. If anything goes real good, then you did it. That's all it takes to get people to win football games for you.

-Paul "Bear" Bryant

BEHAVIOR CHANGE THROUGH ATTITUDE

A great illustration that points out the tremendous affect attitude has on behavior is found in the following story:

> **A man lived by the side of the road and sold hot dogs. He was hard of hearing, so he had no radio. He had trouble with his eyes, so he read no newspapers. But he sold good hot dogs! Boy, did he sell good hot dogs. He put up a sign on the highway, telling people how good they were. He stood by the side of the road and cried, "Buy a hot dog, Mister." And people bought. He increased his meat and roll orders. He bought a bigger stove to take care of his trade. He got his son home from college to help him. But then something happened. His son said, "Father, haven't you been listening to the radio? If money stays tight, we are bound to have bad business. There may be a big depression coming on. You had better prepare for poor trade." Whereupon the father thought, "Well my son has gone to college. He reads the newspapers, and he listens to the radio, and he ought to know." So the father cut down his meat and roll orders. Took down his advertising signs. And no longer bothered to stand on the highway to sell hot dogs. And his hot dog sales fell almost overnight. "You're so right, my son," the father said to the boy. "We are certainly headed for a depression–business is so bad lately."**

Hopefully, you are now convinced of the importance of the development of the proper attitude. As pointed out, attitude determines a person's behavior. Another crucial point is that a person's attitude can also influence another person's behavior. It should be the goal of every person to encourage positive and healthy behavior in other people. The starting place for this is in your own mind, through the development of a proper **winning attitude**.

One of the people admired throughout my life is the late Vince Lombardi, coach of the Green Bay Packers of the National Football League. During a practice session for the Green Bay Packers in the early 1960s, things were not going well for Vince Lombardi's team. Lombardi singled out one big guard for his failure to "put out." It was a hot, muggy day when the coach called his guard aside and leveled his awesome guns on him as only Lombardi could. "Son, you are a lousy football player. You're not blocking; you're not tackling; you're not putting out. As a matter of fact, it's all over for you today; go take a shower." The big guard dropped his head and walked into the dressing room. Forty-five minutes later, when Lombardi walked in, he saw the big guard sitting in front of his locker still wearing his uniform. His head was bowed, and he was sobbing quietly.

Vince Lombardi, ever the changeable but always the compassionate leader, did something of an about-face that was also typical of him. He walked over to his football player and put his arms around his shoulder, "Son," he said, "I told you the truth. You are a lousy football player. You're not blocking, tackling, and just not putting out. However, in all fairness to you, I should have finished the story. Inside of you, son, there is a great football player, and I'm going to stick by your side until the great football player inside of you has a chance to come out and assert himself." With these words, Jerry Kramer straightened up and felt a great deal better. As a matter of fact, his attitude did a complete turnaround and his behavior out on the playing field changed completely. Jerry Kramer's proper attitude and changed behavior aided him in becoming one of the all-time greats in professional football. He was voted the all-time guard of the all-time greats in the first fifty years of professional football.

That was Lombardi. He saw things in people that they seldom saw in themselves. He realized that the most important value an individual has is the value of self-worth. He had the ability to inspire his people to use the talent they had and improve their personal worth. As a result, the players of Lombardi gave him three consecutive world championships at Green Bay. Lombardi developed the win/win attitude and was willing to sacrifice for his players. Every player who had the privilege to play under Lombardi indicated the strong love and care they felt from the man. Later, when Lombardi moved from Green Bay to Washington, many people wondered how he would handle Sonny Jurgensen, the talented but undisciplined quarterback. They didn't wonder very long. On the first day of practice, one of the reporters baited him with a question about Jurgensen. Lombardi called Sonny to his side, put his arm around him and said, "Gentlemen, this is the greatest quarterback ever to step on a football field." That year Jurgensen had his best year ever. Lombardi`s win/win attitude always looked for and found good in others.

DEVELOPING A WIN/WIN OR SWAN-LIKE ATTITUDE

This great American nation of ours has survived unbelievable challenges and remains a world leader today. Wars, plagues, floods, pestilence, disease and hurricanes have not been able to break the will of our people. Even with the challenges of economic hard times, recessions and depressions, the principles of the Free Enterprise System will provide the means for survival and once again will overcome! The fiber of the people has enabled them to always conquer the greatest obstacles through individual commitment and caring.

Something is happening today in our country, especially in the selling profession, that is impacting everything from the Free Enterprise System to our education system, and even our very homes and families. All areas of life have come under attack from the most deadly virus that this country has ever seen. Imagine, if you can, each person being infected by a deadly virus and slowly falling victim and gradually being destroyed. This demon of destruction carries in its bite the feeling of laziness and a "don't care" attitude. People all around us are beginning to exhibit the fatal symptoms of this national epidemic.The symptoms are easily recognized and can be cured if the victims are warned. The focus of this message is to help you determine if you have fallen victim to the dreaded **FADES** virus and teach you the simple yet effective cure.

The FADES virus is very similar to the AIDS virus. As you know, AIDS attacks a person's immune system and will eventually bring about physical death. FADES attacks a person's service system and brings about a death in any desire to provide service for other people. A person that experiences FADES eventually feels like an **Ugly Duck** because of poor self-image, lack of confidence, and low self-worth. In fact, the FADES carrier has no success in building positive and powerful relationships with other people. The "Ugly Duck" simply Doesn't Understand Caring, Kindness, and Service as the crucial elements in building positive relationships and first impressions.

Definition of FADES

Failure to
Acquire the
Desire for
Excellent
Service

To control this FADES epidemic, we must use the same approach that the **American Cancer Society** uses in controlling cancer. The society puts out a pamphlet called ***Cancer Facts*** and this information points out that the key in controlling cancer is basically YOU! The pamphlet teaches that you can protect yourself against cancer by some simple changes in lifestyle, learning the seven warning signs, looking daily for the warning signs, and when a sign appears, going immediately to a doctor for a medical check-up. You are now going to learn the five warning signs of FADES. By learning the signs, looking for them daily, and obtaining immediate help when a FADES virus sign appears, you will prolong and improve the service you give to other people and also become masterful in nurturing healthy business relationships.

Warning Sign #1 - Loss Of Eye-To-Eye Contact

Regardless of where the virus enters a person's body, it travels first to the area of the eyes, moving slowly from the left eye over to the right eye, leaving the victim with a semi-glazed look in the eyes. You can easily recognize this first symptom in people who will greet you and not look at you. In the more advanced stages of infection, people will actually develop a high sensitivity to contact with other human eyes. Infected employees work with customers and never look them in the eyes when they speak to them. This causes the customer to feel that the employee would rather not look at them, or worse yet, that the employee doesn't really care if they do business with the customer or not. See the danger? Eye contact is a "must" for effective communication. Only through the eyes can we communicate our real interest and concern for another human being, and especially potential customers. Only through eye-to-eye contact can we register sincere concern and interest in our customers.

FADES Warning Sign #1 - Loss of Eye Contact

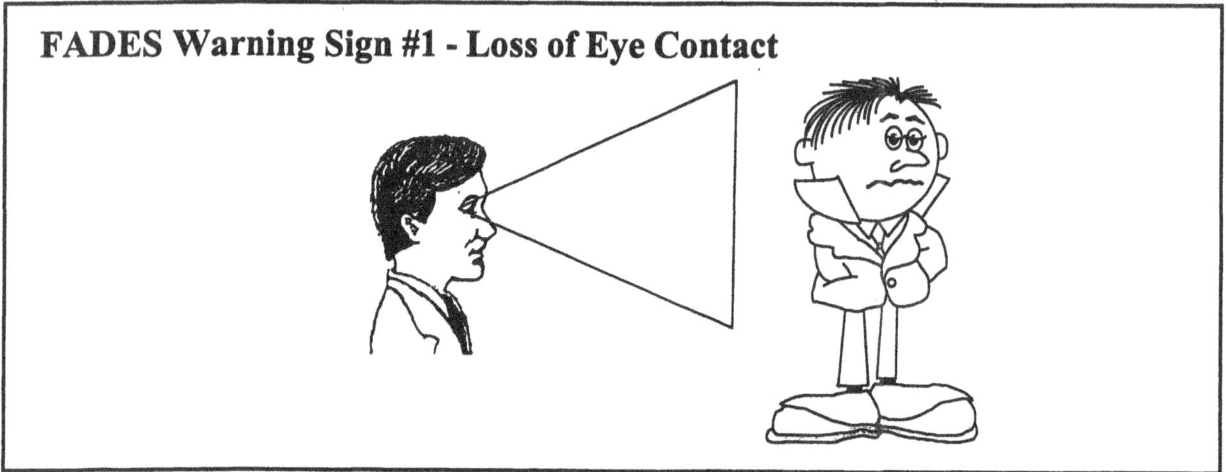

Warning Sign #2 - Disappearing Smile

Once the virus has shut off the power of eye-to-eye contact in communication, it now travels through what has been referred to as the **Trickle-Down Effect**. The virus trickles down from the eyes into the muscles of the face and affects the facial ability to project a spontaneous smile. Almost a **Sour Puss** look is registered to anyone who happens to see the victim's face. A smile is so basic and universal in the communication process; it is literally the light of the face. Again, the danger with this symptom is a negative feeling being projected and communicated to others. An individual's demonstration of this symptom projects an **I don't care attitude** and rudeness instead of kindness. In individuals demonstrating this symptom, a feeling that no one cares dominates social contacts. Can you see the danger this symptom can bring to your potential customers?

FADES Warning Sign #2 - Disappearing Smile

Warning Sign #3 - Negative Verbal Communication

Now that the light of the face is turned off and the sparkle of eye-to-eye contact is gone, the FADES virus moves on down the anatomy and collects itself around the vocal mechanism. The voice is now coated with the deadly power of the virus which manifests itself through two different ways. The first way finds the victim having nothing to say. All the positive thoughts about colleagues and customers go unexpressed because the desire to speak is gone. Is it any wonder that communication problems begin to plague the organization, not to mention the negative feelings that the customer receives from this? The second way the virus is manifested is when the victim eliminates the positive comments in a conversation and concentrates only on negative and critical comments of other people. These victims can be identified by listening to their social conversations during breaks, lunch or just in passing. A dramatic increase in the frequency of negative or critical comments and observations is apparent. Negativism will dominate the entire conversation of the victim. The real tragedy is that this form of conversation has become so commonplace that people expect and accept it. Some people enjoy negative conversation to the degree that it is entertaining. Several popular comedians use "put-downs" as the focus of humor. We pay substantial amounts of money to listen to the criticism of people, races, religions, institutions, and our political leaders. Put-downs have become a popular form of communication with the young people of today. Negative comments create negative feelings and add to the already serious feeling of "not caring" that exists so strongly in the world. Customers hearing such comments become more convinced that this company is not the place to bring their business. Whether it is a lack of verbalization or an overabundance of negative criticism, the effect and end result to the company is lost sales and unhappy customers.

FADES Warning Sign #3 - Negative Verbal Communication

Warning Sign #4 - Negative Nonverbal Language

The virus now moves from the vocal cords towards the back and trickles down the spinal column. Every nerve in the body that controls body movement passes through the spinal cord. The virus first manifests itself here by filling the victim with a powerful feeling of constant fatigue. The victim starts each new day feeling tired. The person walks, sits, steps with an appearance of tiredness. The victims are easy to spot in a meeting or in a store. They are the ones who appear to be fighting an urge to horizontalize. They lean on counters and tables. They slide forward or backward in their chairs looking for someplace to prop their feet. If they do not fight this urge, they will ultimately end up on the floor in a perfect horizontal position–the same position you are in when you sleep at night. Some researchers in the area of nonverbal communication have discovered 800,000 different forms of nonverbal communication. When the nonverbal communication contradicts the verbal transmission, the nonverbal message is the one that is remembered. Imagine the impact of nonverbal transmissions to our customers that we don't care whether or not they do business with us! The power of 800,000 nonverbal messages of indifference and not caring will tell all people to take their business elsewhere! One of the truly frightening things about this nonverbal communication is that the human being has the capacity to receive all 800,000 forms in just seconds. Many experts believe it only takes 30 seconds or less to make a positive or negative first impression. Can you imagine that it takes only seconds to receive the impact of nonverbal messages we send out to other people? Is it any wonder that customers leave because of over-powering feelings of negativism and rudeness projected to them by the personnel of the organization?–those people paid to generate business? Customers are turned off when they feel we don't care.

FADES Warning Sign #4 - Negative Nonverbal Language

Warning Sign #5 - Me-First Attitude

The virus next travels directly to the individual's **service center (The Heart)** and to the individual's **attitude center (The Mind)**. The victim's heart and mind lose all desire to be of service to the customer. The only item that concerns the salesperson is the commission of the sale instead of the relationship or friendship of the customer. Instead of being motivated to go the extra mile or to render any goodwill or compassionate service to others, the victim is motivated by a **me-first** and a **self-centered attitude.** The individual starts asking questions when called upon to do something for another person. Two of these self-centered questions are, "What's in it for me?" (WIIFM) and "How will I benefit?" Self-gratification and self-satisfaction become the major motivators. At this point, the victim is actually destroying business and generating none. All people interacting with the victim are affected in a negative way. The victim is dissatisfied with work, people, the company, and with life in general.

During this fifth stage, the victim will eventually become terminal. Once the victim's service center is destroyed, the individual gives the frequent expression and verbalization of the words, "I don't care!" This utterance is most often heard when the victim has been asked to do something for someone else. For example, a person might be asked, "Why didn't you vote in the last election?" "I don't care!" or, a boss might say "We need the support of every employee in the company on this issue." "I don't care!" Victims! Victims! There are thousands of victims from the virus of **FADES** presently working in industry and for your company. Without doubt, this virus is one of the greatest threats that has ever appeared in our country. The only obstacle that the American Free Enterprise System can't overcome is a state of the union where a majority of the workers and leaders no longer care about what's happening around them.

FADES Warning Sign #5 - Me First Attitude

The Cure - Turning The Ugly Duck into a Swan

A cure does exist for the person who has fallen victim to the poisonous bite of the **FADES** virus, and a person can begin a process that will remove all of the five warning signs. The simple cure can restore the sparkle in eye-to-eye contacts, smiles on the face, excitement and enthusiasm in the tone of voice, spring in the step, and confidence in the posture of the victims. This simple process will remove negative thoughts and comments from the dialogue of the American worker and create 800,000 positive transmissions from the nonverbal communication network that tell people that someone cares! The cure is really the greatest miracle in the world and turns ugly ducks into swans. The cure can be found in the following simple saying found in the illustration below.

The Cure

To the degree you give others what they want, they will give you what you want.

The ugly ducks of the selling world can develop the attitude of trust, care, love, service, kindness, and sacrifice. The ugly duck victim goes through the simple process and learns to become a **SWAN**–meaning the victim begins to **Sense What Another Needs!!!** If a salesperson can realize that all customers want to be treated in a caring way that demonstrates respect and the knowledge that all people have worth, the customer will respond by providing repeat business. As it says in the book ***The Ugly Duckling***, by Hans Christian Anderson, "It doesn't matter about being born in a duckyard, as long as you are hatched from a swan's egg."

The Ugly Duckling Miracle

It doesn't matter about being born in a duckyard, as long as you are hatched from a swan's egg.

By developing the **Swan-Like Attitude** of win/win, a person learns to look for positive things in the world and in other people. As the famous saying states, **"You find what you look for."** By looking for positive things in others, and realizing that all people have worth, an individual truly develops the skill of giving to other people what they really want: to be treated as if they are important, have value, and are something special.

I know what you are thinking! You're saying that the solution to the problem is so simple and too simple to work. Well, just think of the story of the bumble bee illustrated below. The experts state that it is impossible for the bumblebee to fly, but fly he does.

The Bumble Bee Can Fly!

The bumble bee cannot fly. According to the theory of aerodynamics, and as may be readily demonstrated through laboratory tests and wind tunnel experiments, the bumblebee is unable to fly. This is because the size, weight, and shape of his body, in relation to the total wing-spread that he has, make flying impossible.
But fly he does!!!

AN EXAMPLE OF A SWAN-LIKE ATTITUDE

Are there any organizations that exhibit this swan-like attitude? Yes! As I spend time doing seminars throughout the United States, I am constantly looking for prime examples that indicate a win/win relationship. Extraordinary customer service can still be found, even though it requires a harder search than it did 30 years ago, due to the trend of more self-service groups. Lew Young, editor-in-chief for ***Business Week*** magazine said, "Probably the most important management fundamental that is being ignored today is staying close to the customer to satisfy his needs and anticipate his wants. In too many companies the customer has become a bloody nuisance whose unpredictable behavior damages carefully made strategic plans, whose activities mess up computer operations, and who stubbornly insists that purchased products should work."

All business success rests on something labeled a "sale" which at least momentarily weds a company with the customer. I have found an organization that exhibits an attitude that the customer is a friend instead of a nuisance. Ten years ago I was returning from a workshop in California. I usually fill up my car with gas in St. George, Utah, but for some reason I traveled right by the Dixie area. By the time I noticed the gas gauge, I was on empty. The first available gas station I found was the Beaver Valley Chevron in Beaver, Utah. Like many modern consumers, I pulled into the self-service island desiring to save money by pumping my own gas. A service attendant came running towards my car as if it was on fire or a bomb was visible on the roof. Surprised and a little spooked, I quickly rolled up my window, fearing that a problem was occurring. The attendant then tapped on the window, and I slowly rolled the window back down. The young man, smiling from ear to ear, said, "What a beautiful day, sir. Can I fill it up?" Knowing that I was in the self-service island, I said, "No thank you; I will do it because I don't want to pay full service prices."

"It doesn't matter," he said, "if you are in the self-service or full-service island; we will fill it up." I certainly hadn't anticipated this type of service. After the young man began filling up my gas tank, he then cleaned my windows. He came back to the car window and asked, "Can I check the oil?" Again I was reluctant. I had heard terrible stories of service attendants raising the hood and sticking a screwdriver through one of the hoses. Because the attendant was so eager to perform these additional small acts of service, I allowed him to do this. Of course, I stepped out of my car and watched him carefully to make sure he did exactly what he indicated he would do. He then proceeded to check the air in all four tires and noticed that my rear left tire was low, so he filled it to the proper level. After the young man finished these tasks, he gave me the price of my gas and processed my credit card. He expressed his appreciation for my business and smiled.

I drove away from the Beaver Valley Chevron station in shock. I discussed this unusual behavior exhibited by the attendant with my wife when I arrived home. I concluded that whenever a customer receives good service, it seems to be unusual behavior instead of normal behavior. Isn't it a shame that we are surprised when we are served well? Shouldn't all of us expect good service all the time? During the past five years, I have visited the Beaver Valley Chevron at least 30 times and have always received excellent service. In fact, last November, another college professor and I parked our car across the street and observed the station for 15 minutes. During this time, five cars pulled into the station and all cars were approached within a 30-second time frame. I have told my students to check out this remarkable service station when they travel home during the quarter breaks. I always get back positive reports. The Beaver Valley station is the highest rated Chevron station within the state of Utah.

What attitude is exhibited by this service station? A win/win, or swan-like attitude! This station simply has learned to sense what another needs. This station also performs those routine tasks that are no longer performed by its competitors.

Practical Application Exercise–Selling Yourself Presentation

The purpose of this exercise is to provide you with a unique experience in selling yourself as a product. As you know, one of the major skills required by employers in the world of business is the ability to sell yourself to others. This ability to sell yourself is also a major tool of success that you will need throughout your life. Specifically, you are to prepare and present a **five-minute presentation** in which you will sell yourself as a product to a group of buyers. Your buyers will consist of three to five people who you know. It is suggested that you take the "third person (he/she)" or "I (first person)" approach when you sell yourself. Each member of your group will fill out an evaluation form on you, which will ask for your strengths and weaknesses as they see you. This presentation is to be carefully planned and rehearsed and should persuade your group members to purchase you. A sample evaluation form is found with this exercise that you can copy and use for feedback during your presentation. A suggestion that will help you in preparing for this presentation is to follow the steps shown below:

STEP ONE: List at least three skills and talents that you have.

Example:

1. Type 60 words a minute.
2. An ability to budget.
3. Good bargain hunter.
4. Great organizer of time.

STEP TWO: Turn your skills and talents into benefits that other people can receive from you.

- Type 60 words a minute: I can save others time by typing their reports and assignments. This will improve the appearance of their work and improve their grade.
- An ability to budget: I can help others save money; live within their income; avoid financial burdens.
- Good bargain hunter: I can save others 10-50 percent on items they purchase. I can save people time because I know where and when to buy.
- Great organizer of time: I can help other people become more productive. I can save them time and provide them free time to do what they want.

STEP THREE: Now prepare some visuals that represent the talents and skills you will be selling. Some examples are: A plate of cookies if you bake well, something you have built if you do woodworking; a picture of a car if you rebuild automobiles; a tennis racket if you love to play tennis. If you can't bring an object then put together some charts, pictures or other types of visual aids.

STEP FOUR: Practice giving this presentation in front of the mirror at least three times before you present it to your group. You will find out that you will tend to speak faster than you usually do. This will give you some extra time to work out your presentation. You must spend five minutes in front of your group in the class.

STEP FIVE: Review and become acquainted with the evaluation sheet that will be used by your class members as it is found below. Your evaluators will use it in providing you feedback.

SELF-PRESENTATION EVALUATION SHEET

Please circle your personal response to each of the seven areas. Below the response write some general comments that will help the seller in future presentations.

1.	**Interesting and catchy opening.**	**Poor Fair Good Excellent**
2.	**Held interest of group.**	**Poor Fair Good Excellent**
3.	**Kept good eye contact.**	**Poor Fair Good Excellent**
4.	**Organization.**	**Poor Fair Good Excellent**
5.	**Modulated voice.**	**Poor Fair Good Excellent**
6.	**Identified at least three talents and skills.**	**Poor Fair Good Excellent**
7.	**Moved group to want product.**	**Poor Fair Good Excellent**
8.	**Overall impression of the presentation.**	**Poor Fair Good Excellent**

GENERAL COMMENTS:

FOUR

THE SEEDS OF SUCCESS

Learning Objectives

When you finish studying the material in this chapter, you should be able to:

1. **Identify the three obstacles that prevent success.**
2. **Discuss the difference between success and achievement.**
3. **Discuss several examples of the definition of success.**
4. **Summarize the FEED process of success.**
5. **Explain the relationship between expectations and behavior.**
6. **Describe several examples of the self-fulfilling prophecy.**
7. **Describe the "Act as if" principle of enthusiasm.**
8. **Explain Franklin's sixth-step process of habit change.**
9. **Discuss ten ways to nurture the seeds of success.**

Success begins with in the mind!

It is important to keep a positive outlook even when things look difficult and grim. Before David was to fight the giant Goliath, his friends, fearing for the worst, came to pay their last respects. "What makes you so sure that I will not return?" asked David, surprised at their pessimistic appraisal of the situation. One of his friends was quick to reply. "David," he said, "Goliath is so big! How can you possibly expect me to win? David just smiled. "If he is so big and I use my slingshot," he asked, "how can I miss?" Now that is a positive view on the situation.

THE SEEDS OF SUCCESS

Success in life seems to depend heavily on attitude and other personality factors. A small difference is found between the top achievers in occupations and careers and those who merely do well. This chapter goes into several key elements of success that seem to formulate the small difference found between these two categories of people. The success seeds discussed in this chapter contain principles of thought and healthy behavior that will give you the winning edge in all aspects of life in addition to success in the selling profession.

Before we discuss the seeds of success, some ground work must be laid so that you can better understand the successful elements that must be incorporated in your life to feel like a winner. This chapter will begin by covering the three obstacles that prevent an individual from obtaining success and then will identify the four success seeds found in every successful person.

THE OBSTACLES THAT PREVENT SUCCESS

Before defining success, isolating reasons why so many people turn out to be unsuccessful is necessary. People that feel they are unsuccessful in life seem to be leading toward a type of **living death**. They seem to be suffering from three obstacles that prevent a person from feeling successful. When a person suffers from a living death feeling, one immediately has low self-esteem. This low self-esteem affects one's level of confidence which prevents an individual from attempting new challenges and risks, therefore developing a fear of failure. The three obstacles of a **lack of self-confidence**, a **fear of failure**, and **low self-esteem** create a slow, but progressive, personal death in the heart and mind of a person.

The three obstacles contribute to the living death of many people with whom we associate. One of my favorite books is ***The Greatest Miracle in the World*** by Og Mandino. In his book, Mr. Og Mandino discusses this idea of **living death**. Let me quote from his book the following passages that will help explain the concept of living death.

> **Most humans, in varying degrees, are already dead. In one way or another they have lost their dreams, their ambitions, their desire for a better life. They have surrendered their fight for self-esteem and they have compromised their great potential. They have settled for a life of mediocrity, days of despair, and nights of tears. They are no more living than living deaths confined to the cemeteries of their choice. Yet they need not remain in that state. They can be resurrected from their sorry condition. They can perform the greatest miracle in the world. They can come back from the dead.**
>
> **Most of us build prisons for ourselves and after we occupy them for a period of time we become accustomed to their walls and accept the false premise that we are incarcerated for life. As soon as that belief takes hold of us, we abandon hope of ever doing more with our life and of ever giving our dreams a chance to be fulfilled. We become puppets and begin to suffer living death.**

The Three Obstacles of Success

- ⇨ **Lack of self-confidence**
- ⇨ **Fear of failure**
- ⇨ **Low self-esteem**

Again, this living death feeling seems to cause people to have a lack of self-confidence in their personal potential, low self-esteem, and fear of failure. The way to bring yourself back from this death is to learn and implement in your life the seeds of success and become success oriented. Will Rogers made a comment about this type of living death in his very last speech he ever gave: "Lord, let me live until I'm dead!" He was referring to those "walking zombies" whom he had become familiar with during his lifetime.

SUCCESS BEGINS IN THE MIND

The majority of national sales trainers, motivational speakers, and human development consultants tend to agree on one major idea: **"We become what we think about!"** Before you can win in life, you must first win in your own mind. In essence, a change in your attitude must take place. A change of mind can turn a boring task into an exciting adventure. This concept brings back to memory a childhood experience I had as a young boy on the farm in northern Utah.

As a boy, I had the daily chore of taking food out to the hogs each morning. This activity was referred to as "slopping the hogs." As I would take the two silver buckets, filled to the brim with the family leftovers, to the hogs, our family's large and lazy creatures would wander slowly over to the trough and quickly consume all that was placed in front of them. The hogs would never look up at me as I lowered the contents of the bucket down toward them, and no appreciation was ever displayed on their fat, pointed faces as I provided them with daily nourishment. I developed a strong dislike for this chore, as I had to encounter the smell and dirty surroundings each day. This dislike turned into a depression. I hated the job, the surroundings, the unappreciative ugly creatures. This negative attitude had a large impact on my self-esteem and confidence. I indeed felt a "living death".

This negative attitude and the feeling of low self-worth was reinforced every day, as the hogs never seemed excited when I approached them with their daily meal. My attitude toward this duty quickly changed upon the arrival of nine baby **"piglets"** one summer morning. One day, as always, I proceeded to pick up the two silver buckets in my hands. As the morning sunlight reflected off the buckets, the baby piglets quickly gained focus of the reflection that meant nourishment was soon arriving. Moving slowly towards the pen, I noticed something I had never seen before in my "slopping the hogs" experience. I identified a self-generated enthusiasm, a natural hunger that created excitement on the Rodney Dangerfield look-a-like faces of the piglets. As I walked closer to the pen, the baby piglets began to run, while stumbling over and falling on top of each other, toward me. As I moved closer toward the fence, the piglets proceeded to leap towards me and ended up leaning on the first rail of the wooden fence. As the two buckets were lowered, I wasn't allowed to drop the contents into the trough. The nine baby piglets leaped head-first into the trough; and while lying on their backs, proceeded to consume all the contents that would fall from above. From that time on, each day started out with excitement and enthusiasm as I took out the morning leftovers to the baby piglets, because I knew they would anticipate with passion my daily delivery. At that time, I stopped using the phrase "slop the hogs" and started saying "feed the pigs" because this chore, which was earlier referred to as a burden, now became a pleasure. This attitude change improved my self-esteem, increased my self-confidence, and allowed me to once again take on new challenges and not be fearful of failure.

Feeding the Pigs

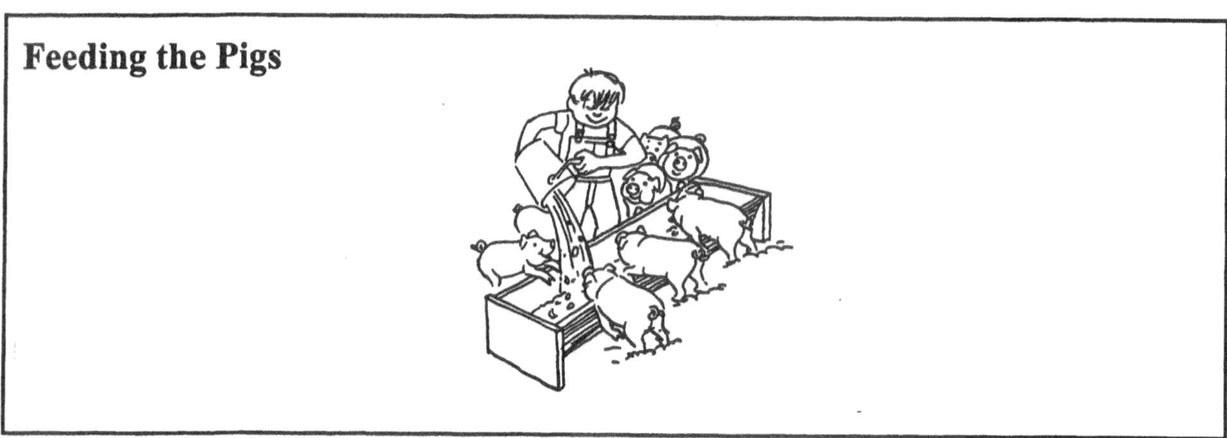

This experience reminds me of the single most important concept I learned during my undergraduate years in college. Dale Carnegie made a statement in his book, ***How To Win Friends and Influence People*:** **"The deepest drive inside all people is the desire to succeed, to be great, and to excel."** This is a universal urge found in every individual. We must constantly "FEED" this drive so that we can obtain and enjoy the benefits of success.

In fact, the word **FEED** identifies the four basic success seeds that are found in all people. All the books I have read and the tapes I have listened to point out four elements or characteristics that are found in people that are successful. Each of these four "success seeds" will be discussed in great detail. Success seems to be totally dependent on how the individual nourishes or feeds the four success seeds that have been planted in the heart of each person. These success seeds can be a two-edged sword. What they do for you entirely depends on the type of growing process you provide for them during your lifetime. You have complete control and free agency in determining the process in how you nourish, develop, and use these seeds of success. One of the major goals for this chapter is to discuss the four insights that will help you feel successful–or experience a process that will now be called **"Feeding the Pigs."** In fact, these insights or success seeds can instill in all of us the same enthusiasm and love for life that the baby piglets had on my farm many years ago. I think a good term to call ourselves would be **PIGS**! PIGS meaning gaining personal insights that will guarantee personal success. The next illustration points out the transformation of hogs into pigs results when a person gains personal insights that guarantee success. The rest of this chapter will teach you the four personal insights, or success seeds, that if applied, will guarantee the feeling of success in all that you do.

Personal Insights that Guarantee Success

Personal
Insights that
Guarantee
Success

FOCUS

The letter "**F**" in **FEED** represents the term **Focus**. The dictionary defines focus as the "ability to develop a central point." The more we focus in on specifics, the greater will be our chances for success. Most success builders and trainers agree that a person must learn to focus in on the true meaning of success. Studies done by the ***Neuropsychology of Achievement*** state that the number one dominant characteristic of high achievers is the ability to focus, or visualize their goals in vivid detail. They "pre-live" certain specific goals down to their sights and smells. This pre-living of goals has been called **imaging**. Many athletes improve their skills by watching idealized performances on videotapes. By focusing better on specific, positive points, success is encountered at an earlier and faster pace.

Confusing Success With Achievement

We all have grown up in an achievement-oriented society and associate success as simply being the completion of an achievement or an accomplishment. We tend to measure the success of a person by a measuring stick that consists of the number and the types of achievements obtained. Wealth and material possessions seem to be important measuring tools. In addition, awards, recognitions, certificates, trophies, and other tangible items become very important and necessary in order to feel successful. We seem to be conditioned to this idea from childhood. As a child, we receive rewards for jobs and small tasks performed and completed. As we enter grade school, class grades become an important symbol of success. We learn the importance of awards through the scouting program as we obtain all the ranking advancements and merit badges available.

Achievements become more important in junior high and high school. We desire to obtain membership in school organizations, trophies for athletic events, medals, letters, scholarships, and other honors through our involvement with school and civic clubs. Our mind begins to be programmed towards achievements, and we tend to forget that the process of improvement, development and learning is as important as the final reward or goal. Even though achievements and accomplishments are important, continual progress is also important. We must constantly attempt to strive for higher goals, improve past performances, and make improvement a daily habit. For this reason, achievements should be like goals that you shoot for instead of the only obsession or focus of your everyday activities.

As discussed above, achievements are important; but more important is the process that leads up to achievement. This process is called **success**. We must learn to focus as much on the process as we do the destination. Earl Nightingale, in his tape ***The Greatest Secret in the World***, defined success as the "progressive realization of a worthy ideal.

Earl Nightingale's Definition of Success

The progressive realization of a worthy ideal.

In other words, success is simply progressing towards worthy goals. If you set worthy goals to obtain, and actively seek and move towards those goals, you can be considered a success. **Achievement is like the destination, and success is the journey towards the destination**. A person does not have to obtain worldly awards and honors to be successful. If a person is constantly improving and moving towards worthy goals, he/she is a success in life. By progressing, a person is doing the best that he/she can do with what they presently have. By focusing more on success instead of achievement, we will feel daily the satisfaction of moving closer to meaningful goals. The Japanese call this concept of continuous improvement **kaizen**! The process of an on-going, step-by-step movement of self-improvement is big in the Japanese work culture. One never stops improving and learning.

You can see by now that success will naturally lead one towards achievements in life. The next illustration provides some examples of success and achievement–notice the difference between the two.

Success	Achievement
Success is the process of losing weight every day and learning how to watch what you eat and exercising daily.	**Achievement** is losing 30 pounds of weight in three months.
Success occurs every semester, taking and passing classes.	**Achievement** is receiving your graduate degree in business.
Success is the process of getting into shape by running, lifting weights, and preparing for tryouts	**Achievement** is making the school's football team.
Success is attending classes, doing assignments, studying, and passing exams	**Achievement** is passing this selling class with a good grade.
Success is the process of learning the steps and process of obtaining financing, finding a location, hiring and training your new employees.	**Achievement** is when you obtain your small business loan to start your own business.
Success is doing your research, writing your draft, editing, revising, and refining the novel until it reaches the stage in which it can be published.	**Achievement** is publishing your first novel.

To sum up our discussion, look at the illustration that further defines the difference between success and achievement. We now have a good definition of success. We know that it is the progressive realization of a worthy ideal, or in other words, **progressing towards the worthy goals we set in life**. It is important to understand that success is a very personal thing and means different things to different people. To some people, success is a big paycheck at the end of a work week. To others, it is a shiny new car. To a salesperson, it may be breaking a sales quota by earning extra commissions. And, to a young business executive, it is that big promotion after many long years of dedication to the company. Again, realize that these examples show achievements that have been accomplished. The process involved in each of these goals is where success is truly found. Success can generally be stated as that deep, indescribable pride in doing the best at one's job and in having one's life in order. Success is the **journey** and achievement is the **destination**.

The Difference Between Success and Achievement

Success is like the journey–A goal in the process of being accomplished.

Achievement is like the destination–A goal that is accomplished.

Becoming More Success Oriented

In an early 1980s edition of ***Success Magazine***, a survey was conducted to find out how today's Americans answered the proverbial question, "What is success?" A study was done by the Gallup Organization in which they asked the general public to choose from a list of 12 factors the three factors they considered most important as criteria for judging personal success. The breakdown of the 12 factors indicates the frequency with which each factor was named. Recent research studies on the topic of success have validated this survey.

Personal Success Factors

SUCCESS

Personal Success Factors	
1. Good Health	58%
2. Enjoyable Job	49%
3. Happy Family	45%
4. Good Education	39%
5. Peace of Mind	34%
6. Good Friends	25%
7. Intelligence	15%
8. Unlimited Money	11%
9. Talent	7%
10. Luck	6%
11. Luxury Car	2%
12. Expensive Home	1%

Two things are identified from this survey. First, the old symbols of success like money, large homes, and luxury automobiles have slipped to the bottom of the list. When this same survey was conducted 30 years earlier, these items were the top-rated items. Second, the new criteria for personal success have become the intangible factors like health, enjoyable job, family, education, and good friends. These items were on the bottom of the list 30 years ago.

This new personal definition of success supports the idea that it is possible for every person to be successful. I like what Howard Whitman said in his book ***How to Fashion Your Own Brand of Success***. Whitman gives two main criteria of success and an example.

Whitman's Two Criteria of Success

TWO CRITERIA OF SUCCESS

1. **Do others think you are a success?**
2. **Do you think so?**

He states that these two questions are as related as the straw is to the ice-cream soda. If you want to fully enjoy an ice-cream soda, it is nice to have both the straw and the soda. But, if you are to have only one, it is certainly far better to have the ice-cream soda than to have only the straw because the straw is quite worthless alone. And it is quite worthless and futile, also, to have the whole world thinking that you are a success if you do not think so yourself. The ice-cream of success is your own inward knowledge of it. Given that, you do not necessarily need the acknowledgment of the outside world.

We now can conclude that success is a personal thing, and in order to achieve it, you only have to establish some worthy personal goals and be in the process of actively moving towards those goals. A worthy goal is a goal **that enhances one's self worth and value.** Every person can become a success. Again the important question is brought up, "Why do so many people fail instead of succeed?" The answer seems to be that people only associate success with achievements and don't understand that the limitation of success seems to lie within each of us. It is totally dependent on how the individual nourishes the four success seeds that have been planted in the heart and mind of each person.

Focus On The Keys Of Opportunity

Successful people develop the ability to recognize and take advantage of opportunity. Successful people realize that opportunity results from hard work, intelligence, and preparation. They believe that each individual is an opportunity, and people can create their own opportunity and develop capacities to move toward opportunity. In essence, **YOU** are the key element in opportunity. Opportunity does not come from luck. Opportunity will not come knocking at your door, so don't sit waiting with the hope that you will hear the knocking. You must put yourself in the position of recognizing the opportunities that will come your way. If you are prepared to recognize opportunity, you will identify those situations that are passed over by people who have not developed the sense of success. Preparation must precede opportunity. Opportunity does not come to the lucky; it comes to the prepared and hard working–those people who are able to put themselves in a position to win in life. These people recognize an opportunity because they are looking for it every day–once they see it, they grab it.

In summary, your success in taking advantage of opportunities in life will increase as you understand four principles of opportunity. The understanding of these four principles will allow you to better implement yourself as the key element in the opportunities of your life.

The Four Principles of Opportunity

Principle 1: Preparation must precede opportunity.
Principle 2: Position yourself to meet opportunity.
Principle 3: Look out for and learn to recognize opportunity.
Principle 4: Reach out and grab opportunity when opportunity finally presents herself.

Focus On The Lessons Learned From Failure, Not On The Failure

A person's daily feeling of success is strongly related to how an individual handles the failures that will come his way. One of the biggest pitfalls all people fall into is to assume the following:

**Because I have failed at one thing,
I have failed at all things.**

Some of the greatest people in the world have been able to meet failure face on and use it to their advantage. Did you know that

- **Walt Disney** was fired as a newspaper editor because he had no good ideas? He also went broke seven times and had a nervous breakdown.
- **Leo Tolstoy** flunked out of college?
- **Pablo Picasso** could barely read or write at the age of 10 and was considered a hopeless pupil because he refused to learn mathematics?
- **Sir Isaac Newton** was allowed to get an education only because he proved to be a complete failure in running his family's farm?
- **Theodor Geisel's** first manuscript was rejected 43 times before a publisher seriously considered printing it? He is today known as Dr. Suess, and his first manuscript was ***I Think I saw It on Mulberry Street.***
- **Admiral Richard Byrd** had been retired from the Navy as "Unfit for Service" when he flew over both poles?
- **Henry Aaron**, the greatest home run hitter of major league baseball struck out more times than 99 percent of all major league baseball players?
- **Sir Winston Churchill's** father considered his son so "dull" that he doubted whether he could ever earn a living? Churchill failed the entrance exams at Sundhurst College twice and was taken out of another university so that he could study with a tutor.
- The well-known example of **Abraham Lincoln** who failed at being a businessman, a politician and thirteen attempts at being elected to political office before finally becoming the President of the United States?
- A young man's lifelong dream was to attend West Point. He was twice turned down but applied a third time and was accepted. His name was **Douglas MacArthur**.

How do successful people look at and handle failure? These people realize that failures are simply potential half-steps toward the future. Losers look at failures as missed opportunities. People who know how to nurture the seed of failure realize that they can learn from failure and receive growth. Losers look at failure as a heavy burden to carry around for the future. Those people who can't handle failure have a hard time of freeing themselves from the memories of the negative experience and become discouraged and eventually depressed. A successful person who uses failure as a tool in molding a better product for the future will also understand that yesterday's problems are over with. Successful people also realize that they can even **win in failure**. When faced with a situation in which they have lost or failed, they still look at it as a positive experience if they do one of the three things found in the next illustration.

How to Win in Failure

- **You learned something to improve your future performance.**
- **You improved on your past performance.**
- **You were able to reach a new personal best.**

An individual can use lessons of failure for an advantage or let failure become a dark shroud of dejection and defeat. One must focus on the lessons learned from failure and not on the failure itself. Also, if one fails at one thing, one does not fail at all things. As inventor Charles Kettering put it, "**Failures, repeated failures, are finger posts on the road to achievement. The only time you don't fail is the last time you try something and it works. One fails toward success.**" Look at another perspective from Alexandria Dumas. He states that "**A person who doubts himself is like a man who would enlist in the ranks of his enemies and bear arms against himself. He makes his failure certain by himself being the first person to be convinced of it.** Failure is indeed conquered in one's own mind, in how an individual copes with the failure, and in how he/she uses it for the future Look at the next illustration that reflects the ideas of Tom Hopkins, a nationally respected sales trainer. His five attitudes toward failure are built upon his philosophy that "**I am not judged by the number of times I fail, but by the number of times I succeed, and the number of times I succeed is in direct proportion to the number of times I fail and keep trying.**"

Tom Hopkins's Five Attitudes Toward Failure

1. **I never see failure as failure, but only as a learning experience.**
2. **I never see failure as failure, but only as the negative feedback I need to change course in my direction.**
3. **I never see failure as failure, but only as the opportunity to develop my sense of humor.**
4. **I never see failure as failure, but only as an opportunity to practice my techniques and perfect my performance.**
5. **I never see failure as failure, but only as the game I must play to win.**

EXPECTATIONS

The second letter of "E" in the **FEED** process is **Expectations.** A popular statement is, "If you want to get the best out of a man, you must look for the best that is in him." Expectations is defined as "anticipation of future good." Expectations can influence behavior; therefore, people may get a better performance if they expect a better performance. Historically, this behavioral phenomenon is called the Pygmalion Effect or the **Self-Fulfilling Prophecy**. The Pygmalion effect has roots deeply planted in Greek Mythology. Pygmalion was a sculptor who hated women but ended up falling in love with one of his most beautiful carved statues of a women. Pygmalion became so obsessed and infatuated with the statue that he prayed to the goddess Aphrodite to bring this statue to life. After Pygmalion's repeated prayers to the gods, Aprhodite gave life to the statue. The concept rests on the premise that what we see reflected in many objects, situations, or persons is what we put there with our own expectations. We create images of how things should be, and if these images are believed, they become self-fulfilling prophecies.

Thus, the self-fulfilling prophecy occurs when people become what others expect them to become. Negative expectations can bring about a lower level of performance in some people while positive expectations can bring about a higher level of performance in others. When people act on a false belief, the false belief turns into a true reality. R. K. Merton, Professor of Sociology at Columbia University, elaborated on this concept by stating that, "When one predicts an event, the expectation of the event changes the behavior of the person in such a way as to make the event more likely to happen." The next illustration shows several examples of this concept in daily life.

Common Self-Fulfilling Prophecies

- **The postal worker who is afraid of dogs eventually gets bitten.**
- **The lion tamer who loses his or her nerve is most vulnerable to get attacked.**
- **A young man whose parents do not trust him and continually accuse him of stealing eventually figures he might as well get punished for the real thing.**
- **The student with "examination neurosis" is convinced that he or she will fail, spends more time worrying than studying, and does poorly on the exam.**
- **The teacher expects a minority student from a lower socio-economic background to be an underachiever so the teacher fails to challenge and develop the student and the student turns out a poor performance.**

According to Merton, the self-fulfilling prophecy is, in the beginning, a false definition of a situation. This false definition causes a new behavior that makes false conception come true. This creates a circle of error, for the person will cite the actual course of events as proof that one was right from the very beginning.

In the 1960s, Robert Rosenthal and Leonard Jacobsen tested the **self-fulfilling prophecy** in an elementary school in a lower-class neighborhood. At the beginning of the school year, tests were given to all the children in the 18 classrooms–these tests were nonverbal IQ tests. They disguised the test as one that would predict "intellectual blooming." After the test, they randomly chose 20 percent of the children in each room and labeled them intellectual bloomers. Rosenthal and Jacobsen told the teachers that these children could be expected to show remarkable gains during the coming year on the basis of their high test scores. In actuality, the difference between these experimental children and the control group was solely in the teachers' minds.

The children were retested eight months later. The experimental children (intellectual bloomers) showed an overall IQ gain of four points over that of the control children. Their excess in gain was two points in verbal ability and seven points in reasoning. It made no difference whether the child was in a high-ability or low-ability classroom. Rosenthal and Jacobsen's data indicated that there was no difference in the amount of time teachers spent with the students. This suggests that the quality of interaction that took place between the teachers and their students determined the IQ gains.

Perhaps the most remarkable finding was that the teachers' personal attitudes had also been affected. They thought the brighter students were more appealing, more affectionate, and better adjusted than the other students. Of course, there were some students who had gained in IQ even though they had not been designated as intellectual bloomers. Ironically, the teachers believed these students were not as well-adjusted, interesting, and affectionate as even the students who had not done well. Thus, it was not the increased IQ that caused the teachers to like or dislike their pupils, but whether or not they had done what had been expected of them.

Psychologists have long realized the necessity of creating management patterns that bring motivation, increase productivity, and increase communication. According to Rensis Liker, a well-respected researcher in the behavioral area, "If a high level of performance is to be achieved, it appears to be necessary for a supervisor to have high performance goals and a contagious enthusiasm as to the importance of these goals."

The importance of what managers believe about their employees and their ability to train and motivate them is illustrated by "Sweeny's Miracle," an example of the self-fulfilling prophecy. In the 1960s, James Sweeny, a professor of industrial management and psychology at Tulane University and director of the Tulane Biomedical Computer Center, believed that he could teach even a poorly educated person to be a capable computer operator. George Johnson, a black janitor at the center, was chosen for the study. During the morning, Johnson performed his custodial duties, and Sweeney tutored him in computer operations in the afternoon.

Johnson was doing very well in his training program when someone in the Personnel Department decided that it was necessary to have a certain IQ score in order to be a computer operator. Johnson was tested, and his IQ indicated that he would not be able to learn to type, much less operate and program a computer. Sweeney persisted. He threatened to resign unless Johnson was permitted to continue his training. Sweeney prevailed, and he is still directing the computer center. Johnson is now in charge of the main computer room and is responsible for training new computer operators. Sweeney's expectations were based on what he believed about his own teaching ability and Johnson's ability to succeed.

Another example of the self-fulfilling prophecy happened in the great sport of football. Football has always been a great teacher on what expectations can do to an individual's performance. A crowd, coach, and teammates can bring out the best or worst in a player. Such a thing happened to a place-kicker named Curt Knight. Curt Knight was a young player who played for the Washington Redskins of the National Football League in the early 1970s. One year, Curt Knight led the league in extra points and field goals. This was the result of many things; Knight was a talented athlete, but he had one other important element going for him, a coach who had confidence in him and knew how to bring out his best.

Vince Lombardi goes down in history and the record books as one of the greatest and most successful coaches of all time. While at Green Bay, coaching the Packers, he brought a team of losers to league and world championships. After his glory years at Green Bay, Lombardi took a new coaching position at Washington. Lombardi had an unusual style of coaching. He expected his players to give their all. If a player was later than 15 minutes "early" to practice, he was considered late. This idea of being 15 minutes early for everything was called **Lombardi Time**. Also, Lombardi did something unusual when reviewing past game films with his players. He spent most of his time pointing out the good things on the rookie ball players instead of going over all the mistakes. He would always praise a good block, tackle, pass, or run. Every time a player did well, Lombardi would comment on it. Many experts of the game of football say that he had a talent of bringing out 100 percent in his players. The main reason, people feel, was his constant positive reinforcement.

During Lombardi's year at Washington, Curt Knight excelled above all other kickers in the National Football League as the number one kicker. Lombardi would always speak highly of Knight when talking to the press. Whenever the Redskins were in a kicking situation, Lombardi would not hesitate in using Knight. He said he knew Knight could do the job. These expectations brought about a high level of performance and an outstanding year for Curt Knight.

Vince Lombardi died a year later, and George Allen was chosen to succeed Lombardi as head coach of the Redskins. Allen also had a very unique style of teaching and coaching. His style was a 180 degree shift from Lombardi's style. Instead of concentrating on positive reinforcement, he would use negative reinforcement to bring about high performances. He would make a ball player so mad that the player worked harder to prove Allen wrong.

Allen was known to literally embarrass and chew out players who made blunders in public. Because of his negative comments, some players had a hard time adapting to the change of leadership style. Curt Knight had a harder time than most players. Curt Knight's performance on the football field began to falter. During one particular game, the Washington Redskins were in a "must" situation to score with only a few seconds left. They were in a field goal situation, which would allow them to score three points and win the game. George Allen elected to go for the touchdown instead of the field goal. His comment after the game was, "I felt that Curt couldn't do the job." An amazing thing happened to the performance of Knight. The following games, he not only lost his motivation, but also missed many easy field goals and extra point attempts. We learn from the previous examples four basic ideas about the self-fulfilling prophecy that are illustrated below.

Four Conclusions of the Self-Fulfilling Prophecy

- **We can become what we think about.**
- **We can become what others expect us to become.**
- **Positive expectations can bring about a higher level of performance.**
- **Negative expectations can bring about a lower level of performance.**

The key is the relationship between expectations and performance. Successful people know that life is a self-fulfilling prophecy. They know that a person usually gets what he or she actively expects. A person's fears and worries can turn into anxiety. Also, if a person's mental expectancy is healthy and creative, his or her body will seek to display a condition of well-being. **The body manifests what the mind harbors.** Positive expectations must begin in your mind. As you prepare your mind to start expecting positive things, positive things will start happening. As mentioned in the previous chapter, you find what you look for.

As the well-known sales trainer Zig Ziglar states often in his seminars, "You find what you look for in life." You can go into Atlanta, New York, San Francisco, Salt Lake City, and even beautiful Deweyville, Utah, and find problems like crime, drugs, and some of the most negative people in the world. Or you can go into the same cities just mentioned, and find some of the most loving, caring, and dedicated people in the world. You will find what you look for.

You can take the most outstanding student in this school, nitpick him/her to death, and manage to find some fault with the person. Or you can take the average person and start looking for good qualities and find them in abundance. Again, it depends on what you are looking for. In essence, accentuate the positive by looking for what you want in life instead of what you don't want in life.

To close this success seed of expectations, I would like to relate to you an experience I had with a person who is employed at the same college where I am presently teaching. I gave a customer service seminar for all the secretaries, custodians, and staff personnel during the spring of 1989. A school custodian, who was in attendance during my entire presentation, came up to me afterwards and said, "I enjoyed your presentation, but I still hate my job." This person didn't look too happy. In fact, he could have easily fulfilled the job as the Cruise Director for the Titanic! He went on for several minutes telling me everything he hated about working at the school as a custodian. I got the feeling that this person was very frustrated and was looking to change jobs. All of a sudden, I remembered listening to a tape cassette of Zig Ziglar and decided to use a technique he has applied with great success.

I told the custodian, "Your situation doesn't sound very good, and the unfortunate thing is that it's probably going to get worse!" I just hit him in the face with a bucket of ice water and the man became surprised. "What do you mean?" he said. "It's very simple. Your present situation and future situations will get worse because there is a good chance that you will lose this job, and future jobs, even bad jobs. As you know, jobs in this area aren't that easy to find." "What are you saying, Dave?" "Sir, there is not a company anywhere that can have so much negativism in one employee and survive." As you probably now can see, this employee was very attentive. I had to take his present situation and make something positive out of it.

I then proceeded to tell the man that I had an idea if he was really interested in hearing it. The custodian was so shocked by our conversation that he said, "I'm ready to hear anything." I said, "The first thing I want you to do tonight is to go home and take out a sheet of paper. On this paper, list everything you like about your job and your company." The custodian said, "That will be easy because I don't like anything about it!" I continued by saying, "Do they by any chance pay you to work or do you just work out of charity." He said, "Certainly they pay me for the work I do!" I then said, "Do you like that?" "Of course I do Dave." "Good", I said. "So you like being paid for your job, go ahead and write that down. Let's continue right now to start your list."

I went on and said, "Do they give you time off for vacation time?" "Of course they do Dave, you know that." I then said, "Do you like that?" "Of course I do Dave." Again I said, "Then write that down too!" I now was noticing a change on the custodian's face. Again I said, "Do you have a retirement program here?" "You know they do Dave!" "Write that down also," I said. As we continued our discussion, we discovered several other things the custodian liked. In fact, we came up with ten items he liked about the job which he ten minutes earlier hated and liked nothing about just ten minutes earlier.

As you can see, a person can take his job or company and find many good things about it, or a number of bad things about it. It depends on what you want and expect out of life, because you are going to find what you're looking for. A few weeks later, as I saw this custodian in the hallway at school, I asked the question, "How are things going?" His response was, "Great!" This person's world seemed to change because his attitude changed.

ENTHUSIASM

The third letter of "**E**" in the **FEED** process is **Enthusiasm**. It is interesting to know that the etymology--the derivation of enthusiasm--comes from three Greek words. The first Greek word of "Theos" means **God** and the other two words "En-Tae" means **with you**, so enthusiasm literally means "God within you" and also "divine inspiration." We associate words like enjoyment, fun, inspiration, passion, and dynamic with enthusiasm. A turned-on employee who has a passion for a specific job is a powerful asset in today's selling world.

If you think back on your life, you will agree that whenever you lost your enthusiasm for any activity, you also lost your desire to keep working at it and when that happened the activity was eventually pushed aside. In today's work world, few drop dead from exhaustion but many quietly curl up and die from dissatisfaction–they lose the love and enthusiasm for their specific job. Enthusiasm can increase productivity, improve morale, and make another person feel physically and mentally better. If you don't believe it, just look at the person at your place of employment who is the most enthusiastic. You will notice major differences in his/her behavior and performance as compared to other employees. Again, enthusiasm in the work place is a rare thing in today's world.

Why is it that people today look more sad than glad? I have been told by students that if you are smiling during an examination, it is a clue to the instructor that you are cheating! I have been told by city workers that when you are happy, smiling, and singing on the job, it is a tipoff to the boss that the worker is not putting out. In fact, look happy on the job and your co-workers will get angry with you and say comments like, "Why are you so happy?", "Boy, you sure are kissing up to management!" or "What drug are you on!" I have walked into many restaurants early in the morning for breakfast singing, whistling, and looking happy. Often, I see many people hold up their knifes with angry and hateful feelings, "Who gave you the right to look so happy in the morning." The look of misery, pain, and sadness is common today in many organizations.

The "Act As If" Principle

Most sales trainers agree that enthusiasm is one of the most important factors necessary for success in selling. Enthusiasm is something that can be acquired. A principle that I believe in with all my heart is the **Act As If** principle. It is simply "**Act the way you want to feel and soon you will feel the way you act.**" Most of us know that actions follow emotions. We feel a certain way and that feeling governs our behavior. But it is also true that emotions follow actions. So, if you want to feel glad, act glad.

In the selling profession the "Act As If" principle has also been called the **fake it till you make it** concept. Many salespeople believe that if you want to look successful in the eyes of other people, dress and act successful. If you want to look confident, then act confident. You can feel and look enthusiastic by applying the three key ingredients found in enthusiastic people. I called the three keys the **TRIPLE As** and they are found in the next illustration. The "Triple As" refer to the three people skills that show enthusiasm:

The Triple As

Acknowledgment	**= Eye contact**
Acceptance	**= Smile**
Approval	**= Positive Verbal Statements**

Acknowledgment is created through the eyes. A person's eyes have been called the "windows of the soul." Eye contact with another person is the universal sign of acknowledgment. When you come in contact with another person, look at them, eye-to-eye, and the person will feel that you are interested, attentive, and happy to see them. A person feels **acceptance** through the "light of your face," or through your smile. A smile makes a person feel accepted. Whenever you approach a person on a sidewalk, a smile from the other person brings about a feeling of warmth. I'm not talking about staring, just simply smiling. **Approval** is felt from a person when a positive verbal statement is given. The statement must be specific, sincere, and deserving.

Think back on the last family reunion you attended. Let's all be honest; no one loves family reunions except those people who are close to passing on from this earth life. Look at what people do to each other in an attempt to create the feelings of acknowledgment, acceptance, and approval. Relatives will approach each other and have eye contact, smile, and then verbalize something positive. If you want a person to think that you like them, simply apply the "Triple As" which are acknowledgment through eye contact, acceptance through smiling, and approval through positive verbal statements.

You need to understand one important concept dealing with the "Act As If" principle. This principle will **prime your pump** and **recharge your battery** for the day by creating initially, self-generated enthusiasm. It is your duty to keep the "water flowing" once the pump has been primed. As one of our favorite sayings is found below.

Recharging My Battery

I am like a storage battery constantly discharging energy. And unless I am recharged at frequent intervals, I will soon run dry.

All of the great positive mental attitude books, motivational seminars, cassette tapes, and self-improvement programs are great in creating or generating motivation and enthusiasm, however, they are short-lived unless you are able to apply specific success principles, through discipline, every day of your life. This is why successful people are always listening to motivational tapes, attending seminars, reading positive books, and associating with other success-oriented people. These people believe "like attracts like" and if you expose yourself constantly to uplifting messages, you will be able to keep that storage battery of enthusiasm recharging daily.

Your Individual Enthusiasm Chamber

Let's end this section on enthusiasm by suggesting a simple but effective way to start every day of your life feeling better through charging up your battery of enthusiasm. In every house there is a room called the reading library, water closet, or bathroom. I give this special room the name of the **PALACE OF PRESTIGE**. The "POP" room, as I like to call it, is a very special place for all people. No matter how much money you make, how many honors you have received, or how many initials or titles you have in front of your name, all people enter this room in basically the same manner each day. Even our present President of the United States, starts off his day in the same type of room you entered first thing in the morning.

Make this individual "Palace of Prestige" be the beginning point each day for charging up your battery of enthusiasm. Many psychologists have determined that your first encounter of the day has a more direct bearing on your attitude and mental health for that day than all your other encounters combined. Also, William James, the father of American psychology, concluded that "we become how we act, so if we wish to conquer undesirable emotional tendencies in ourselves, we must go through the outward movements of the kind of tendencies we wish to cultivate." Again, William James is simply verifying the power of the "Act As If" principle we have discussed. In this special room, you can make your first encounter a positive one and you can cultivate the feelings you want for the day.

When you go to bed at night, turn your "opportunity clock" on. An opportunity clock wakes you up to music, not an alarm. Don't start your day with an alarm clock, because it will make you feel tense and shocked. The reason is that memories of your childhood will come back. While in grade school, whenever you heard an alarm you thought of a fire, robbery, or an emergency. This early morning shock will cause your stomach muscles to squeeze down and inhibit the digestive process. Intense emotions have been known to cause a stroke or heart attack. Set your opportunity clock to a mellow station with music you enjoy. After the clock goes off, slowly roll out of bed. If you jump out of bed you might cause an overwhelming rush of blood to the head and develop a headache.

As you move from your bed, go to the closet and put on a robe. The reason for this is that you only want to see your face in the bathroom mirror. Females are very smart and have mastered this technique because the mirrors they carry in their purses are small in size in order to show only the face. If you saw your entire body early in the morning, you would become discouraged to view what Father Time has done to your beautiful body. With your robe on, walk into the bathroom and immediately **acknowledge** yourself through eye contact. After just fifteen seconds, you will quickly learn that God has a sense of humor because of the funny creatures, like you, he has created. You will immediately smile. When we make ourselves smile, we actually feel like smiling. In our face, we have 90 separate muscles. Muscles necessary to frown number 72. Only 18 muscles are needed to smile. This

acceptance through smiling will exercise these 18 muscles. After you have started smiling, keep the 18 muscles working for a minimum period of two minutes. The December 1988 edition of ***Success Magazine*** states that the medical profession is agreeing today that **"the mere act of smiling produces a flood of brain chemicals that sets you on the road to feeling good."** As you maintain this smile, you will begin to feel the release of "good feeling" brain chemicals.

Brain Chemicals Create the Old Smiling Face

Let those brain chemicals and endorphins come!

After you have acknowledged and accepted yourself, end this recharging moment in the Palace of Prestige by **approving** yourself with several positive verbal affirmations. Simply say several verbal statements that state something positive that has already happened. Don't say that "I am going to have a good day." Say, "I am having a good day." After several affirmations, you will feel better and will have a better outlook towards the day and for life. What this process simply does is allows you to use the greatest gift you have. Our greatest gift is **the ability to choose the way we think, act, or feel**. The ultimate personal put-down is when we permit someone or something to take charge of our lives and our attitudes. The greatest power and gift we have is the power to choose. As you leave your house, you will physically and mentally feel better, have positive expectations, and your chances of success will be greatly enhanced. Use the power of your individual enthusiasm chamber, or the Palace of Prestige, every day to generate positive feelings and thoughts.

DISCIPLINE

The fourth letter in the **FEED** process, **"D,"** is **Discipline**. The dictionary defines discipline as "control gained by training and obedience." In essence, we all have seen discipline in our life in the form of the habits we have willfully accumulated during our life. As you look at yourself, your friends, and other people around you, you will notice something interesting: People become slaves to the habits they develop. The well-know writer John Dryden said, "We first make our habits, and then our habits make us. The great educator Horace Mann wrote, "Habit is a cable. We weave a thread of it every day, and at last we cannot break it." And Samuel Johnson stated, "The chains of habit are generally too small to be felt until they are too strong to be broken." Let's look at a powerful saying dealing with our habits found in the next illustratrion.. This popular saying illustrates how habits can be a two-edged sword. They can be for our good, or they can be a hindrance that encourages slavery and failure.

As illustrated in the habit statement, a habit can be nurtured as a seed of success or it can develop into a seed of failure. Every individual has the choice of developing good or bad habits. **The successful people of the world seem to gain the habit of doing those things that unsuccessful people don't like to do.** They become slaves to good habits such as dedication, promptness, quality work, positive attitude, responsibility, and going the extra mile on every task.

Who Am I? I Am Habit!

I am your constant companion.
I am your greatest helper or your heaviest burden.
I will push you onward or drag you down to failure.
I am completely at your command.
Half of the things you do, you might just as well turn over to me
and I will be able to do them quickly and correctly.
I am easily managed, you must merely be firm and show
me exactly how you want something done.
After a few lessons I will do it automatically.
I am the servant of great men and the laughs of all failures as well.
Those who are failures, I have made failures.
I am not a machine though I work with all the precision of
a machine plus the intelligence of a man.
You may run me for profit or run me for ruin,
it makes no difference to me.
Take me, train me, be firm with me and I will
place the world at your feet.
Be easy with me and I will destroy you.
Who am I?
I am habit!!!

–Author unknown

Let's look at an example you can really relate to. As a student, you already have learned the powerful impact of habits through your studies. Good study habits will improve your performance on test scores and written homework. For example, some good study habits include studying a little bit each day, studying in a designated area with good lighting, reviewing work each day after class, and becoming involved in a study group. Some bad study habits include cramming the night before a test, studying on your bed which is made for sleeping, reading assigned readings and doing homework at the last possible moment before they are required, and never using the resources available with other students. Once again, every individual will determine through hundreds of daily choices and decisions whether the success seed of habit is developed into a healthy success seed.

The process that replaces a bad habit with a good habit is one that requires constant application. Most behavioralists believe that a minimum of twenty one days is necessary to replace a bad habit with a good habit. Probably the greatest expert on habits that has ever lived is Benjamin Franklin. He had a unique style in breaking the chains of his own bad habits. He felt that bad habits were the greatest obstacle for any person to reaching a high level of stature. Let's look at how Benjamin Franklin, taken from his own diary and in his own words, substituted his bad habits for good ones.

> **I made a little book in which I allotted a page for each of the virtues I desired. I ruled each page with red ink so as to have seven columns, one for each day of the week, marking each column with a letter for the day. I crossed these columns with thirteen red lines, making the beginning of each line with the first letter of one of thirteen desired virtues, on which line and its proper column I might mark by a little black spot, every fault I found upon examination to have been committed respecting that virtue upon that day.**
>
> **I determined to give a week's strict attention to each of the thirteen virtues successively. Thus in the first week my great guard was to avoid even the least offense against Temperance, one of my desired virtues, leaving the other virtues to their ordinary chance, only marking every evening the faults of the day. Thus, if in the first week I could keep my first line, marked T, clear of spots, I supposed the habit of that virtue so much strengthened and its opposite weakened that I might venture extending my attention to include the next, and for the following week keep both lines clear of spots. Proceeding thus to the last, I could go through a course complete in thirteen weeks and four courses a year. And like him who, having a garden to weed, does not attempt to eradicate all the bad herbs at once, which would**

> **exceed his reach and his strength, but works on one of the beds at a time, and, having accomplished the first, proceeds to a second, so should I have, I hoped, the encouraging pleasure of seeing on my pages the progress I made in virtue by clearing successively my lines of their spots till in the end by a number of courses I should be happy in viewing a clean book after a thirteen-weeks' daily examination.**
>
> **I entered upon the execution of this plan for self-examination and continued it with occasional intermissions for some time. I was surprised to find myself so much fuller of faults than I had imagined; but I had the satisfaction of seeing them diminish. To avoid the trouble of renewing now and then my little book, which, by scraping out the marks on the paper of old faults to make room for new ones in a new course, became full of holes, I transferred my tables and precepts to the ivory leaves of a memorandum book on which the lines were drawn with red ink that made a durable stain, and on those lines I marked my faults with a black lead pencil, which marks I could easily wipe out with a wet sponge. After awhile I went through one course only in a year, and afterward only one in several years, till at length I omitted them entirely, being employed in voyages and business abroad with a multiplicity of affairs that interfered; but I always carried my little book with me.**

In his own words, that takes a person some time to understand due to his unique writing style, Benjamin Franklin basically pointed out that changes in habits are a daily task. During your lifetime you have accumulated thousands of habits. Hopefully, most of them are good ones. Along with those good habits, you have many that are harmful and if you were pressed, you could compile a fairly complete list of them like Franklin did. Based upon the discussion of Benjamin Franklin, personal experiences, and suggestions of well-known human development trainers, it is suggested that you do the following six steps.

- Identify the specific bad habit that is undesirable.
- Identify the specific good habit that will replace the undesirable habit.
- List and write down the specific steps that can be accomplished daily to create the habit change.
- Practice the new habit for a minimum of 21 days by applying the specific steps of the new habit.
- Keep a daily record of how well you do on a notepad, small book, or note cards.
- Repeat this process by working on a second bad habit and continue this as a part of your life.

It is also suggested that you make the elimination of bad habits an on-going process. Successful people who have been interviewed commonly suggest that you should pick someone who you admire for a specific behavior. Observe that person in the specific behavior and identify characteristics and traits found in the person. Apply those characteristics and traits individually, one by one, over a long period of time. Eventually, you will begin to demonstrate the exact behavior you originally admired. The keys tend to be **observation** and **application**. Observe what you desire, and apply it through specific steps of change for 21 one days. This form of discipline will bring about a feeling of confidence and understanding that change is enhanced based upon the person's desire and persistence.

MOVING TOWARDS OUR PERSONAL POTENTIAL

All four of these success seeds blend into one concept. Better self-awareness is created and a person's capacity is increased. Self-awareness is a thorough understanding of one's own identity and own weaknesses and strengths, and sets the stage for improvement. People must always keep in mind where they are and where they are going. Self-awareness creates patience and establishes a solid foundation for progression towards worthy goals and one's own potential. Once a person has a healthy and true understanding of his or her present situation, then a focused-in view of the future road of travel towards worthy goals becomes clear. The old saying, "If a person is not moving forward, then he is moving backward" seems true. An individual must constantly move forward, progressing towards the established worthy goals in order to be headed in the correct direction. Focus, expectations, enthusiasm, and discipline are required tools to move us in the right direction to reach our personal best. In essence, we must constancy feed our self-worth and value. This "spirit" of always attempting to improve oneself is very important if a person is to continue in the direction of self-actualization. If a salesperson had the greatest sales year ever in 2003 and was named the company's top salesperson, he will have to prove himself all over again in 2004. Many people have said that it is easy to get to the top in their profession; the hard part is staying there. If there is not continued progression, then the true potential of the person will never be accomplished.

The "Feed the Pigs" Spirit

Focus
Expectations
Enthusiasm
Discipline

Knute Rockne, the legendary coach for Notre Dame, was an inspiration in many people's lives. In fact, he had the ability of helping young men realize their greatest potential. Most particularly, Rockne coached and inspired George Gipp towards his potential. George Gipp, with the coaching of Knute Rockne, became one of the most dedicated and brilliant players of all time. In fact, he was so loved and committed to the game of football, that he eventually died for the cause. He kept moving toward personal improvement till he died.

This is told of George Gipp.

> "At Notre Dame George Gipp came under the influence of the immortal coach, Knute Rockne. Gipp absorbed the spirit of this great coach to a point where he breathed Rockne's rhythm and lived his enthusiasm. It was only natural that effective play execution came in turn. Gipp learned to do everything well. He blocked and kicked and passed and ran and tackled better than any other college player who ever played the game. Many sports writers indicated that he was the total and complete performer–closer to perfection than all other players to ever play the sport. He truly was able to maintain and play to his full potential every day. Gipp had no bad playing days. He was constant like a fixed star. He was always in good physical condition, yet came out of the game drained of every ounce of energy and exhausted from having given everything he had. This was the way Gipp did things. He was in the game all the way, and he fought for the glory of Notre Dame rather than for personal applause. He was indifferent to publicity. The only satisfaction he asked was to know he was accomplishing something, being productive, making a contribution. Rockne learned to trust Gipp, to place confidence in Gipp's confidence, and to rely on him to pull the team through tough spots with his own ingenuity.
>
> In the latter part of the 1920 season, Gipp fell sick. Rockne later said: "In our final game against Northwestern at Evanston, Gipp got out of the sick bed to make the trip. I used him very little that day. We were winning. The final score was 33 to 7. But, in the last quarter the stands chanted Gipp's name so loud and long that I finally sent him in for a few plays on the ice-covered field with the wind off Lake Michigan cutting us all to the bone. He played brilliantly. After the fans had been appeased, I got him out as soon as I could. But, he returned to school with a raging fever. Gipp went back to his sick

> bed, from which he never got up. Pneumonia had him backed up against his own goal line. He lived barely two weeks."
> Rockne sat at his bedside as Gipp lay dying. Someone said, "It's pretty tough to go." "What's tough about it?" Gipp smiled feebly. "I have no complaints, Rock," he said, "I know I'm going. It's alright; I'm not afraid." His eyes brightened with their flames of pallor. "But," he added, "I would like to make one last request. Sometime, Rock, when the going isn't so easy–sometime when the team's up against it and things are going wrong, when the odds are against the team and the breaks are beating the boys, then tell them, Rock, tell them to win one for the Gipper. I don't know where I'll be then, Rock; but I will know about it and I will be happy." A moment later Gipp was gone.
>
> In a 1938 game, Army and Notre Dame were playing to an overflow crowd. At the half the score was 0 to 0. The members of the Notre Dame team were badly battered and bruised, hardly being able to drag themselves to the dressing room at the end of the half. It was then that Rockne granted Gipp's wish and for the first time told the boys what Gipp had said. The rest is history. A sobbing band of Fighting Irish raced out onto the field to meet Army for the last half. Grantland Rice later said: "When Notre Dame lined up for the kickoff, I knew they were playing with a 12th man, George Gipp. Then, I watched that inspired team as they went smashing, clawing, passing, driving, 80 yards to victory. And, somewhere, the great heart of George Gipp must have been happy."

The spirit of George Gipp is really no different than that of any individual who realizes his potential and is constantly aware of his present situation. We learn from George Gipp that we must constantly improve ourselves as we climb a rung of a ladder long enough to grab the next rung up. Successful people really learn to understand themselves in terms of talents, skills, strengths, weaknesses, and habits. They learn to constantly push towards their potential. Every time they attempt to accomplish something, they try to improve on their past performance and move closer towards their potential.

NURTURING THE SEEDS OF SUCCESS

It was mentioned in the previous section that a **success seed** is like a two-edged sword. If not nurtured properly, the seed can enslave us as well as strengthen us. Here are some helpful hints that will allow you to nurture your success seeds so that you will become a successful person.

- **Take Inventory**: Take a pencil and paper and list all of your talents, skills, and assets. Do a strength chart, and you will find out that you are far from being broke.
- **Read Success Stories**: Read the biographies of men and women from every walk of life and every race of life who used what they had to build a successful life.
- **Listen and Read**: Listen and study speakers and teachers who build mankind–Norman Vincent Peale, Zig Ziglar, Dale Carnegie, Napoleon Hill, and Og Mandino among others. You'll find that the attributes and ideas that they promote have a way of fitting easily into everyday life and will mold us into successful people.
- **Build in Steps**: Start in an area where you know you can succeed–remember that **success breeds success**. Once you have accomplished success there, move another step and then another.
- **Service**: Do something, a small act of service or kindness, for someone else. This involves the same principle of **what you give out comes back to you**. In becoming a millionaire, Andrew Carnegie made 38 other men millionaires.
- **Selection of Associates**: Remember, it is a proven fact that you acquire much of the thinking, mannerisms, ideals, and characteristics of the people you are around, whether they are good or bad influences.
- **Accentuate the Positive**: Look for good in other people and develop the habit of giving sincere praises and "strokes" to others. In a world filled with negative, everyone needs a positive extra boost now and then.
- **Victory Journal**: Keep a diary of all your successes and good experiences. Periodically review and update this journal. Add on to this book until you have filled it up--when this happens, start another. As you keep these successes in a journal, you will be reminded that you have succeeded in the past and that you can do it again when things become difficult and discouraging.
- **Filter**: Watch carefully what you put in your mind. Negative, positive, good or bad, is recorded in your mind, and it will build and repair or reduce and tear down your self-esteem and worth.
- **Join A Group**: Join a group with worthwhile goals in which you meet for an hour each week to discuss goals, dreams, and motivation, and to be just uplifted.

These are some of the gardening tools we have use to nurture and constantly feed my success seeds. Try a few of them or try them all–you will be pleasantly surprised with the outcome. You will also enjoy the satisfaction that comes as you learn how to "Feed the Pigs."

Practical Application Exercise–Achievement Paper

Read the following paragraphs first. Answer the questions in order. There are no wrong answers. Do not answer these questions for your instructor's approval but do answer all of the questions honestly. Take the time needed to think about your answers.

Everyone with ability finds a challenge in completing this paper. Most people are willing to admit and study their mistakes; but few are willing to risk admitting and studying their achievements. When you take this risk, you will come to know the best that is in you and recognize opportunities faster. Whenever you have done something well, enjoyed doing it, and were proud of it, you have made use of the best that's in you. Such an experience is called an **achievement** in this questionnaire.

Everyone has had experiences like that, at least once in a while–at school, at home, in social activities, in community life, perhaps through hobbies, athletics, and other activities. In early childhood, your achievements may have seemed small, but you have had greater and lesser ones since then. Some of the things you feel are achievements might seem like "nothing" to other people; so remember that what really counts is the way "you" feel about your experiences.

Please answer the following questions:

1. What is the achievement that first comes to your mind? Please describe it briefly. What age were you at the time?

2. What activities give you the most pleasure when you are not at work?

3. After leaving high school, which two or three subjects did you study and enjoy most?

4. Outline in the spaces below, in just a few words, as many of your achievements as you can. Reflect over your entire life and identify those major accomplishments. It will help you to remember if you try to think of two or more for each three years of your life. Write them as they come to mind; they probably will not be in chronological order.
   A.

   B.

   C.

   D.

E.

F.

G.

H.

I.

J.

K.

L.

M.

5. Now, place checks at the left of those you feel are your five greatest achievements. Go back to question four.

6. Now re-examine the five you have checked. Which is the greatest of them all? Identify the five and put the greatest next to the letter A and the next by the letter B and so on.

A.

B.

C.

D.

E.

7. What is the earliest achievement you can recall? This should be something done before the age of 10, perhaps even when you were around 5.

8. Between the ages 12 and 18, while in or out of school, what was your greatest achievement?

9. Look back to question six in which you identified your five greatest achievements. Now, in the space provided below, describe the top achievement in sufficient detail to show what you actually did, where it took place, and the results which made the achievement important to you.

10. Your family is raised successfully; you have a guaranteed income of $75,000 per year; everything you want is paid for; your children are happily married and financially independent. What would you like to do for the next 20 years?

11. If you could be someone other than yourself, of all the people who have ever lived on the earth, who would you most like to be? Why?

12. If you were to leave this community and had to leave an object behind which you felt represented you, what would you leave? Why?

13. Given an opportunity to write the engraving on your headstone or monument for use after your death, what would you write?

14. What are your three greatest strengths? What are your three greatest weaknesses?

FIVE

FACTORS IN SELLING YOURSELF

Learning Objectives

When you finish studying the material in this chapter, you should be able to:

1. Explain how first impressions are developed.
2. Describe the elements of nonverbal communication.
3. Discuss the three body language rules.
4. Describe the elements of verbal language.
5. Describe the elements of surface language.
6. Identify the five dress guidelines.
7. Explain how the personality is developed.
8. Identify ways to build a persuasive personality.

Impressions–You are the company!

A corporation may spread itself over the whole world... may employ one hundred thousand . . . yet the average person will form a judgment of the corporation through contact with one single individual. If this person is rude or inefficient, it will require a lot of courtesy and efficiency to overcome the bad impression. Every member of an organization who, in any capacity, comes in contact with the public, is a salesperson; the impression made is an advertisement, good or bad!

–Author unknown

FACTORS IN SELLING YOURSELF

Most of us are quick to make judgments of our fellow humans based on very little information or inaccurate information. We tend to judge each other on first impressions and are slow to change our mind. Because of the impact we can make on people in the first couple of minutes during a social encounter, it is important that salespeople make a favorable positive first impression.

Like it or not, lasting impressions are formed in the first few seconds of an interaction with another person. Usually, the first 30 seconds is all it takes to formulate either a positive or negative impression. If a positive impression is made, you have a good chance to continue the conversation. If you make a negative impression, chances favor the person not wanting to further the discussion, and the person will attempt to cut off the discussion as soon as possible. It should be your goal to make a positive impression with everyone you meet, especially those you meet in a selling situation and remember the important points found in the next illustration.

The First Encounter

- **Initial emotional judgment.**
- **Formed in 30 seconds or less.**
- **Four-minute barrier.**
- **Lasting impact.**

Think of what happens when you meet someone for the first time. Part of your impression is formed from subconscious assessments of tone of voice, firmness of a handshake, types of gestures and mannerisms, style of walk, type of dress, physical makeup, and type of personality. The purpose of this chapter is to teach you what you must do to be able to create positive first impressions during your social encounters with other people, especially in selling situations. Learning to package yourself will be a great tool during your lifetime.

CONTACT–THE FIRST FOUR MINUTES

One of the best books written on developing first impressions is ***Contact: The First Four Minutes*** by Leonard and Natalie Zunie. The authors state that the first four minutes are the most crucial, or the average time in which strangers interact before they decide to continue or end their encounter with other people. This four-minute concept applies to everyone, especially people in the selling industry. We have all been somewhere and wanted to talk to the individual next to us. We search for a way to open the conversation. When we do this, we are faced with the **four-minute barrier**, or the amount of time it takes to be received or rejected. **Contact** is the way a person meets and relates to other people during this initial interaction. When we meet someone for the first time, many things help contribute to what the person says to us. In fact, gestures, posture, facial expressions, and other nonverbal communication contribute 58 percent of what is said to others. We will now discuss all the crucial elements that help form the image we give to other people during our first encounters.

First Impression Factors

- **55% comes from what we see.**
  - **–Facial expressions**
  - **–Body language**
  - **–Dress and appearance**
- **38% comes from tone of voice.**
  - **–Rate**
  - **–Pitch**
  - **–Volume**
- **7% comes from our words.**

NONVERBAL COMMUNICATION-BODY LANGUAGE

Much attention has been given to the importance of nonverbal communication, or body language, during the last several decades. The study of nonverbal communication was first popularized when the book, ***Body Language***, by Julius Fast came out in the 1970s. Fast's research in this area made people aware of the importance of body language but was too simplistic but became a foundation for additional studies. The potential for reading and sending nonverbal signals in interacting with others is very exciting. More than two thirds of communication between people can be nonverbal. Nonverbal communication is **body language–the physical projection of words**. Body language messages that are given off by a person help form the basis of impressions and intentions. By taking advantage and becoming aware of nonverbal body cues, a salesperson can increase the level of success in selling to customers.

Eyes

In the book, ***Contact: The First Four Minutes***, the eyes are referred to as the primary form of nonverbal contact. You can really learn how to read a person from eye signals. A darting look and lowering eyes gives a signal of "I don't trust you." Staring is impolite, and many times increases the possibility of a fight or other threatening feelings. When eyebrows are raised with a smile, this sign shows that there is interest. A wink can suggest that you have a secret.

Especially in selling situations, a salesperson must maintain eye contact with the buyer. A good general rule to follow is the **80/20 rule**. While conversing with the buyer, maintain eye contact 80 percent of the time and occasionally look away 20 percent of the time to avoid coming across as staring which may become threatening to some people. When eye contact is interrupted for a long period of time during a sales presentation, the buyer may develop feelings that are negative. Some of these feelings may be that the salesperson is lying, being deceptive, lacking confidence, or simply not caring and showing no interest. Eyes can smile, and many emotions are conveyed by eye contact. Experience will help you learn how to use the messages from the eyes as an aid and information source.

Body Messages

Besides concentrating on the eyes for revealing information about others, spend time in noticing the body messages that are given off. By body messages we mean postures, positions, movements, hands, gestures, mannerisms, touching, and space.

Postures and positions: When people are tense, defensive, and just unreceptive, they give off specific body gestures. When a person crosses the legs, he/she could be giving a sign that the person is relaxed and receptive to what you are saying. The important concept with body messages is that people speak in clusters of signals, therefore learn to recognize the compatibility that is found among the various messages given off at one time. Leaning forward in a chair can indicate that the person is interested in what you are discussing.

Salespeople attempt to get products in the hands of buyers to prevent them from crossing their arms, a sign that could mean defensiveness or appearing to be unreceptive. Generally, any change of position may indicate a change of mind. Salespeople are very concerned about body postures and positions because of the old saying **actions speak louder than words**.

Another good body message is the tilting of the head. When a buyer nods the head up and down, he/she may be agreeing with what you are saying. Moving the head closer to you generally indicates interest in you. When the prospect is busy or out of time, one may move back and forth or move around. One of the most obvious movements is when a person looks at the watch; this shows that a person is concerned about time–he/she may be in a hurry or has an appointment.

One of my favorite movements of the body to observe deals with the hands. Hands help us communicate and draw pictures to express size, shape, or direction. Hands also can express authority and acceptance. Clasped hands can indicate tension or anger. The tapping on a desk suggests restlessness, boredom or impatience. We have all seen people hit their foreheads when they forget something. Some people who have studied body language say that when people touch their nose, this indicates that they don't believe what you are saying. A person may stroke his chin when one is evaluating what you are saying.

You need to learn how to read the body messages given off by your buyers. When I was selling in the retail environment, I remembered many people reaching for their checkbook or wallet and how this sign often led to a commitment to buy because the buyer was determining how much money he had. If you do not remember anything else about body language in this chapter remember what John T. Molloy said in his book ***Dress for Success***–**"Although you cannot control other people, particularly strangers, by reading their body signals, you can control the way other people will react to you if you control your own body signals."**

A person's private bubble: One of the most interesting concepts that I have been exposed to in selling is that all people prefer certain distances with the people with whom they are communicating. Every person has an invisible bubble around them. The distance that exists between two people can result from their personalities, purpose of discussion, and how well the two people know each other. Impersonal business or discussions are usually conducted with a distance of 3 to 5 feet. Close friends or family usually are less that 2 feet apart. The more friendly the climate, the closer two people will be towards each other. Larger distances indicate that the situation is very formal or that the two people feel a bit uneasy or uncomfortable with each other. All of us have our own **personal bubble** around us. We do not like people to enter this private bubble unless we give them permission to do so. If this bubble or personal space is invaded without permission, we tend to give off the warning signs that can easily be picked up. Some people become nervous, avoid looking others in the eye, and some even start to perspire. It is a good rule to let the other person know when your space has been invaded. We generally start giving off messages like moving back, stiffening up, or becoming a bit offensive. Introverts tend to have a larger personal bubble than extroverts. It is helpful to know what personality type your buyer is so that you won't create an uneasy buying atmosphere from the beginning.

Touching: Touching should be done with extreme caution. We all tend to do a bit of touching in shaking hands with others. A firm handshake indicates friendliness and confidence. If it is too long, it may come across as too forward and intimate. On the other hand, a limp or loose handshake shows unfriendliness and maybe a lack of self-confidence. Some people like to put their hand on the shoulder or back of others. This may relax a person, but generally can embarrass others or give off the wrong signals. A general rule of thumb to follow in selling situations is to limit any amount of touching to a handshake.

Mirroring: Every salesperson should build an atmosphere during the selling situation that is positive and comfortable. One way to do this is to assume the same body postures, gestures, and positions as the customer. This concept called **mirroring** helps establish a level of trust and rapport between the salesperson and the customer. In establishing a positive buying environment, the seller can often assume the same body angle as the customer. If, when seated, the customer leans back, the salesperson can also lean back and relax. The seller can take the lead in mirroring and give off body signals to promote more of a open and friendly environment. Leaning forward, opening up your arms, and nodding your head will suggest cues to the buyer and often the buyer will mirror the same signals. By exhibiting positive body signals, and through assuming the same signals given off by the buyer, the selling atmosphere can become more friendly and make the buyer feel more at ease.

Guidelines In Understanding Body Language

To summarize our discussion on body language, four general guidelines should be followed to avoid any misunderstanding. These guidelines will assist you in understanding what other people are really saying with their body gestures.

Four Body Language Rules

- **One signal can have multiple meanings.**
- **We speak in clusters.**
- **When there is a contradiction, believe the body signal.**
- **Avoid annoying body signals.**

Rule One: **One body signal can have multiple meanings**. To think that "crossing the arms" always means a person is closed or defensive can be wrong. People also cross their arms when they relax and when they are cold. The same is true when a person is looking at his/her watch. A person isn't always showing impatience. Looking at your watch could also show that you are just interested in the time, or checking to see how much time you have left before you have to make a departure, and sometimes it is just a habit. Based on the person's background and body language habits, one signal can have multiple meanings.

Rule Two: **People speak in clusters**. To understand what a person is really saying nonverbally, look for multiple signals or clusters. If a person looks at one's watch, begins to yawn, and backs away from you, you can generally come to the conclusion that the person wants to leave you. One body signal can fool you, but several signals in a cluster usually are reliable in signifying a specific message or idea.

Rule Three: **When a contradiction occurs, believe the nonverbal message**. Again, actions speak louder than words. Whenever a person verbally says one thing and then gives off nonverbal signals that contradict the verbal message, you are usually safe in believing the nonverbal signal. People find it easier to mask their voice and words, but find more difficulty in masking their body signals that exists below the neck.

Rule Four: **Avoid annoying body signals**. Every person has one or several mannerisms that may annoy another person if they appear often within a short period of time. It would be wise for every person to videotape him/herself often to identify those body signals that are dominant in his/her body language. Also, every person needs to avoid obvious annoying body actions. In ***Successful Selling Strategies,*** Charles L. Lapp identifies the most common annoying mannerisms that every salesperson should avoid.

The Twenty Most Annoying Mannerisms–Charles L. Lapp

1. **Scratching of the head.**
2. **Running hand or comb through hair.**
3. **Screwing at an ear.**
4. **Raising eyebrows.**
5. **Picking nose or teeth.**
6. **Clearing throat often.**
7. **Chewing lip or chewing gum vigorously.**
8. **Constantly adjusting tie.**
9. **Cracking knuckles.**
10. **Hitching at the pants.**
11. **Cleaning fingernails while talking.**
12. **Pacing around while talking.**
13. **Slapping the buyer on the back.**
14. **Pointing continually.**
15. **Pushing right to the face while talking.**
16. **Coughing without covering mouth.**
17. **Butting in when the buyer is talking to someone else.**
18. **Doodling with a pencil or pen.**
19. **Fingering a card or paper.**
20. **Scowling when an order isn't obtained.**

VERBAL COMMUNICATION

A person's verbal communication can create a positive buying atmosphere and give the salesperson selling power. In this area of verbal communication, we will discuss the persuasive tool of words and also touch on areas like voice characteristics and tone.

Elements of Verbal Language

- **Tone of voice**
  –Pitch, volume, and rate.
- **Words**
  –Positive and persuasive.
- **Figures of speech**
  –Simile (like, as)
  –Metaphors (is)

Tone: The tone of your voice can show positive or negative attitudes to the listener. If you increase your voice pitch, you tend to keep people's attention and seem more alive and enthusiastic. A monotone voice is boring to most buyers. It is good to fluctuate your tone of voice during a conversation. You need to find a happy medium between soft and loud, as loud can be offensive, and speaking too softly may lose the listener.

I had the privilege of listening to Dick Nourse, the anchorman for KSL News of Salt Lake City. He indicated that when he started broadcasting nearly 40 years ago, he was told that the best way to establish credibility and authority was to lower your tone of voice and speak a little slower. This is something to think about as you prepare your next sales presentation.

Voice characteristics: Using proper voice characteristics with appropriate timing can aid you in a successful conversation. **Zig Ziglar**, one of the top sales motivators and trainers in the country, says that **the most persuasive tool a person has is his own voice.** Timing in speaking is very important. Interrupting may indicate a desire to dominate and is often rude. Few people like to be interrupted. Long pauses before answering a question may indicate that the answer may be false, as the person is thinking of something to say. Some characteristics that are distracting are mumbling, mispronouncing words, overuse of slang, and a lack of enthusiasm in the voice. It is a good tool to use modulation and fluctuation of the voice throughout the presentation.

Words: Using words that stir up positive meaning in customers are usually best for achieving your selling goals. You should use words that are persuasive and positive. The 12 most persuasive words in the English language today, based on research done by Dorothy Leads and found in the October 99 issue of ***Sales Doctors Magazine***.

The Twelve Most Persuasive Words

You	**Results**	**Love**
Easy	**Discovery**	**Proven**
Money	**Free**	**Health**
Guarantee	**Save**	**New**

You should avoid words that convey meanings of unhappiness or unpleasant events, such as mistake, problem, wrong, damage, error, and failure. Also, avoid words that sound unpleasant to the ear, such as itch, bloody, sticky, guts, creepy, sloppy, and grime. Generally, be careful about the words you use and avoid using slang.

In summary, use words that have positive meanings. There may be a few times in which you need a strong word that gives emphasis; a negative word may be appropriate, but this is seldom the case. Always attempt to be simple and speak on a level that can be understood by the buyer. Use words that create a good atmosphere with the buyer.

Figures of speech: Certain figures of speech can aid you in your selling situations. They can help you describe or explain the product to the buyer. Two common figures of speech are **similes** and **metaphors**. A simile is comparing the familiar qualities of two items. For example, you would say, "This car is as quiet as a burning match," or "He works like a horse." The key is using the words “like” or “as.” Another example of a simile is, "This electric hot-water heater is so well insulated that it is just like a big thermos bottle." Again, you compare two qualities of two different items or objects.

A metaphor is very similar to a simile but the words like or as are omitted. Taking the example from above, you would create a metaphor by saying, "He is a real workhorse." Another example is, "This idea is a real penny pincher." Using figures of speech brings in creativity and helps create a picture for the buyer. A metaphor is using a word to literally connote an object or idea.

One of my favorite figures of speech is called a **euphemism**. A euphemism is when you substitute a more pleasant word for the one that may offend or suggest something unpleasant. Some examples are found in the illustration below.

Euphemism Examples

Next to new instead of used.
Inexpensive instead of cheap.
Sanitary engineer instead of garbage man.
Custodian instead of janitor.
Unattractive instead of ugly.
Associate instead of salesperson.
County landfill instead of county dump.
Domestic engineer instead of housewife.

Figures of speech can strengthen your presentation, but care must be used not to overuse them and not to replace important information that the customer should know.

APPEARANCE OR SURFACE LANGUAGE

We have discussed several items that must be considered in developing a persuasive package of yourself. The area of appearance is of great importance. When you meet a person for the first time, the first thing that is noticed is your appearance: your clothes and grooming habits. If you do not have a good appearance, you can lose the opportunity to further your interaction with the other person even before you open your mouth. When I say appearance, I refer to a person's grooming, dress, and physical makeup. We can't do much to improve our physical features, like a large nose, but we can improve our appearance by concentrating on good grooming habits and learn some basic guidelines on dress. We all know basic grooming rules like clean fingernails, clean hair, pressed clothes, and a clean body. I want to concentrate on developing positive surface language, which is the combination of grooming and dress. Surface language can play a major role in your ability to formulate a positive first impression. Today, there are some unwritten rules as to how a person should dress. We need to be aware of what is accepted because **what we wear will immediately establish our credibility and likeness.** Ego Von Furstenberg says in his book ***The Power Look***, **"In the business world, discrimination by appearance is a fact of life."** Let's look at what some authorities say about dress so that we will not be hindered in getting the jobs and meeting the people we want in life.

Dress

The key word for your dress is **appropriate**. It is possible to overdress and to underdress. Your dress can be too stylish, too far out of style, too formal or informal. Especially in the selling profession, a well-managed appearance will communicate positive feelings and establish credibility. Some salespeople are told to dress as if they are a success--in essence "fake it till you make it." Be sure you have good taste and good sense when it comes to what you wear. There are five general guidelines that can be used in assisting salespeople in their dress preparation. These five guidelines are **desired image by the firm or industry, products or services sold, type of customer served, physical characteristics and body makeup**, and **unwritten dress rules by dress authorities.**

Desired image by the firm or industry: The first thing a salesperson should do is to look at the competition, the industry, and the desired look of the seller's company. If you are in a very professional, businesslike atmosphere, selling data-processing equipment or computers, the unwritten dress code in the industry is at least a shirt and tie; more appropriate would be a sports coat or suit. IBM had a company dress code for years stating that their salespeople must wear a white shirt, blue sports coat, and a tie. Surveys that have been done with IBM's competition and customers state that the white shirt is an asset to IBM's salespeople, and the white shirt gives them moral superiority over their competition. IBM wants their salespeople to maintain this image. Even IBM's competition believes that they should adopt the white shirt if they are to successfully compete with IBM. Other industries like the automotive, agricultural and discount retailing industries allow people to dress more casually. Once again, take a look at your competition and industry and be sure to dress so that you fit in and don't look out of place.

Five Dress Guidelines

- ➩**Desired image.**
- ➩**Product or service sold.**
- ➩**Type of customer.**
- ➩**Body make-up.**
- ➩**Dress rules and guidelines.**

Products and services sold: If your products are very expensive and complex, your dress should be more on a formal basis, (suit and tie) than informal. Salespeople in retail clothing sales usually wear a shirt and tie. A salesclerk in an automotive parts store can get by with a clean, colored shirt and no tie. Many salespeople in industrial sales who sell cleaning supplies have to adjust their dress based on the type of buyers they work with. If they are selling to large organizations, a suit may be more appropriate than a sports coat.

Type of customer served: Much of this area has been covered in the first two topics of industry and type of goods sold. One item that must be mentioned is your customer. If your customer is very shy, reserved, and feels uncomfortable with authoritative figures, you may be wise to "dress down" or be a bit informal. Instead of wearing a pin-stripe suit, wear a sports coat. If your customer is very businesslike, professional, or authoritative, dress in a dark suit so that your desired image is more professional and businesslike.

Physical characteristics and body makeup: This area is very crucial because you want to dress according to what your body allows. You don't want to emphasize the negative and you do want to emphasize the positive. Many people dress for failure because they wear clothing that conflicts with items like color or physical build. Husky or overweight people tend to look better in darker colors or stripes because these colors and patterns tend to trim their appearance. Short people look taller in pin-stripes and tall people look shorter in mild plaids. Large people should be careful wearing dark pin-stripes, as this pattern tends to look more authoritative, especially to people who feel uncomfortable with figures of authority.

Written dress rules by dress authorities: The original research on dress was put together during the 1970s and is found in the book ***Dress for Success***, by John T. Molloy. Molloy stimulated the interest in dress and how it can assist you in becoming more successful. His early research still provides some sound guidelines on how to effectively package yourself. Molloy has been called America's first wardrobe engineer and below are some of his general rules accepted by most industries.

- Avoid high fashion and exaggerated styles of clothing. These constantly changing fashion swings suggest instability, immaturity, and undependability to your client, customer, or prospect.
- Never wear double-knit suits, sport coats, pants, or shirts. Double-knit material has an unmistakably inexpensive look. Double knit has the tendency to say all the wrong things about you. Wear wool or wool blend fabrics and cotton shirts.
- Wear dark brown, burgundy, or black shoes for business. Anything else is too flashy and destroys your credibility. In addition, wear over-the-calf socks to avoid showing your legs when you cross them.
- Wear darker clothing for more serious selling or business situations. The more serious the situation, the more serious the color of the suit. Remember, lighter colors, although friendlier and not intimidating, must be reserved for less serious sales calls or business meetings.

- Make sure all your accessories, such as watches and jewelry, are simple and tasteful. Gaudy, flashy accessories give you the untrustworthy and shifty air of the proverbial "honest John" used-car salesman.

Most of Molloy 's early research and suggestions are for the male gender, however, he has come out with guidelines specifically for the female gender that can be found in his book ***The Women's Dress for Success Book***. Additional experts have come out with helpful information that can provide some sound guidelines today in effectively packaging yourself for dress success in business. Mr. Molloy's research originated with the questions he asked 100 top executives throughout the country. They are found with their responses below.

100 TOP EXECUTIVES ARE ASKED ABOUT DRESS

The following information is taken from a survey of 100 top executives of major corporations by John T. Molloy, author of ***Dress for Success***.

Question: Does your company have a written or an unwritten dress code?
Answer: Ninety-seven said yes. Three said no. Only two had a written dress code.

Question: Would a number of people at your firm have a much better chance of getting ahead if they knew how to dress?
Answer: Ninety-six said yes, four said no.

Question: If there were a course in how to dress for business, would you send your son or daughter?
Answer: All 100 said yes.

Question: Do you think employee dress affects the general tone of the office?
Answer: All 100 said yes.

Question: Do you think employee dress affects efficiency?
Answer: Fifty-two said yes, forty-eight said no.

Question: Would you hold up the promotion of a person who didn't dress properly?
Answer: Seventy-two said yes, twenty-eight said no.

Question: Would you tell a young person if his dress was holding him back?
Answer: Eighty said no, twenty said yes.

Question: Does your company at present turn down people who show up at job interviews improperly dressed on that basis alone?
Answer: Eighty-four said yes, sixteen said no.

PERSONALITY

When choosing people for sales work, most sales managers would prefer a workable personality over specialized training. Many companies have a policy for hiring salespeople as they seek people with certain fundamental personality characteristics, then proceed to furnish the necessary sales training. We have discussed in this chapter several factors to consider in developing positive first impressions. Your personality can help you maintain this positive first impression or change the impression if it is a negative one. A person's personality is unique because it distinguishes one person from another and it is that which makes an impression on others. A personality can help determine if people like or dislike you. You should know that there is no such thing as an ideal personality, but there are some things you can incorporate in your life that will make your personality more persuasive and appealing. Before we discuss those things that will give you a persuasive personality, let us first define exactly what makes up your personality.

Key Points of the Personality

- ➪**Consists of many things.**
- ➪**First five years are crucial.**
- ➪**Can be reprogrammed during life.**
- ➪**Many strategies exist to improve it.**

Personality is a sum total of many things

Your personality is very complex and is a sum total of several things. Among the most important elements that make up your personality are your traits, attitudes, personal experiences, physical characteristics, attributes, and your environment. Your personality determines how you will react and interact to the world around you. Personality is the outward expression of an individual's personal worth, which is made up of all the things that are learned and acquired throughout life. As mentioned before, personality includes the qualities and traits that people like or dislike about you.

A personality is developed throughout life

People have wondered, "When do we develop our personality?" Most psychologists will agree that our personality is starting to form from the day we are born. The years that seem to be most crucial are ages 1 to 5. Our family has a great influence on us, but our personality continues to develop as we grow because of our relationships that are developed and the experiences we have. Our minds are very complex and are very similar to a tape recorder. From day one, we record everything we see, hear, and experience. Even though our conscious mind can't recall all this information, our subconscious mind stores all the information that we acquire. Every time we experience something, it is just like entering a new program into our computer-like tape recorder. We draw on these stored programs whenever we are faced with a situation. Past experiences will often determine how we meet the situations we are faced with in the future. These programs in our mind determine how we handle life's situations and how others will act towards us.

We can reprogram our mind

We discussed how we develop our personality early in life, but we must realize that we can change parts of our personality by going through a reprogramming process. We can program our minds with thoughts of failure that will instruct us to produce failure. We can also reprogram our minds by entering thoughts of success that will produce healthy productivity. Ben Franklin teaches us a simple way of reprogramming ourselves. His method of doing this is simply to select a trait to improve on and write it down on a card with specific instructions on how to put the desired change into practice. Keep this card in your pocket for quick and easy reference and practice this desired behavior trait for a week. By making a conscious effort, you actually begin to alter an undesirable behavior trait into a desirable trait that will improve your personality. We all should spend time in reprogramming our mental computer. The following guidelines contain some areas that you may want to concentrate on in developing a more persuasive personality.

TEN WAYS TO BUILD A PERSUASIVE PERSONALITY

1. **Learn to be socially sensitive**: Learn to practice good manners, respect opinions of others, and avoid offending others by using profanity, dirty jokes, interrupting, and smoking without permission.
2. **Call people by their names**: The most magical sound in any language is a person's own name. Learn to pronounce names correctly. Develop a system so that you can remember a person's name and call the person by his/her correct or desired name. Any conversation becomes warm and personal when names are used.
3. **Make others feel important**: Learn to give recognition and encouragement to others. Learn to speak well of all people and look for the good in all people. Develop the talent of giving sincere praise that is specific and deserving.

4. **Learn to project a spontaneous smile**: Smiling makes you a pleasant person to be around and it also promotes a positive atmosphere. A smile can open doors and reduce tension.
5. **Develop a genuine interest in others**: Learn to be a good listener and encourage other people to talk about themselves. Attempt to see things from the other person's point-of-view before making any judgments. Talk about things that interest other people.
6. **Keep appointments and follow through**: Develop the habit of always being early or on time. Follow up on what you do and say and always meet deadlines. If you are going to be late or miss an appointment, please be courteous and call the person in advance.
7. **Be careful with humor**: Avoid dirty and sacrilegious stories based on race, religion, sex, or national origin. Develop an ability to tell jokes well and respond to humor. Remember that humor can relax people and be a great sales tool for breaking the ice and warming up people.
8. **Learn to look people in the eye**: Maintaining good eye contact shows self-confidence, interest, and concern. The skill of good eye contact can provide you great information as you look over and read your buyer during a sales presentation.
9. **Develop good health habits**: Obtain the necessary rest and exercise–this will keep your mind fresh and productive. Good health habits help avoid burn out. A healthy body enhances your ability to think and solve problems.
10. **Watch your appearance and grooming**: Develop the habit of wearing clothes that compliment your physical makeup. Always wear clean and pressed clothing. Always look clean by bathing and watching personal body odor.

Self-Discovery Experience–Do You Make A Good First Impression?

A QUIZ
By Jane Sherrod Singer, M. A.
University of California

Let us grant the fact that the most important thing to do is to "wear well" over a long period of time. However, the impression you make on someone you meet is often a lasting one and very difficult to change. Indeed, there are many times when, if the initial introduction is not satisfactory, there is never another chance. Here are some keys. How many do you have on your chain to unlock the doors of acceptance and friendships?

QUESTION	YES	NO
1. Do you smile readily and often?	❑	❑
2. Are you neatly groomed at all times?	❑	❑
3. Do you have a firm handshake rather than offering what feels like a dead fish?	❑	❑
4. Is your posture naturally straight, shoulders back, head high?	❑	❑
5. When talking to a person do you look into their eyes?	❑	❑
6. Do you speak clearly and audibly instead of mumbling?	❑	❑
7. Do you show special respect, by standing, opening doors, etc. for people who are older than you?	❑	❑
8. Can you stand still instead of shuffling your feet?	❑	❑
9. Do you keep your hands away from your hair and your face?	❑	❑
10. Are your actions free from nervous mannerisms, such as chewing on something, biting on nails, clearing your throat, scratching head?	❑	❑
11. When a person is talking, do you give him/her your undivided attention?	❑	❑
12. Are you genuinely interested in other people?	❑	❑
13. Do you have a number of interests or hobbies?	❑	❑
14. Is your language free from flagrant errors, profanity, and an over-use of slang?	❑	❑
15. Is it habitual for you to use courteous expressions, such as "please" and "thank you?"	❑	❑

ANALYSIS OF "DO YOU MAKE A GOOD FIRST IMPRESSION?"

SCORING: Give yourself **2 points** for each **yes** answer.

YOUR SCORE __________

This is a difficult quiz to score, for a no on any one of these questions might be enough to discourage certain critical people. In general, however, we have found the following analysis to be true.

26-30 Points: You make a very good impression; one that encourages people to want to know you better. It is not difficult for you to land a job and, if you have the necessary qualifications, you will keep it.

12-24 Points: Like many of us, you are no paragon of graciousness. People tend to brush past you In their first meeting, and you have to prove their eyes. A little more polish as indicated by these questions would help you a great deal.

0-10 Points: You are licked before you start and are indeed masterful in driving people away from you. You can help yourself by practicing good manners and self-confidence, the keys to making a good impression.

Assess Yourself–Does Your Body Language Really Give You Away?

Take a few moments and take this body language quiz that will determine how much you really know about the power of body language and its meaning. The answers are found on the next page.

1. When taking leave of someone you want to impress favorably, you'll score more points if you give him or her a friendly pat on the back.
   _________True _________False
2. When a woman touches a man the reaction is quite different from when a man touches a woman.
   _________True _________False
3. If the person you're talking to nods frequently while you're talking, it means that he or she agrees with everything you're saying.
   _________True _________False
4. A facial expression is the most reliable form of nonverbal communication.
   _________True _________False
5. You can control a conversation nonverbally with just one gesture.
   _________True _________False
6. Your clothes can speak louder than you do.
   _________True _________False
7. Looking steadily at the person to whom you are talking affects the way that person sizes you up.
   _________True _________False
8. If you're trying to determine whether the person talking to you is being deceptive and attempting to hide something, there is one gesture that can often tip you off.
   _________True _________False
9. Individuals who often touch other people--putting their hands on their arms or shoulders, patting them on the back--usually lack self-esteem.
   _________True _________False
10. It's easy to tell how much someone likes you by simply observing his or her gestures and movements.
    _________True _________False
11. Women are more inclined than men to overlook the significance of gestures when talking with another person.
    _________True _________False
12. When a person meets you, his/her first impression is more likely to be influenced by your facial expression than how good-looking you are or how you've dressed.
    _________True _________False

ANSWERS TO BODY LANGUAGE QUIZ

1. **False**: In a study at the University of Missouri, male and female subjects had a series of short, get-acquainted sessions with a researcher's associate. In some cases the associate was instructed to touch the person's arm or pat him or her on the back at the end of each session. When the associate left the room, each subject was asked to rate his liking for the associate on a scale of 1 to 5. The results were reported as follows: When the subject and the associate were of the opposite sex, liking for the associate was much greater when the subject received an arm touch rather than a back pat. But liking for the associate was not affected by the type of touch in a same-sex interaction.
2. **True**: A Purdue University study cites research indicating that "tactile closeness (touching) facilitates psychological, interpersonal closeness." Further finds reveal interesting sex differences. On one hand, it was found that when a woman's touch conveys to a man even the slightest suggestion of sexual desire, he considers the touch pleasant and indicative of warmth and affection. And the more she touches him in ways suggestive of sexual desire, the more affectionate, loving and pleasant he interprets it to be. But when a man touches a woman in this way, instead of communicating love, affection, or friendliness, it is likely to convey nothing more to her than sexual desire itself.
3. **False**: A psychiatric study at the Albert Einstein College of Medicine explored the various implications of head nodding, which is an effective, but ambiguous, form of conversation. The researchers explained that a listener's occasional nodding helps keep a conversation going, whereas repeated nods by a listener suggest a lack of interest and often lead the speaker to hesitate or change the subject. Nodding can also be used by the listener to send a "hurry up and get to the point message" or by a speaker to intimidate others.
4. **False**: Body movements of the hands, arms, legs, feet, shoulders, or a person's posture often reveal more about someone's feelings and emotions than do facial gestures, according to studies sponsored by the National Institute of Mental Health. A facial expression can be controlled to give a desired impression, but body movements are seldom contrived or affected and the subject is not likely to be conscious of what the movements reveal to the observer. For example, a person's facial expression may cause him to appear calm and self-confident while his hands and fingers may be twisting nervously.
5. **True**: An Oxford University study of the psychodynamics of gestures and body cues found that when a person speaking keeps his hands in mid-gesture at the end of an utterance, he is indicating there is more to come and thus prevents interruption. The researchers also realized that the last person at whom a speaker looks before ending his utterance is most likely to speak next. This eye contact not only synchronizes thoughts and wishes, but also passes the floor to a particular member of the group.
6. **True**: You can say nothing, but your clothes will still speak for you, or you can be quite talkative and loud and wear plain clothes that may contradict your speech. As such, clothing is likely to play an integral part in social encounters and is an important channel of nonverbal communication.

7. **True**: Studies of the effects of nonverbal behavior conducted at the College of Charleston show that those who gaze steadily at a person during some interaction are judged to be more sincere. And at North East London Polytechnic, a team of investigators using 80 men and women, between ages 20 and 60 as subjects, studied the effects of a steady gaze in real life settings in which a person soliciting money for charity either looked a possible donor in the eye or looked at the money tin. Significantly more money was donated in the former situation.
8. **True**: The gesture is the "hand shrug"–the spreading of the hands with palms upturned in the you-see-I-have-nothing-to-hide gesture. In psychological tests at the University of California, it was found that the "hand shrug" increased to a marked extent in interviews in which subjects were trying to deceive or withhold information.
9. **False**: According to the findings of a study of 80 male and female college students which showed that the "higher the subject's self-esteem the more intimate the subject was in communicating through touch, especially when communicating with a female."
10. **True**: Dr. Albert Mehrabian, Associate of Psychology at the University of California, has this to say: "Greater liking is conveyed by standing close to another person instead of far; by leaning forward instead of back when seated in a chair; by facing the person directly instead of turning to one side; by touching; by extending bodily contact, as during a handshake and prolonged good-byes."
11. **False**: As evidenced by University studies which show that women are much more attentive to, and affected by, gestures and other nonverbal signals than men are. And it's noted that a woman's greater sensitivity to this form of communication will often cause her to accord it more significance than words.
12. **True**: Studies in nonverbal communication conducted at Ohio State University show that facial expression clearly dominates the perception of liking or disliking. And it follows that the expression on your face when another person sees you is likely to carry more weight in influencing a positive or negative reaction than how you rate in the good-looks department or how well-dressed you happen to be.

The Body Message Quiz and the answers are taken from a series of original research found in quizzes from ***Family Weekly***, the editions of November 7, 1976; February 13, 1983; June 19, 1983, January 23, 1983.

Practical Application Exercise–Idea Presentation

We discussed in the first chapter about selling power and what selling power can do for you. It was pointed out that selling power can help you get your ideas and messages across to other people. This exercise gives you the opportunity to develop your selling power by preparing a **five-minute** presentation in which you sell an idea to a small group of buyers of your choice. This idea is to be well developed and receive the acceptance from your group. You are encouraged to use some type of visual aids to support your presentation. Some examples of ideas that have been used by other students are as follows:

1. Honesty
2. Caring for others
3. Proper dress
4. Good Nutrition
5. Eating habits
6. Discipline
7. Goal Setting
8. Organization
9. Attitude
10. Exercising
11. Good grooming
12. Any idea that you feel is important.

This idea must be presented in such a way that your group will start implementing the concept in their daily lives. Your evaluators can use the evaluation sheet that is found below.

IDEA EVALUATION SHEET

	AREA				
1.	**Organization**	**Poor**	**Fair**	**Good**	**Excellent**
2.	**Enthusiasm**	**Poor**	**Fair**	**Good**	**Excellent**
3.	**Persuasion**	**Poor**	**Fair**	**Good**	**Excellent**
4.	**Poise/Confidence**	**Poor**	**Fair**	**Good**	**Excellent**
5.	**Modulation of Voice**	**Poor**	**Fair**	**Good**	**Excellent**

Additional Comments:

SIX

THE BUYING AND SELLING PROCESS

Learning Objectives

1. Describe the five stages of the buying process.
2. Explain the four factors that influence buyer behavior.
3. Describe the three types of consumer products.
4. Identify several types of buyers and their characteristics.
5. Discuss the three types of buying motives.
6. Explain the self-concept theory and explain its four components.
7. Describe the AIDCA selling formula.

And you think selling for a living has its tough days!

How would you like a job where if you make a mistake, a big red light goes on with a loud noise and 18,000 people start booing you?

–Jacques Plante
Former professional hockey goalie

THE BUYING AND SELLING PROCESS

In order to understand why buyers buy, one must understand their behavior and the influences that encourage them to buy. This chapter will concentrate on several factors that will give you a better understanding when working with customers.

When a customer purchases a product, it is not an instantaneous act but a series of activities. Buying is a process that is made up of a series of minor decisions. Whatever the type of buying decision, the decision itself is really a collection of decisions involving things like needs, wants, products, service, price, and time. The buyer goes five stages: (1) need identification, (2) information search, (3) evaluation of alternatives, (4) purchase decision, and (5) post-purchase evaluation.

STAGES IN THE BUYING PROCESS

Stage One: Need or Want Identification

The buying process begins when an individual recognizes a need or want. This may be triggered by sales promotions of a seller, advertiser, a salesperson's persuasion, a close friend, or any other influence within the buyer's environment. After the buyer recognizes a need or want, the buyer begins to move towards purchasing a product or service that will satisfy this need or want.

A salesperson can play an important role in the need identification stage by suggesting and arousing awareness of the need or want that the prospect was unaware of and encourage the buyer to take action. People seem to have difficulty in discerning between their needs and wants. Our wants outnumber the needs we have in life. A **need** is that which is necessary for survival or to keep on living. The only basic needs we really have in life are for food, shelter, and clothing, which are items that help us sustain life. A **want** is a drive, wish, or demand for something not necessary for survival. As we obtain extra income or a surplus of money, we begin to desire things that are beyond the realm of our needs. Our minds tend to play games on us as we begin to believe certain things are necessary to survive in life. For example, we feel like a new car is needed as the present one begins to get old. Even though the old car still gives us the needed transportation to get from one place to another, we are no longer satisfied with it and believe that we must have a new one. This want, when driven by strong emotions, tends to take on the appearance of a need which must be satisfied to obtain any inner peace. By rationalizing wants into needs, we buy things that make life more comfortable. It is not enough just to get by with the essentials; we want to live in more comfort than we did the year before. This is one reason why many people buy products they can't afford.

Stage Two: Information Search

Some needs and wants can be satisfied immediately by a purchase, and the buyer will obtain the product with little thought. This is common with inexpensive items like a hamburger to satisfy hunger, or a candy bar for a snack. When the need or want involves something that the buyer has had little experience with and is higher in price, the buyer may embark upon a lengthy search for information. This search involves all the activities involved in looking for ways to satisfy the recognized need or want. If this search involves looking for a car, the buyer will learn more about the different makes of cars available, the differences between these makes, and about the dealers who sell them. The buyer will also look at past experiences, talk to friends, associates, family, and business companions and maybe even look through some consumer publications that contain information on car ratings. A general rule of thumb most consumers follow is to spend more time in researching information when high price, value, or risk is involved. After acquiring this information, the buyer may test drive several cars.

Stage Three: Evaluation of Alternatives

The information search stage leads to a desire to identify several alternatives that can be evaluated and studied. Numerous alternatives are looked at, and a process of weighing and deciding takes place. The buyer may take into consideration the feelings of others when looking at costs and benefits. If deciding on a car, the buyer will consider the financing alternatives, and how much a dealer will give for the old car when used as a trade-in. Many factors are considered, and the salesperson must have an emphatic understanding of the various feelings and influences that may lead to the buyer's feelings of uncertainty and risk. The buyer is careful about the specific product that will be chosen to satisfy the need or want. Once a specific product is identified and studied, the buyer is then ready to seek out a seller who is carrying the product.

Stage Four: Purchase Decision

After several alternatives have been looked at and studied, the fourth stage of purchase decision takes place. The customer is finally ready to make a decision and select a product for purchase. The choice is based on the outcome of the evaluation stage. Product availability may influence which brand is purchased. During this stage, the buyer determines which seller and company would be best to buy the product from. Issues like price, delivery, warranties, installation, and credit arrangements are discussed with sellers and settled. Finally, the actual act of buying occurs.

Stage Five: Post-purchase Evaluation

The final stage of the buying process is the post-purchase evaluation of the product. After using the product, the buyer will experience either satisfaction or dissatisfaction with what was purchased. The level of satisfaction will determine if a repurchase will ever be made. Salespeople must pay attention to how the product is used and evaluated by buyers. Favorable impressions and evaluations will be the first step in buying another product from you. Feedback from satisfied buyers can help develop new and better selling points, and unfavorable satisfaction from customers can pinpoint factors that can be corrected.

The Five Stages of the Buying Process

Stage 1: Need or want identification.
Stage 2: Information search.
Stage 3: Evaluation of alternatives.
Stage 4: Purchase decision.
Stage 5: Post-purchase evaluation.

FACTORS THAT INFLUENCE BUYER BEHAVIOR

Several factors must be considered in attempting to understand the buyer's behavior. Let us place these factors into four major groups. The four groups are **seller, product, situation,** and **buyer** and are identified in the next visual.

Four Key Factors

- **Seller**
  - –Person or organization.
- **Product**
  - –Convenience, shopping, or specialty good.
- **Buyer**
  - –Individual characteristics.
- **Situation**
  - –Time, need, weather, and psychological factors.

Seller

Different characteristics of the seller can play a major role in the behavior of the buyer. Some buyers are turned off because salespeople are too talkative and apply too much pressure. Characteristics like service, friendliness, and location can help the buyer feel comfortable and develop positive feelings about the store. The seller in this case can be an individual salesperson or a store. Some buyers keep going back to the same store because they like a specific salesperson. Other people shop at a specific store because they like the variety of products, the quality, and the store's atmosphere.

Product

Product characteristics such as features, style, and price influence the buyer. Some people will buy even though they do not like the salesperson. They see a product as "too good to pass up" because the price is low, so they go ahead and purchase the product. It is very important that the salesperson explain the product to the buyer and overcome any obstacles like price by justifying the value of the product and by creating financing alternatives.

The salesperson must also realize that products are different and that some products require more creative selling and persuasion than others. There are basically three major categories of consumer products and each product category will require a different approach in the selling strategy.

Three Types of Consumer Goods

- **Convenience goods**
  - –**Low priced items found everywhere, purchased frequently with minimum effort.**
- **Shopping goods**
  - –**Items purchased after comparisons are made.**
- **Speciality goods**
  - –**Items high in price, found in few locations, and can require extra mile effort to obtain.**

- **Convenience goods:** This first category of products consists of low priced items that are purchased frequently and with minimum effort. These goods are found at numerous outlets. Impulse goods like gum, soda pop, magazines, candy, and newspapers fall into this group. Very little personal selling is needed for convenience goods, as national advertising and other promotional tools take care of influencing the buyer.

- **Shopping goods:** The second category of products consists of those goods that the buyer will purchase after shopping around and comparing factors like style, quality, price, color, and brand. These goods require creative selling and persuasion on the seller's part. Examples of products in this category are furniture, used cars, appliances, jewelry, and clothing.

- **Specialty goods:** The last category of consumer goods is called specialty goods. These products are special because buyers will go out of their way to obtain the item. These products are usually high in price and found in very few locations. Some examples of this group are original oil paintings, fancy sport cars, and well-known expensive brand goods.

Situation

Various "situational" factors can play a major role in buyer behavior. Items like pressure of time, time of day, weather, or the psychological factors of the buyer and salesperson can play a major role in the selling situation. A salesperson must be aware of the situation. A customer may have had a hard day, so the customer is very grouchy and picky. The customer may only have 20 minutes to buy a product during lunchtime so the customer is in a hurry. The salesperson knows that patience and understanding are very important, as the buyer may be quick-tempered for reasons unknown to the salesperson. In general, customers tend to exhibit different moods based on the type of weather. A salesperson with a skill in asking good questions to obtain helpful information can assist the buyer in any type of situation.

Buyer

A buyer is anyone who might purchase a product. A buyer must have interest in the product and the means to buy it. Although you qualify all your prospects on items like money, authority, and desire, customers will have many different personality types. A salesperson must learn how to adapt and adjust to different customers and know the best strategy to use with each one. A salesperson should learn to put him/herself in the customer's shoes; by doing this, the seller can use the best approach and techniques to provide good service.

A salesperson will usually encounter a variety of different types of buyers in a single working day. We will look at eight specific types of buyers based on characteristics and then look at some simple strategies that can be used in dealing with each type of buyer. Remember, the key is to adjust and adapt to the variety of buyers.

Argumentative type. This first type of buyer has some general characteristics that are quite obvious. The buyer is insincere, likes to argue, makes unreasonable demands, and is likely to talk loudly. A salesperson deals with this type of buyer by showing respect, allowing the buyer to talk, and being good-natured.

Silent type. The characteristics of this type of buyer are an unexpressive face and no desire to answer questions. A salesperson should ask questions that can be answered with more than a yes or no answer. Be more personal than usual and demonstrate the product by encouraging the buyer to handle and touch the product–in essence, becoming personally involved in the presentation.

Talkative type. This buyer dominates a conversation and discusses personal affairs. A seller should be courteous with this buyer and always remain businesslike. The seller should also learn to lead the buyer back into the presentation.

Hurried type. This buyer is impatient and nervous. The buyer constantly looks at a watch and is very busy. When you notice this type of buyer, you should be rapid in your presentation and get to the point in a hurry. Concentrate only on important points and listen carefully to the customer.

Just-looking type. The general characteristics of this well-known buyer is the appearance of "I'm just looking," and seeming undecided or fearing sales pressure. This type of buyer starts to move away when approached and can't be rushed. Some reasons for the behavior may be that the person is buying unfamiliar merchandise or may be in your store for the first time. A salesperson should invite the customer to look, give facts about the product, use short sales talk, ask few questions and make the customer at ease by helping only when invited.

Procrastinator type. This buyer wants time to look and think everything over and waivers between one product and another. The person is slow and leisurely in motion. When you identify this type of buyer, avoid overpowering pressure and summarize the benefits the buyer will lose if a purchase is not made today. This type of buyer fears making a bad decision, so be rational in explaining the product.

Ego-involved type. General characteristics of this type of buyer include questioning the salesperson, displaying personal knowledge of the merchandise, being argumentative in nature, and contradicting many points given by the seller. A salesperson should welcome this buyer's opinions and ideas, be very patient and courteous, and agree with the buyer on some points.

Average type. This group of buyers will make up the majority of the customers you will deal with. These people have a fairly well-formed idea of what they are looking for, are pleasant and courteous, and offer few objections. A salesperson should make an attempt to gain their attention through a pleasant approach, explain the merchandise, and use goodwill to bring the customer back in the future. This group of buyers doesn't mind being asked a few qualifying questions.

BUYING MOTIVES

The seller, buyer, product, and situation can be greatly affected by the buying motive found or created in the mind of the buyer. A buyer's feelings and actions can greatly change at any time by a set of motives, or the inner states that moves a person towards the purchase of a product. Motives drive us towards our goals. A person who is purchasing a sofa might be attracted by the color and fabric. However, when the seller encourages the buyer to sit down on the sofa and actually feel what the sofa is like, the buyer may become emotionally involved and become more persuaded to buy it. All buying motives fall into one of three different classifications as identified in the next illustration.

Buying Motives

- **Rational buying motives.**
  - **Decisions based on logical reasons.**
- **Emotional buying motives.**
  - **Decisions based on impulse and emotions.**
- **Patronage buying motives.**
  - **Decisions based on loyalty and past experiences.**

Rational Buying Motives

Rational buying motives result when a person makes a buying decision based on concrete reasons and logic. The buyer will only make a purchase decision after comparisons of price, quality, style, color, brand name, durability, and financing have been discussed.

Emotional Buying Motives

Emotional buying motives result when a person makes a buying decision based on impulse or emotions. These decisions are made without any prior thought or planning. These motives are strong and sellers spend most of their efforts in attempting to stir up these emotional appeals to a level that rational thinking can't take place.

Patronage Buying Motives

Patronage buying motives should be the long-term goal of every salesperson. This group of motives results from loyalty to a specific store or to a specific salesperson. Customers put much trust in a store or person when patronage buying motives are used. Past positive experiences and consistent excellent service are keys to winning over a customer. This is the ultimate goal every seller wants to achieve–developing a list of good, regular customers who will return time and time again.

THE SELF-CONCEPT THEORY

All of us possess a mental picture of ourselves. People's actions, including their purchase decisions, are related to this mental concept of themselves. This mental picture is called the **Self-Concept Theory**. The self-concept theory consists of four separate selves: **real self, self-image, looking-glass self,** and **ideal self.**

The **real self is you as you really are**. This self is an objective view of the total person. This is who you really are. Some people will never find their real self and others spend their entire life striving to discover their real self. As you advance in years, you are discovering more of your likes, dislikes, strengths, and weaknesses–those items that make up your real self.

The Self-Concept Theory

***Looking glass self*: The way you think others see you.**
***Self-image*: The way you see yourself.**
***Ideal self*: The way you want to become.**
***Real self*: The way you really are.**

Your **self-image is the way you see yourself.** This is the way an individual views oneself at the moment, and the perception may be distorted. Our self-image can change because of the many different types of experiences we encounter.

The **looking-glass self is the way you think others see you**. This is the way individuals think others see them and can be quite different from their self-image. This self is of great concern during a person's teenage years. At this time in life, one values highly the opinion of friends and peers.

The last self is called the **ideal self, which is the way you would like to become.** The ideal self serves as a personal set of objectives and is the vision of what you would eventually like to become. You will spend your life aspiring towards your ideal self.

In buying goods and services, people are likely to choose those goods and services that will move them closer towards their ideal self. Those who see themselves as intellectual are more likely than others to join literary book clubs, for example. Young people who see themselves as athletes will buy brand name products endorsed by famous athletes. The young businessman who is on his way up the corporate ladder will take up golf, having determined this is the sport of executives. Advertisements use beautiful, sexy, and attractive people to promote soft drinks. Salespeople should attempt to identify the ideal self in customers, then appeal to this self.

THE SELLING PROCESS

Buying is the complement of selling. While the customer is involved with buying, the seller is involved with selling. The salesperson has to understand how the customer's mind works when making a purchase. With this knowledge, the salesperson will be able to use his persuasive powers more effectively to influence the customer in making a favorable buying decision. To move the customer through the buying process, a helpful selling strategy is a psychological process called **AIDCA.**

Five Stages Of A Sale–AIDCA

In persuading the customer to make a purchase, the seller can use an effective strategy that consist of five stages: (1) attention stage, (2) interest stage, (3) desire stage, (4) conviction stage, and (5) action stage. This is a process is called **AIDCA**. The creative salesperson leads the customer through these five mental stages of a sale. Each stage has definite characteristics. When the salesperson recognizes that the customer has reached a particular stage, he should try to lead the customer to the next stage.

Attention Stage

When the customer becomes aware of a need or a want, the first stage has been entered, the **attention stage**. The customer's attention may be drawn by a need or want for the product from an advertisement in a magazine, by a commercial on a television or radio program, or through the seller's opening approach statement. The awareness of a need or want for a product may arise abruptly or develop over a long period of time. For example, a woman may turn on her washing machine and watch it sputter and grind to a stop. Suddenly, she needs either service or a new machine. She may have ignored ads on television by an appliance dealer for several months but now realizes the message and may become persuaded to go to the store and purchase a new washing machine.

It is obvious that the salesperson cannot begin selling until the customer's attention has been focused on the product. If the customer does not have any need or want that the product could satisfy, the customer will not even start to think about buying it. The direct-to-home salesperson appreciates this fact because many times the door gets slammed in his/her face before he/she has finished the opening statement in the presentation. The person on the other side of the door simply has no interest in the product and is therefore unwilling to give the salesperson his/her attention.

Because the salesperson must first get the customer's attention, the salesperson makes an approach. The salesperson hopes that a buyer will provide an opportunity to go with the sales presentation. Some of the best suggestions in gaining the customer's attention are to promise benefits, provoke curiosity, and mention favorable selling points and benefits. If the approach is successful, or if the customer's attention is drawn to the product in some other way, the salesperson can lead the customer to the next stage.

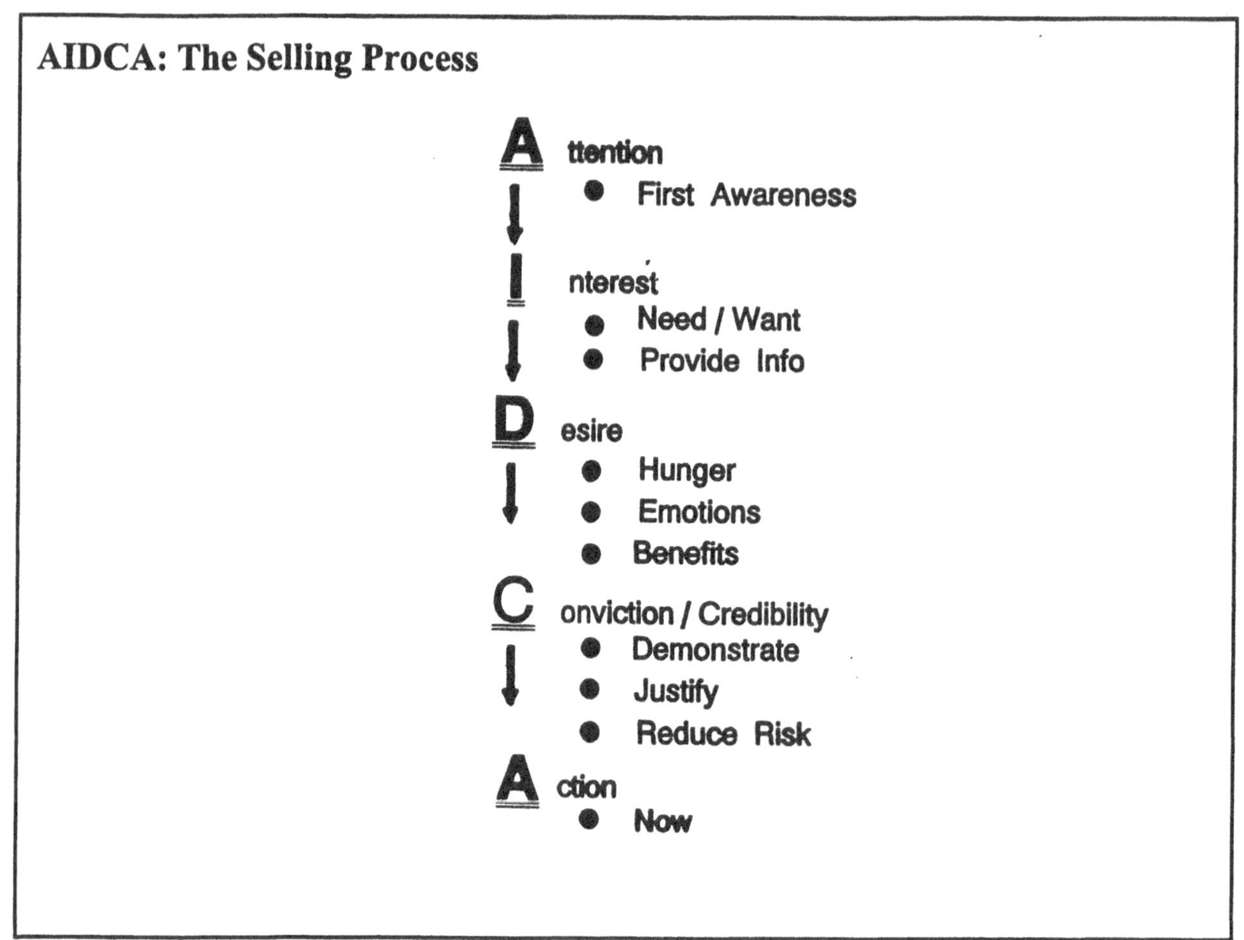

Interest Stage

After the customer focuses attention on the product, the next step is progression towards a purchase in the **interest stage,** when the customer begins to look at the product as a way of satisfying a personal need or a want. The insurance salesperson knows that many people realize the need for life insurance, but they have not developed any interest in satisfying that need. They feel that they are in no danger of losing their lives for a while, and consequently they do not need to think about buying life insurance just yet.

The customer who has developed interest will pay attention to ads about products and services that will satisfy his/her need. The customer will shop around and talk to friends to acquire information. Most importantly, close attention will be given to the salesperson's presentation.

Notice how a salesperson of electric ranges and appliances gains the attention of a customer and then arouses interest in the product.

Salesperson: Hello! I see you are looking at our newest range. We think it is one of the most smartly styled ranges we have ever carried.

Customer: Yes, I do like the design.

Salesperson: Have you noticed the computerized controls that make cooking so easy? This range practically does the whole job for you. Very little effort and time is needed.

Customer: Yes, but it looks a little complicated; I'm not very high tech.

The customer's attention was caught by the product itself, but her attention was focused and strengthened by the salesperson's opening statement. In the second statement, the salesperson tried to arouse the customer's interest in the automatic controls as an attractive feature of the range. The customer showed that interest had been sparked by saying, "It looks a little complicated, but I'm not very high tech." It would seem that the customer was interested enough to want the salesperson to provide assurances. This should lead directly into a demonstration by the salesperson of how easily the controls can be used. In fact, it could be a verbal closing signal that might encourage the salesperson to proceed in attempting to close the sale.

Desire Stage

The next stage in the customer's progress towards a purchase is the **desire stage**. In the desire stage, the customer wants the product and begins to hunger for it. It is possible for a customer to develop an interest in a product and yet not develop a desire for it. Customers are usually led towards the purchase of a product because they have needs or wants that the product can satisfy. But if customers have no strong feeling about their need, or consider their need to be trivial or unimportant, they may easily give up the idea of making the purchase. However, if customers deeply feel their need or want and the product appears to be a likely answer for the need or want, then a desire will be generated for the product. The salesperson can strengthen the customer's desire for the product by appealing to the five senses and emphasizing benefits instead of features. Some helpful suggestions in arousing interest and creating desire are to immediately enlarge on the promise of several major selling points, clearly tell the benefits that buyer will gain, show how easily the product is to use, use sex and prestige appeals, and customize and personalize your presentation to the individual buyer.

Conviction/Credibility Stage

If the salesperson's demonstration and sales talk prove to be effective, then the customer moves toward conviction. In the **conviction or credibility stage**, the salesperson must be prepared to explain a benefit again, to demonstrate a feature of the product again, to handle the competition objection, or to offer proof of earlier statements about the product to convince the customer that the particular product best suits his/her needs. Much summarizing and reinforcing is done in this stage.

But, even if the customer is convinced that the product is the right one to buy, the customer may not feel that he should make the purchase. The customer may be unsure about the company's credit arrangement, salespeople's reputations, service reputation, or whether the company will be able to make delivery by the time the product is needed. When a salesperson notices that the customer seems convinced that the product is right but is still hesitating, the salesperson must try to discover the reason for that hesitation. Experience is an important tool to the salesperson at this time. Arrangements can be made to satisfy the customer, within the limitations of company policy. Helpful ways to create credibility are to tell of the product's popularity, give testimonials, provide assurances, proof, and warranties, and convey and accentuate the value.

Action Stage

When the customer has decided to satisfy his need by making the purchase, the customer is in the **action stage** and the sale is made. Sometimes, however, the customer may be completely convinced that the product is right yet still hesitates to make the purchase.

The process of completing a purchase requires making a decision, and most people are concerned about making the right decision. If the decision involves a good deal of money, it is often particularly hard for the customer to decide. A good knowledge of effective closing techniques comes in handy at this time.

The salesperson must help the customer to decide whether or not to take action. You can do this by saying, "Mrs. Taylor, I would suggest the lamp with the blue base. It would fit into your color scheme perfectly. Do you want to take it with you, or would you like to have it delivered?" Or you might say, "Mr. Thompson, if you place the order now, we can guarantee delivery by Friday." At this point, the salesperson should always consider whether there are additional sales that could be made. If the customer has reached the action stage, the customer is in a receptive frame of mind. The salesperson can take advantage of the situation and make a multiple sale. This can be done by using a selling technique called **suggestive selling** which is suggesting related, added-on items once the customer has committed to buy the major product.. The experienced salesperson, however, knows not to push a customer too hard at this point–or at any other point. Each customer must be handled individually. Pushing for an initial sale or for additional sales must be timed right, or it can alienate a customer. If the customer shows no additional interested in any additional purchases, the salesperson should concentrate on making sure the customer completes the original purchase and leaves happy.

Several helpful suggestions in bringing about action include making the choosing easy by giving yes/yes alternatives, tell how, when, and where to get the product, provide financing alternatives, name terms that are easy for the buyer, and point out the benefits that will be lost if the purchase is not made today.

Practical Application Exercise–AIDCA Selling Presentation

The purpose of this presentation is to provide you an opportunity to apply the five mental stages of a sale, AIDCA, in a presentation. You are to prepare a **five-minute** presentation selling a convenience good to a small group of buyers. Like the previous two presentations, this presentation also will require that you use visual aids to assist you in the presentation. The product you select should cost less than two dollars and it is recommended that you sell something that is consumable–or that can be eaten. Students in the past have chosen a simple product like a candy bar. As you prepare for the AIDCA presentation, answer the questions below in preparation for your presentation. Use the evaluation sheet at the bottom of this page to obtain feedback from your evaluators who will act as buyers.

1. Identify the product you will be selling for this presentation.
2. What will you do to catch the **attention** of your group?
3. List those things you will do to create **interest** in your product.
4. What will you do to stimulate **desire** for your product?
5. List those things you will do to establish **credibility** and establish **conviction** in your product.
6. What will you do to prompt **action** from your group?
7. What types of visual aids will you use to assist you in the presentation?

ADICA Presentation Evaluation Sheet

Please circle your personal response to each of the areas below. Below your response write a few comments that will help the student in future presentations.

1.	Did the student gain your **attention**?	Poor Fair Good Excellent
2.	Did the student create **interest**?	Poor Fair Good Excellent
3.	Did the student stimulate **desire**?	Poor Fair Good Excellent
4.	Did the student establish **credibility** and **conviction**?	Poor Fair Good Excellent
5.	Did the student prompt **action** for the product?	Poor Fair Good Excellent

SEVEN

PRODUCT KNOWLEDGE

Learning Objectives

When you finish studying the material in this chapter, you should be able to:

1. **Identify four problems that will happen with inadequate product knowledge.**
2. **Define product.**
3. **Describe key company knowledge information.**
4. **Describe key product knowledge information.**
5. **Identify seven useful sources in acquiring information.**
6. **Explain the mental risk barrier and describe how to overcome it.**

The Power of Knowledge

Therefore I say, know the enemy and know yourself. In 100 battles you will never be in peril. When you are ignorant of the enemy but know yourself, your chances of winning or losing or equal. If ignorant both of your enemy and of yourself, you are certain in every battle to be in peril.

–Sun Tzu, *The Art of War*

PRODUCT KNOWLEDGE

In scanning over a ranking by selected marketing executives of major firms dealing with qualities needed for selling, one quality always was listed in the top five. The quality is **product knowledge**. If salespeople don't spend the necessary time doing their homework or learning about the products and services of their company, they will eventually be another number added to the high turnover that exists in the selling industry. Why is it so important to know your product? Why should you know information about your company? If you don't, the following things will happen to you in your selling experience:

- You will lose sales and encounter more than average sales resistance.
- You will lack self-confidence.
- You will find selling unenjoyable because of the fear and stress that will emerge.
- You will give poor sales presentations.

A salesperson becomes a very important source of information to the buyer during the buying process. Necessary time should be spent learning about the products, services, and company information so the salesperson can fulfill the role of an assistant and consultant to the buyer.

PRODUCT DEFINITION

This first item of discussion is, "what really makes up a product?" When customers buy a product, they buy much more than a physical, tangible item; they buy a package of benefits. People buy products that will make their life more comfortable and satisfy their wants and needs–in essence, products provide personal benefits. People also buy numerous services. Customers expect their life to be benefitted from their purchases. Besides receiving a physical product or service, the customer also purchases credit, delivery, installation, guarantees, warranties, advertising, customer service, maintenance, and all other services that are involved in selling the product or service. Customers may not initially realize it, but they pay for all these additional items when the product is originally purchased.

Product Definition

What is a product?

- ⇨**A package of benefits.**
- ⇨**A tangible, physical good.**
- ⇨**An intangible service.**
- ⇨**Any value-added services.**

COMPANY KNOWLEDGE

Potential customers want to know a little about the company standing behind the product that will be purchased. Having company knowledge is very important to buyers who purchase expensive or industrial products that require much servicing. Customers who buy products that may have to be returned in the future or intangible items like investments or consulting services also want to know information about the company. Company reputation and credibility are very important to the sale–sometimes more important than the individual product being purchased. For this reason, a list of information items should be researched and learned by new salespeople when hired by a selling organization.

✔The company's standing in the industry.

✔The history and past performance of the company.

✔The size of the company and the growth that has taken place in the last several years.

✔The various products or services that are sold by the company.

✔The reputation of the company's service department and sales personnel.

✔The location of service facilities and distribution offices.

✔The various policies of the company like discounts, credit, delivery, exchanges, financing, and order procedures.

Most large selling organizations have training programs established for newly-hired salespeople to educate them with all the crucial information about the company. Some companies publish written information that goes into great detail about the history of the company, the mission statement of the company, and the philosophy of the company's operations. If an organization doesn't have anything formally set up, then the sales manager should spend some time and educate the new salesperson with key and pertinent information. With so many companies selling the same product, a good salesperson needs to know his/her company well enough to help establish credibility in the sales presentation.

PRODUCT KNOWLEDGE

A thorough knowledge of your products and services is essential for sales success. The most successful salespeople are those who can communicate the value of their product offerings to their potential customers. Customers depend on salespeople for information. Salespeople of all industries and products should acquire product information in the areas that are listed below.

■ **Research and development history of your product.** Many companies spend a great deal of time and money in the development of their products. Products are researched, developed, tested, modified, and retested many times before they finally are ready to hit the marketplace. This information can be useful in assuring the customer that your products are well-suited to the customer's needs and problems.

■ **Manufacturing facts.** You will need to know exactly how your products are made, what materials are used, and what characteristics they possess. The materials in the construction of your products can often be translated into important selling points and features.

■ **Product warranty and guarantee.** Learn what your product's warranty and guarantee really consists of and educate your customer in this area. This can be one of the strongest selling tools you have to reduce the risk in the mind of the buyer.

■ **Know the performance characteristic of your products.** When customers buy a product, what they are really buying is the performance of the product. Successful performance examples should be solicited from happy customers through case histories and testimonial letters. A customer will be more confident in buying your product knowing that it has a successful performance history for other users.

- **Know the servicing and follow-up support of your company.** An important concern for many customers is what the company and salesperson will do after the purchase has been made. If your products require servicing over time, your customers should be informed of service contracts and assistance that are available. Know the company policy regarding repairs, replacement parts, and returns. Your customers will want to know this information, especially if your company excels in these areas. When customer assistance is needed after the sale, you should not pass the buck; customers expect you to have all the answers.

- **Know the features, benefits, and advantages of your products.** Know how to translate the features of your products into benefits that the customer can understand and enjoy. Know how your products compare with the product offerings of your competitors. Know exactly the "competitive niche" your product has to give over the competition.

- **Personal use of the product.** Besides talking to customers and other salespeople who have used the products you are selling, take the time and use the product yourself to become familiar with what it can do. It is impressive to any customer to find out that the salesperson is actually using the product that is being sold.

INFORMATION SOURCES

Now that you are aware of the information that should be acquired to assist the customer, know where you can find answers to questions that will be brought up when dealing with product and company knowledge. There are many sources available to obtain the information you will need. Although it is impossible to identify all available sources, the most commonly used will be given. The successful salesperson will stay in contact with these, as well as other information sources that are important to his/her individual company.

- **Company literature.** Every company should have training manuals, visual-aid materials, newsletters, annual reports, and cassettes available for the salesperson. Most companies take care of this in training programs for new recruits, but every salesperson should be involved in an on-going program to keep up on the new information that is available in the industry.

- **Sales supervisors and other salespeople.** Your sales manager and experienced salespeople with your company represent one of the best sources of knowledge. Be a good listener and ask questions to take advantage of their insight and understanding.

- **Sales meetings and conferences.** Most sales organizations have weekly or monthly meetings. One of the purposes of these meetings is to answer any questions salespeople may have. If you have had difficulty in obtaining the answer to a specific knowledge problem, bring it up in this meeting.

- **Trade magazines and professional journals.** Business publications that are tailor-made for your industry provide an excellent source of current information on new product knowledge. Most industries have a specific publication that addresses specific issues in your industry.

- **Manufacturing representatives and selling agents.** Frequently make contact with those professionals that provide your company with the products. These professionals have direct contact with the makers of the products. Use them as an important information source.

- **Past and present customers.** Make it habit to solicit information from your customers. They will be honest with you and will provide the most important information. Customers will let you know if the product or service is providing benefits and satisfaction. Since the customer is generally called upon by your competitors, they often will provide you with good competitive information also.

- **Testing bureaus and trade shows.** The last area consists of those independent organizations like ***Consumer Reports*** that test products and provide performance information. Also, visit trade shows and talk to salespeople from all levels concerning the products that are in your industry.

MENTAL RISK BARRIER

Product and company knowledge are important because they help reduce any risk that is present in the buyer's mind about product purchases and decisions. A **mental risk barrier** exists between every salesperson and potential buyer and with every product as illustrated in the next illustration.

The Mental Risk Barrier.

A certain amount of risk exists in the buyer's mind with every product purchase and decision.

A certain amount of risk is involved in buying every new product. Of course, the risk is small for a thirty-cent candy bar. If you purchase a candy bar that is old or not too fresh, you don't spend much time reflecting on the poor product purchase. But, as the product increases in value or price, more risk becomes attached to the purchase decision. Items like cars, homes, and other expensive products require much time and information before finally being purchased by the customer. Because of this risk barrier that exists in every sale, it is important for the salesperson to acquire sufficient knowledge to help lead the people to buy and to handle any questions or concerns that may arise in the sales presentation. By knowing the product and industry in depth, a salesperson can work out the fears and answer the questions that are expressed by the customer.

A good background in product knowledge is very helpful in handling price and credibility questions that tend to increase the mental risk barrier. This barrier becomes thinner as the salesperson increases his product knowledge. As the salesperson gains experience and product knowledge, he can handle all concerns of the buyer during his presentation.

EIGHT

PROSPECTING

Learning Objectives

When you finish studying the material in this chapter, you should be able to:

1. **Describe how prospecting is like detective work.**
2. **Identify the two major purposes of prospecting.**
3. **Define four common prospecting terms.**
4. **Describe and provide examples of the twelve most common prospecting methods.**
5. **Discuss how to develop a personal prospecting system.**

A key for prospecting success:

There are three simple rules I use for prospecting success in the competitive insurance industry:

1. **Get out and see the people.**
2. **Get out and see the people.**
3. **Get out and see the people.**

–Raymond J. Gorzinski

PROSPECTING

The first major step in the sales process is the step of prospecting. Prospecting is a process of looking up and checking out all possible sources for leads. Some salespeople in the industry classify prospecting as one of the least appealing tasks of the selling process because they have not practiced this step properly and have not learned the its value. Salespeople must learn that the step of prospecting is essential for their growth and survival.

PROSPECTING IS DETECTIVE WORK

Prospecting is very similar to detective work. A detective learns to consider everyone associated with the crime as a suspect; each person is potentially a valuable lead in finding the person who committed the crime. Salespeople also must look at everyone in the realm of their activity as a suspect or a lead. Detectives gather information and clues to find their suspect list so that time will be spent on the alibis and motives of those with the greatest chance of having committed the crime. A salesperson refines and reduces a list of suspects to create a good list of prospects with a better than average chance of buying. Prospecting creates a list of potential buyers that will later be reduced through the second step of selling, which is "qualifying."

REASONS FOR PROSPECTING

Prospecting is not only the first step in the sales process, but is also a very important step. The first illustration of this chapter points out that prospecting accomplishes two main tasks: First, prospecting develops a list of new leads or potential buyers. Most companies lose between 15-20 percent of their customers each year. Some reasons for this reduction are customers that go out of business, move away, switch to a competitor, cease to qualify financially, go into another line of business, or simply no longer has the need, want, or desire. A salesperson must replenish the list daily so that he or she can spend time giving presentations. If you do not make prospecting a daily habit, your prospecting list will soon dry up. Second, prospecting produces a steady stream of sales for the future. The continued use of prospecting is a "must." Your attention to this step will provide you a work schedule for the future. Prospecting takes time and must be worked into your weekly schedule to help secure prospects for future presentations and sales. Successful salespeople commit one hour a day to prospecting so that a constant list of sales are generated.

The Two Purposes of Prospecting

- **Develop a list of potential buyers.**
- **Produce a steady stream of sales.**

PROSPECTING TERMS

As you become engaged in the step of prospecting, there are several terms that will become part of your daily vocabulary. The term **prospect** generally refers to any person who is interested in your product. The term **lead** refers to one who wants, can afford, and can benefit from your product, but is not yet qualified. Whether you use the term prospect or lead, you are referring to a potential buyer who may be interested in your product. The term **referral** simply means a lead or prospect given to you by someone else. The last term, a **hot prospect**, is a qualified person who is ready to buy. A hot prospect would be a car buyer who has just walked into a dealership and quickly identifies the car he/she wants and has the cash to pay for the car on the spot. These types of customers are the ideal ones that come your way every month or so.

THE TWELVE MOST COMMON PROSPECTING METHODS

Company Information

This first method should be the **first tool used** by any salesperson. Before any additional prospecting methods are used, a salesperson should always check present and past customers. Many good leads can be obtained from within your own company. Your best source is always your present customers. Your present customers are a source of reorders. They are also prospects for goods and services you are not selling to them now. Study your sales records to see what your present customers are not buying from you. Make it a point to cover those products on future calls. Check to see if there are other departments or divisions that you are not calling on that could use some of your products.

Company Information

The first place a salesperson should always look.

- **Present customers**
- **Inactive accounts**

Present customers are a source of new prospects through referrals. Check other departments in the company you represent. Check the credit department and the service department. While you are checking on your present customers, go back and make a list of your inactive accounts. Find out why they quit buying and see what it would take to get them back buying from you again. Some changes may have been made since you last did business with them. Don't go digging for gold in another area when you can find it in your own backyard.

Center-of-Influence

A salesperson should get to know prominent people in his community and territory. These people have great influence and a good reputation. Their advice and counsel are usually well respected and received. These people are usually professionals, such as lawyers, doctors, college professors, city officials, and executives in the industry. You simply try to obtain referrals from these individuals. You should only use their names if given permission. If you do not get permission, keep their names confidential. Most salespeople usually like to repay their centers-of-influence for their services with cards on anniversaries, gifts at Christmas, or invitations to dinner.

Always remember that every individual can be a center-of-influence. Each of us is the center of our own little world and can exert some influence on a certain number of people. The more friends and acquaintances you have, the more influence you can utilize in finding prospects. Joe Girard is known as the "World's Greatest Salesman" by ***The Guinness Book of Word Records***. His record of selling retail cars has not yet been beaten.

He has a rule he calls the "Girard's Law of 250." He believes that the average person has positive influence over 250 people and when an individual is in a profession like those we have discussed in the center-of-influence method, who knows where the number will end.

The Center-of-Influence Method

Utilizing influential people like

- ⇨**University Professors**
- ⇨**Medical Doctors**
- ⇨**Lawyers**
- ⇨**Certified Public Accountants**
- ⇨**Politicians**
- ⇨**Corporate Executives**
- ⇨**Media Personalities**

Spotter

This prospecting method is very similar to the center-of-influence method, but the people that you use do not have well-known reputations. Instead of being people in lime-light positions, these people are individuals who daily contact many people because of their professions or careers. Examples of these types of people are service personnel, repair people, taxi drivers, retail salesclerks, inspectors, secretaries, customers, barbers, and hair dressers. Experienced sales people also use junior sales representatives as spotters to relieve them of the prospecting chore so they may spend more time selling by giving presentations. Also, some firms require that their junior salespeople pay their dues in the industry by starting off as spotters for an established salesperson.

The Spotter Method

Utilizing professional people who have daily contact with a high number of people.

- ⇨**Hair care professionals**
- ⇨**Repair and service people**
- ⇨**Retail clerks**
- ⇨**Secretaries**

Spotters keep a lookout for prospects. When they locate a good prospect, they will drop the name off to the salesperson. These people are in a position to gain information about other people. Most salespeople reward their spotters with gifts or money. Joe Girard, who we have already mentioned as the most successful car salesperson in the world, promises his customers money for bringing in other prospects who will buy. Generally, people who get around and hear information about other people make excellent spotters.

Endless-Chain

This method involves obtaining referrals from an excellent source–satisfied customers. Once you have made a sale, or when you follow-up on a buyer who is happy with your product, you can ask for the names of a couple of friends who may be interested in the same product. It is a good rule to only ask for a couple of names, maybe three to five, and always ask permission to use their name. It is also a good practice to ask satisfied buyers if they would give you a written testimonial letter. Tangible feedback, like a letter, strengthens a salesperson's presentation and reduces the risk in the mind of the buyer. Remember the mental risk barrier?

The Endless-Chain Method

Obtaining referrals from happy customers.
- **Ask for a few names.**
- **Only use with permission.**

Two special advantages of this method are that you have names of future prospects, and you have already started qualifying them. "Word of mouth" will soon get around to these referrals, and the sales resistance will be reduced. Products that are sold best by this method are products that are sold door-to-door: books, cookware, vacuum cleaners, and insurance.

Observation

This prospecting tool involves observing items like the local newspaper, club lists, and directories for potential prospects. For example, an insurance agent will spend time looking through the evening newspaper for marriages and births that involve people who are in need of these products. The real estate salesperson will look at the "for sale by owner" signs in front of homes and ads in the newspaper. Who could better use a realtor than a person trying to sell a house? Salespeople should always listen for good leads. This is why many salespeople join several community and civic organizations which require attendance at luncheons and meetings. Conversations with friends and acquaintances and polite eavesdropping can establish prospects and leads. Salespeople should always listen for leads in clubrooms, trade fairs, and other places where potential buyers may gather. Always be looking for additional prospects by watching, reading, and listening.

The Observation Method

How do you find customers?

- ➪**Listen**
- ➪**Observe**
- ➪**Read**
- ➪**Professional Involvement**

Advertising

The advertising method of prospecting involves utilization of the media: placing ads in newspapers, direct mail, trade magazines, bulletin boards, and the yellow pages. Health, insurance, and real estate companies spend great sums of money and time placing ads in newspapers. More recently, doctors, dentists, and lawyers are beginning to use newspaper and television advertising.

Advertising–Utilizing the tools of the media.

- **Television**
- **Radio**
- **Newspapers**
- **Magazines**
- **Yellow Pages**
- **Direct Mail**
- **Outdoor**
- **Specialty Items**

Telemarketing

This method is very direct, personal, and inexpensive. Little time is involved because modern technology allows a salesperson to contact many people in a couple of minutes. This method can demonstrates a success ratio of between five and eight sales out of every 100 calls. Many companies hire people to just call prospects from the phone book, or another prepared list they've obtained, with the hope of setting up an appointment for the salesperson An industry now exists that is in the business of generating prospect lists for telemarketing companies.

Telemarketing

A fast and personal method that talks to the customer where they live.

With the rising cost of transportation and other selling costs, this tool of prospecting is really growing. Telecommunication companies are encouraging more businesses to take advantage of the phone by pushing telemarketing. More firms are spending an increased amount of time using the telephone as part of their daily prospecting strategy.

Cold-Canvassing

This method is sometimes used when leads cannot be uncovered any other way. Even though it is a last resort for some companies, it is the major prospecting device for companies that sell products like vacuum cleaners, cookware, magazines, books, knives, cleaning supplies, and photo albums. This method works best with products that everyone needs. **Cold-canvassing** can be tough, but you will find the least amount of competition there. This door-to-door method requires that salespeople learn how to develop a positive first impression and good door approaches. This method depends on selling percentages and the percentage goes up if the salesperson has a pre-qualified prospecting list to utilize. The old rule still is "If you knock on so many doors, so many buyers will be found–it's the law of averages."

The Cold-Canvassing Method

Door-to-Door selling is an old-traditional approach but still effective for products people need in the home.

Group or Party Plans

Some products are sold best through parties. Almost everyone is acquainted with Tupperware parties. A salesperson asks a person to serve as hostess who will receive gifts and other inducements to hold a small party with a few close friends and neighbors. Demonstrations before groups are very effective because word-of-mouth interaction generates interest. Products that are normally sold through this method are crafts, toys, makeup, and the previously mentioned Tupperware. This is a popular profession for women who want to stay home and work part-time.

Fairs, Shows, and Exhibits

Industrial salespeople set up booths at trade fairs and shows to demonstrate and display products to visiting buyers. These booths are very effective if they show attention-getting displays, multi-media presentations, and products that attract a crowd of people. The goal of this method is simple–to get names and addresses of potential buyers that later can be called. Many sellers that use this method will offer a free drawing for a product if visiting people simply fill out a slip with their name, address, and phone number–the development of an instant prospect list. Some sales do take place at the fair or show, but the main goal is to have your product present at a place where many potential buyers of your product will be visiting.

Contests

This method is used by many food chains, local radio stations, and general consumer magazine clearing houses. Prizes and gifts are offered to those who buy products or visit the place of business. Many sporting good stores will have a "big buck contest" during the deer hunt. To enter, a hunter simply has to go into the store and register. Of course, the sporting goods store hopes that the hunter will pick up some last minute items before the big hunt.

Coupons

Some companies offer coupons that allow the prospect to receive a reduction in the price of a product or service. A very common coupon method in this area is the use of coupon books that contain two-for-one offers. Buy one product at full price, and the second product is free. The goal of businesses that use this method is to have the consumer come back again and pay full price. By offering a coupon, you encourage customers to come into your business and try your product or service at least once. This method is also used by dry cleaners, supermarkets, car service companies and even by doctors.

DEVELOPING A PERSONAL PROSPECTING SYSTEM

You need to consider a couple of items when developing a personal prospecting system for your product and company. A good prospecting system depends on many items like the salesperson, the product, the company, and the territory or environment. When putting together a prospecting system, avoid prejudging prospects. You will be surprised at how many people you have marked off your list that would purchase your product if approached. Attempt to tailor-make a combination of prospecting methods that serve you best. Use trial and error in the beginning, and try all methods and eliminate the unsuccessful ones. Keep accurate records of the methods you use. Find those methods that best fit your personality and product. Converse with other successful salespeople in your industry and determine what is working for them. The most important concept to remember is that the most productive prospecting systems involve using the name of another person. The key element in prospecting is people, people, people. The human influence is the strongest tool you have.

Customize a personalized prospecting system that considers the following:

- ✔**Your personality.**
- ✔**Your selling strengths and weaknesses.**
- ✔**The product you are selling.**
- ✔**The industry you are competing in.**
- ✔**What other successful salespeople are using.**
- ✔**Past history and experiences in prospecting.**
- ✔**Trial and error in experimenting different methods.**

NINE

QUALIFYING

Learning Objectives

1. Define qualifying.
2. Discuss the importance of seeking qualified prospects.
3. Explain the MAD approach in qualifying.
4. Utilize the qualifying process through two exercises.

A young psychology student serving in the Army decided to test a theory. Drawing kitchen duty, he was given the job of passing out apricots at the end of the chow line. He asked the first new soldiers that came by, "You don't want any apricots, do you?" Ninety percent said, "No." Then he tried the positive approach: "You do want apricots, don't you?" About half answered, "Uh, yeah, I'll take some." Then he tried a third test, based on the fundamental technique of providing two possible positive choices. This time he asked, "One dish of apricots or two?" And in spite of the fact that soldiers don't like Army apricots, 40 percent took two dishes and 50 percent took one!

—Taken from *Bits & Pieces for Salespeople*

QUALIFYING

Examining leads and prospects to determine if they might be potential buyers is known as **qualifying**. In all the salesmanship books we have read and reviewed, the area of qualifying customers is one of the selling steps that is least covered. We truly believe that if a salesperson does not spend sufficient time in qualifying his/her prospects, he/she will be wasting valuable time and money. At a selling seminar several years ago, and it was disclosed that the average professional salesperson spends around only one hour a day giving presentations. All the rest of the time is spent looking for new customers and servicing present customers. Many people spend this precious hour giving presentations to people that will not end up buying. To save you time and money and increase your productivity, learn how to qualify your prospects so that the one hour a day giving presentations will be a good return on your investment.

SEEK QUALITY PROSPECTS

The quality of prospects is more important than quantity. Let me use an analogy between a salesperson and a prospector seeking valuable ore. We know that some mineral deposits may be five to ten times as rich as others. This is true with a prospect list–one list may contain 10 percent good prospects while another may contain 25 percent or more. The difference between the two is in the care and intelligence with which the salesperson qualifies each potential buyer on the list. These potential buyers are not merely names–they are people like you and me. They have the same types of needs that we do. We learn later that some are more likely to buy than others. What we want to stress is that successful salespeople will qualify and evaluate each name on their prospecting list before placing it on the list of people to see and then attempt a sales presentation. Qualifying, if done correctly, will save the salesperson valuable time and money.

THE MAD APPROACH

Let us introduce to you to the best qualifying method that is used in selling. This method is called the **MAD Approach.** This approach involves concentrating on three areas in screening your prospects. The three areas are **money, authority,** and **desire.**

The Three Elements of the MAD Approach

Money
- **Cash, assets, or credit.**

Authority
- **Decision making power.**
- **Legal authority.**
- **Age restrictions.**
- **Formal authority.**

Desire
- **Wants or needs the product.**

Money

This first qualifying area of money tells you that your prospect must be able to afford your product. The buyer must either have cash, assets that can be turned into cash, or credit worthiness. It is always nice when the buyer has the money to pay for the product. In some cases, the product costs more than the buyer can presently afford. Some examples are a home, a car, or a type of investment. In these situations, the prospect needs to be worthy of credit in order to make the purchase. Many businesses have become conservative in lending credit, and others have discontinued the practice. Credit allows some buyers to purchase the product who normally couldn't afford the product. This allows you to make additional sales. Many businesses allow prospects to lay products away and pay on them monthly. Remember, money does not have to be in dollars and cents; it can also be in assets and credit.

Authority

A prospect must be eligible or have the authority to buy. Certain products require that the prospect have authority to purchase them. Products like explosives, certain chemicals, and guns are restricted to those who can legally purchase them. Certain drug items must be accompanied by a prescription from a doctor in order to be purchased. In the life insurance industry, unhealthy people who cannot pass the required medical exams and tests are ineligible because they become too high of a risk. As a young boy, a co-signer when was required in order to buy my first car at the age of seventeen. I could not receive credit because I was a minor.

Another interesting item learned in selling products is that some people need to have the confirmation of their partner before making a final decision to buy an item of considerable expense. When selling men's clothing, a common comment or response was that the male buyer had to have his partner's approval before making a purchase of this kind. We see that many men need the approval or informal authority from their spouses before making a purchase decision.

When selling to businesses and industrial organizations, it was found out early that many hours were spent giving presentations to people who did not have the company's authority to make the decision. A seller had to pinpoint the buyer of the organization who was given the authority of the company to make the decision. As experience and wisdom are obtained, a salesperson learns to seek out the person in authority to make buying decisions for the industrial organization and also to recognize the buffers that can stand in one's way.

Desire

The third area of the MAD Approach in qualifying prospects is to find out if the prospect wants, desires, or needs your product. Experience in selling has led us to conclude that many people buy when they apparently have little need for the product. Well-known sales trainer Tom Hopkins suggests that most people buy on emotions and then attempt to rationalize the decision after they have bought the product. Desires, needs, and wants are charged up by buying motives. A customer may buy two expensive suits, even though he was just looking at shirts and ties. People will buy products because they become caught up in the mood of buying. Some experienced salespeople can actually get customers to believe that they must have a certain product, or they won't be satisfied. If you fail to create a desire and hunger in the heart of the buyer, chances are that the customer will not buy your product. The customer has to see a purpose or use for the product.

Desire–Getting the Customer to Want It!

Most people buy on emotions–and desire, want, and need fuel the emotional fire.

Practical Application Exercise–Qualifying Prospects

Instructions: Shown below will be two situations in which you must make a judgment concerning prospects. Based on the information that will be given, indicate on the analysis worksheet whether the prospects meet the **MAD** approach in qualifying. The analysis evaluation worksheet is found on the next page after the prospecting information.

MONEY: Cash, assets, and credit.

AUTHORITY: Decision making, formal, or legal power and age.

DESIRE: Want, desire, or need.

SITUATION A

Assume that you are a sales representative for a major life insurance company. You have received a brief data sheet on eight prospects shown below and on the following page. By completing the analysis worksheet, qualify each prospect.

Prospect 1

Age: 25
Sex: Male
Marital Status: Married
Dependents: Wife just lost first baby with miscarriage
Education: A.A.S. Degree
Occupation: Steel worker
Income: $40,000
Residence: Home
Health: Good

Prospect 2

Age: 45
Sex: Male
Marital Status: Married/Two college-age Students
Education: College Graduate
Occupation: Medical Retirement
Residence: Own Home
Health: Poor

Prospect 3

Age: 28
Sex: Male
Marital Status: Married
Dependents: Wife pregnant with first child
Education: High School Diploma
Income: $40,000
Residence: Apartment
Health: Good

Prospect 4

Age: 45
Sex: Male
Marital Status: Divorced
Dependents: None
Education: M.B.A.
Occupation: Senior Vice-President of a Finance Company
Income: $125,000
Residence: Apartment
Health: Good

Prospect 5

Age: 19
Sex: Female
Marital Status: Single
Dependents: None
Education: College Freshman
Income: $5,000
Residence: Home with parents
Health: Good

Prospect 6

Age: 32
Sex: Male
Marital Status: Married
Dependents: Two children
Education: Two-year degree
Occupation: Department store buyer
Income: $45,000
Residence: Own Home
Health: Good

Prospect 7

Age: 65
Sex: Female
Marital Status: Widowed
Dependents: None
Education: PH.D. in history
Occupation: Retired College Teacher
Income: Social Security/Pension
Residence: Apartment
Health: Good

Prospect 8

Age: 42
Sex: Male
Marital Status: Married
Dependents: Five
Education: College Degree
Occupation: High school teacher
Income: $28,000
Residence: Owns Home
Health: Minor heart attack two years ago, has recovered.

ANALYSIS WORKSHEET FOR SITUATION A: Mark **Yes** or **No**

	MONEY	AUTHORITY	DESIRE
Prospect 1			
Prospect 2			
Prospect 3			
Prospect 4			
Prospect 5			
Prospect 6			
Prospect 7			
Prospect 8			

QUESTIONS BASED ON ANALYSIS WORKSHEET:

1. Who are the two best prospects?

Prospect # _____

Prospect # _____

2. Which prospects would you consider next in line?

3. Which prospects should be eliminated from consideration?

SITUATION B

Assume you are a realtor and a homeowner has just given you an exclusive right to sell his or her home. The homeowner has mentioned that he or she is in a hurry to sell the house and has already made a commitment to purchase another home in the area. The house is situated in a well-kept block in a nice suburban residential community, close to all the major shopping centers. While the seller is asking for one price, you feel that a fair price for the home is about $250,000. The home has the following features:

- Victorian style home with two of the three levels finished.
- Six bedrooms.
- Finished portion of house is 3,200 square feet.
- 90 x 110 plot of land.
- Three baths.
- Eat-in kitchen with an additional formal dining room.
- Oversized two-car garage.
- Large, unfinished basement.
- Large family room with fireplace.

You have information cards on eight prospects. By completing the analysis worksheet, qualify each prospect using the MAD Approach.

Prospect 1
Family: Husband, two children
Age: Adult 33, children 8,15
Occupation: Hardware store owner
Income: $55,000
Down Payment: $8,000
Broker notes: Just went through divorce

Prospect 2
Family: Husband, wife, and two boys.
Ages: Husband 26, wife 25, boys are 4 and 2
Occupation: Mechanic
Income: $30,000
Down Payment: $6,000
Broker notes: Been renting and anxious

Prospect 3
Family: Husband, wife, two children
Ages: Adults in early 30s, children 5, 2
Occupation: Accountant
Income: $45,000
Down Payment: $5,000
Broker notes: Anxious

Prospect 4
Family: Husband, wife, no children but wife is expecting twins.
Ages: 28, 27
Occupation: Electrician
Income: $40,000
Down Payment: $15,000
Broker notes: Very picky

Prospect 5
Family: Single male adult
Age: 35
Occupation: Financial Advisor
Income: $100,000
Down Payment: $50,000
Broker notes: Looking for moderate size home

Prospect 6
Family: Husband, wife, and three children
Ages: 37, 35, 15, 10, 7
Occupation: Husband is manufacturing rep
Income: $60,000
Down Payment: $20,000
Broker notes: Interested in home with lots of room

Prospect 7
Family: Husband, wife
Ages: Mid 20s
Occupation: Owns a nursery school in home
Income: $45,000
Down Payment: $15,000
Broker notes: Seeking home to keep nursery

Prospect 8
Family: Husband, wife
Ages: Mid 50s
Occupation: Teacher and librarian
Income: $60,000
Down Payment: $40,000
Broker notes: No children and want smaller home

ANALYSIS WORKSHEET FOR SITUATION B: Mark Yes or No

	MONEY	AUTHORITY	DESIRE
Prospect 1			
Prospect 2			
Prospect 3			
Prospect 4			
Prospect 5			
Prospect 6			
Prospect 7			
Prospect 8			

QUESTIONS BASED ON ANALYSIS WORKSHEET:

1. Who are the two best prospects?

Prospect # _____

Prospect # _____

2. Which prospects would you consider next in line?

3. Which prospects should be eliminated from consideration?

TEN

THE PREAPPROACH

Learning Objectives

When you finish studying the material in this chapter, you should be able to:

1. **Define the preapproach.**
2. **Identify the objectives of the preapproach.**
3. **Discuss the two types of information needed in the preapproach.**
4. **Describe the sources in obtaining information.**
5. **Develop a preapproach checklist.**

Before I can sell John Jones
What John Jones buys,
I must first see the world
Through John Jones's eyes.

–Author Unknown

THE PREAPPROACH

The third step of the sales process is known as the **preapproach**. This selling step involves the task of collecting information and finding out all you can about a prospect before attempting to set up an interview or appointment. In other words, the preapproach is simply **doing your homework**. A Lawyer will spend days preparing a case before he/she goes to court. Contractors create a bid that includes every nail, board, machine, and the manpower that will be used before they submit a bid for a building job. A student talks to other students to find out the best instructors to take next semester for specific class. Salespeople must also do their homework before beginning a presentation with a potential buyer. The success of your effort depends heavily on the amount of preparation or homework that takes place before the sale.

OBJECTIVES OF THE PREAPPROACH

Like any other step in the sales process, the **preapproach** has some basic objectives. The amount of time and effort spent in achieving these objectives will enhance the success of the salesperson. Three major objectives are:

- To obtain additional qualifying information about the buyer.
- To learn information that will avoid serious errors during the presentation.
- To determine the best approach to use and the best time of day to contact the buyer.

The Preapproach

Preapproach = Doing your homework

TYPES OF INFORMATION

With the exception of special situations like door-to-door selling, you should possess some prior information about the prospect you are planning to contact. All information collected on a prospect should be reviewed before making a sales call. This will serve as a reminder to you about capitalizing on the customer's interests as well as spotting topics that might best be avoided. When doing preapproach work, make sure all information is recorded and written down; don't trust your memory. We will look at two different areas for preapproach work: (1) Company information for organizational buyers, and (2) Personal information for the ultimate consumer.

Company Information

If your customer is an organizational buyer, you will need industry and company information in addition to personal information. With regard to industry information, you should have some insight into the history of the industry, its current status and economic environment, the major competitors in the industry, the relationship between this industry and other industries, and any current problems facing the industry and its member companies. Also, attempt to find out the size of the company, the growth potential, key personnel and executives, the person with the authority to make buying decisions, the financial condition of the organization, purchasing practices, target markets the company serves, the type of management used, and the present suppliers selling to the company.

If you can find out all of the above information, you will probably be the first salesperson in history to do so. Any bit of information is better than none at all. Attempt to find as much as possible. At least find out three additional items about the company with the person who has the authority to make the buying decision as priority number one.. This is the person you will be contacting and persuading to purchase your products or services.

The Most Important Company Information Item

Finding out the key person who has the final decision-making authority is the most important company information item you need to obtain.

Personal Information

You should attempt to find out as much as possible so that you can approach the buyer with confidence and warmth. The personal information to maintain in your customer files should include the customer's name, age, education, occupation, family status, interests, hobbies, memberships, personal traits and characteristics, and anything else that might be of use during your sales approach.

Again, if you can find all the above information then you will be in excellent shape. The better you use your friends and associates for information, the more information you will obtain. Some of the most important topics of information that have been mentioned are first, the buyer's name. Find out the proper pronunciation, spelling, and initials used. In learning about the prospect's family, attempt to find out the ages of all family members, the names, and the marital status of the buyer. As you find out the occupation of the buyer, you can then determine the best time to call on the buyer. If the buyer is a contractor, you'd better contact him before 9:00 a.m.; if the buyer is a banker, you'd better contact him before 10:00 a.m. Knowledge of the customer's occupation can be a significant asset. Remember that the correct pronunciation of the buyer's first and last names is the most important personal item to obtain.

The Most Important Personal Information Item

The correct pronunciation of the buyer's name is the most important personal information item you should obtain.

SOURCES OF INFORMATION

After you have decided on the type of information you want to obtain, the next thing to do is to acquire the information. In gaining preapproach information, be aware that the sources you use should be selected carefully. You should not snoop for information or invade the personal privacy of the prospect. Also, be careful of buffers. A buffer is a person that screens out people for his supervisor or company. A buffer could be a secretary or any company employee. Buffers can also be technological in nature like caller ID and answering machines. Keeping the previous suggestions in mind, the following checklist is excellent to use for acquiring information about your buyer.

Preapproach Information Sources

- ✔ **Centers of influence.**
- ✔ **Trade journals and publications.**
- ✔ **Reference books and business directories.**
- ✔ **Company reports and newsletters.**
- ✔ **Family and friends of the prospect.**
- ✔ **People in the industry.**
- ✔ **People in the community and neighborhood.**
- ✔ **Company employees and associates.**
- ✔ **Members of civic groups and clubs.**
- ✔ **Previous and present customers.**

If you do your homework in the **preapproach stage**, you will become more effective when you enter the sales interview. Keep in mind that your success largely depends upon your preparation. As you gain the needed information on your prospect and his/her company, you will create a more productive climate for your presentation. You will go into the selling situation with more confidence and will find it easier to adapt and adjust to difficult situations. Doing your homework through effective preapproaching eliminates the "cold turkey" feeling that many salespeople experience when they approach the prospective buyer for the very first time. Perhaps another example that all of us can relate to is that first blind date we experienced. Remember the friend who wanted to set you up with a person who you had never seen or met. Without seeing a picture of this person and learning about some personal items like personality, name, interests, and background, you were very nervous and uncomfortable at first until you were able to meet the person, develop rapport, and break the ice. Reliable preapproaching information is a great asset for the successful salesperson.

It is very helpful for the salesperson to create a final preapproach checklist. As the seller reviews this information he/she has acquired before making the sales call, a more effective strategy can be developed that will increase the success of securing an interview for a future presentation. Most sales books and training manuals do not give enough emphasis to this crucial step of the selling process. Look over the checklist of eight items below and make sure all items are checked with a "yes"before proceeding with an sales call.

Assess Yourself–Final Preapproach Checklist

		Yes	No
1.	**Have I obtained at least three information items about the prospect or the organization?**	❑	❑
2.	**Do I know how to pronounce the prospect's name and do I know the key person to contact?**	❑	❑
3.	**Are my sources who provided this information reliable?**	❑	❑
4.	**Have I reviewed my prospect information?**	❑	❑
5.	**Have I organized my presale plan?**	❑	❑
6.	**Have I secured the interview opportunity by determining the right time, place, and approach?**	❑	❑
7.	**Have I checked my image–dress, appearance, and body language?**	❑	❑
8.	**Have I examined my attitude to make sure it is professional and positive?**	❑	❑

ELEVEN

THE APPROACH

Learning Objectives

1. Explain why the approach is a separate selling situation.
2. Discuss the purpose of the approach.
3. Describe and give examples of the nine basic approach techniques.
4. Identify which approach techniques would be appropriate for a variety of different selling situations.
5. Discuss how to develop a customized approach strategy.

Know how to ask the right question!

A group of salespeople, stranded in a motel during a bad storm, wondered impatiently when they could get back on the road to make some sales calls. They grilled everyone who came into the motel in the morning, asking whether the roads were clear enough to travel. One wise person said, "Well, that depends." "Depends on what?" the salespeople wanted to know. "Depends on whether you're on salary or commission."

–Taken from *Bits & Pieces for Salespeople*

THE APPROACH

The fourth step in the sales process is called the **approach**. This step is when the salesperson delivers a brief sales message to the potential buyer. This is the first time in the sales process when the salesperson meets the prospect face-to-face. The approach has been described as doing what has to be done in order to get in to see the customer. A salesperson may have an outstanding product and know that the customer needs the product, but having a good product does not guarantee that the salesperson will have buyers. A salesperson needs to develop a sound approach that will motivate the prospect to want to see the seller. We will discuss in this chapter the purpose of the approach and nine approach techniques that will make it easier to obtain an appointment for the presentation.

THE APPROACH IS A SEPARATE SALE

The approach is a separate sales situation. You must get by buffers and sell yourself successfully to get an opportunity to present your product or service. The approach generally lasts around five minutes or less. Probably the most important time is the first thirty seconds in which you meet the prospect. You will quickly be sized up, so it is very important that you are careful about your manner, gestures, dress, and the opening words that will be used. Any one of the previously mentioned items can destroy the possibility to pursue a sales presentation. If you fail to sell yourself in a positive manner, you may never get the chance to show your product and tell your sales story.

THE PURPOSE OF THE APPROACH

Several things must be accomplished during the approach stage of the sales process. The basic purpose of the approach is to create immediate interest and smoothly move into the presentation. Of course, to do this, you must be able to sell yourself, your product, and your company. It is important to start off on the right foot and gain the attention of the prospect. Also, you must use your preapproach information and find out the right person to contact, select the proper time to call, and determine the best entry–be it a letter, cold call, or by telephone. As you establish rapport and make a good first impression, you are then able to move into the actual sales presentation.

The Approach is a Separate Selling Situation

Before you can sell your product and company, you must first be able to sell yourself.

NINE BASIC APPROACH TECHNIQUES

Because every product and every prospect is different, it is essential to devise opening words and approaches for all types of situations. Every salesperson should be aware and familiar with the following nine approach techniques. After mastering these basic approaches, a salespeople can use their creatively and develop several additional ones that works best for them..

The Introduction Approach

The **introduction approach** is the most frequently used approach technique. It can also be the weakest because it does very little for the salesperson except identify who he/she is and the company that is represented. After identifying him/herself, the salesperson may want to move into one of the other eight approach methods. Basically, the introduction approach is when the **salesperson states his or her name and the company he/she works for**. Also, it is important that the salesperson maintains eye contact and smiles in order to create a positive first impression. A simple example of this approach is "Hello, I'm Dave Smith, representing Hewlett Packard."

The Reference Approach

Using the name of another customer or friend is one good way to start to make the prospect feel obligated to listen. Personally, the **reference approach** is my favorite technique to use because it creates **common ground**. Common ground is simply establishing something in common between two individuals. This technique is especially effective if the potential prospect respects the judgment of the referenced person. This method also reduces the barrier between the salesperson and the buyer because they both have something in common–an individual who they know and respect. An example of this approach is, "Good afternoon, Mr. Davis! Tom Jones, one of your friends, bought a copier from us last week. He indicated that you might also be interested." The referenced person carries more influence in your approach if he/she is a present happy customer of the product or service you are selling.

The Praise or Compliment Approach

This method is when you **sincerely compliment or give sincere praise to the prospect**. You must be specific in your compliment so that the prospect will know that you're being honest and that the compliment is deserving. It is especially effective if the prospect really deserves the compliment or likes to have his/her self-esteem nurtured. If you are not careful in your praise or words of compliment, it could end up in bad taste and create an uncomfortable atmosphere. An example of this approach is, "Good morning, Sir! You are fortunate to have such an ideal location with the high traffic flow."

The Gimmick Approach

When all other approaches seems to be unsuccessful, some salespeople become creative and turn to **unusual ways of getting the prospect's attention**. One type is called the **gimmick approach**. Magazine salespeople use this approach when they pretend to be researchers conducting a survey in the area. By doing a survey the salesperson acquires qualifying information and secures permission to gather information. The salesperson can then make a suggestion based on the survey that involves the purchase of several magazine subscriptions. Another example is when a salesperson lights a dollar bill with a match to show how much money is being lost by not buying a specific product. Some salespeople have even gone to the extent of asking for a glass of water. If you are not careful when using creative techniques, you can hurt the image of the company you represent.

The Question Approach

This popular technique requires the prospect to answer a question that will develop interest in a specific problem that can be solved through purchase of a product. This approach is successful in encouraging early, two-way communication. The questions used can be summarized into four different categories:

- **A qualifying question.**

  "If I could show you a system that would pay for itself within 18 months, would you be interested?"

- **A benefit question.**

  "Your company would need a car that would hold up at least 100,000 miles under normal, driving conditions, wouldn't it?"

- **An image question.**

  "If you suddenly became ill and missed work for four months, how would your family live?"

- **A curiosity question.**

  "Have you ever seen a flashlight work without batteries?"

The key to using the **question approach** is to **ask a question that forces a positive response and also qualifies the buyer for your product**. This is the most popular approach to use in involving the customer.

The Statement or Benefit Approach

This approach is **like an advertising headline**; it attracts the attention and gives exciting news for the prospect. It also is appealing to the prospect's major buying motive. The key to the **statement or benefit approach** is to give some very ear-catching words in the first selling statement. Some examples follow:

"Prices are going up by 20 percent in two days, but you can buy today and save."

"I challenge you to find any cleaner in the world that saves you as much money and that cleans as well as this Clenso cleaner."

"Tom Harris across the street says this product alone has saved him $1,500 during the last year in cleaning costs."

The Premium Approach

This approach appeals to the desire of everyone who wants to get something for nothing. It is used by door-to-door salespeople and supermarkets. The great thing about this approach is that it buys selling time. The **premium approach** is when **you give away a product, small gift, or free sample to a prospect for just listening to a short sales message**. It is more effective if you give away the premium at the end of the presentation. One example of this approach is when a vacuum cleaner salesperson gives a knife set to the potential customer for just listening to a short 30-minute presentation. Also, many direct selling organizations will away a free item to encourage you to buy more. Supermarkets have people, most often beautiful ladies, who stand in the aisles giving away free samples of a new food item the store is promoting. I have even had some ladies come up to me and spray shaving cologne on my hand to encourage me to buy. This technique catches the attention of people and gives the salesperson a few minutes to present a short presentation that will hopefully turn into a sale.

The Product Approach

This approach is tailor-made for **products that are valuable and eye catching**. This is a direct and honest approach in which you get the product in the customer's hands to assist you in the selling message. This technique gains the immediate attention of the product's offerings and benefits. Some examples of this approach are when the tire salesperson shows you a cross section of a steel-belted radial tire or when the shoe salesperson shows you a shoe cut in half to point out the superb construction of the shoe. An office systems salesperson may walk into the office and place the product in the prospect's hands and say, "I want you to see how efficient and easy this office machine is to use."

The Shock Approach

This approach allows a salesperson to **dramatize a scene or situation** that stirs up the emotion and encourages the prospect to take action and buy the product. The **shock approach** is very popular in the life insurance and investment industries. The insurance salesperson creates a scene in which the husband dies in an accident and leaves his wife and children with the burden of paying the bills, making the house payment, and trying to pick up the pieces to start a new life again. The salesperson points out the security and peace of mind that are found in purchasing some life insurance.

This approach is also used by salespeople who are selling big cars. The car salesperson points out how many people die in head-on collisions because they were driving small cars. The salesperson shows you statistics of the deaths that come from people involved in driving small import cars. He/she points out the protection given by a larger car. A large car gives you security and makes driving safe.

DEVELOP A CUSTOMIZED STRATEGY

Which of the basic approaches discussed in this chapter is best to use in selling? Well, the answer is not a simple one because it depends on several factors. Which selling approach technique you use depends on you and your personality, what you are comfortable in using, what product or service you're selling, what works in your specific industry, and what other salespeople selling similar products have had success with. Of course, the most important factor to consider is the buyer and what you think will work best with a specific buyer in a given situation. As illustrated below, you need to develop a customized strategy that is the result of trial and error, research, and your personal observations in your industry of other successful salespeople. Time and experience will help you develop a personal strategy consisting of those techniques that have proven to be most successful in securing an opportunity to give your persuasive sales presentation at a future date.

You Must Develop a Customized Approach Strategy

Key factors to consider in deciding on which approach techniques to use.

- **Personality of the salesperson.**
- **What the salesperson is comfortable in using.**
- **Product or service being sold.**
- **What works well with other salespeople in your industry.**
- **What the specific situation may demand.**
- **Characteristics of the individual buyer.**

Personal Application Exercise–Determining The Best Approach

Instructions: Choose the statement that is most likely to attract the prospect's attention and interest in listening to a future presentation and is the best example of the approach that was discussed in this chapter. The best choices are found at the end of the exercise.

Approach 1: The Praise or Compliment Approach

1. I'm sure that a large company such as yours, Mr. Taylor, is interested in quality products that are being introduced on the market. My company's new plastic tubing is just such a product.
2. Mr. Taylor, it is a pleasure and an opportunity to meet someone with your reputation as an innovator. It is you, and others like you who are leaders of business in our country. I am sure that you will find that my company's new plastic tubing is the type of product that fits your image and philosophy.
3. Mr. Taylor, your company has a reputation in the industry as an innovator. My company's new plastic tubing will permit you to continue your tradition of using quality, innovative products.
4. Everyone in the industry recognizes your leadership in adopting new products. You have maintained this reputation for over 30 years. As purchasing agent for the ACME Company, you must be very proud of the important role you play in maintaining this image and reputation. Our new plastic tubing will permit you to continue your tradition of adopting new quality products.
5. Mr. Taylor! Wow! You have such beautiful office decor. I bet you enjoy looking at those paintings each day. I know you will also enjoy looking at some new plastic tubing I have to show you.

THE BEST STATEMENT IS ___________

Approach 2: The Statement or Benefit Approach

1. This new data processing machine has many advantages over what your secretary is presently using.
2. This new data processing machine will enable your secretary to get more work done in less time, thereby freeing her to do other important work.
3. Your secretary will love the color and bell sounds of our new processing machine. Isn`t that blue color beautiful?
4. There are six main advantages of our new data processing machine over our old one. Let me take some time and discuss them with you.
5. Our company's new data processing machine has saved 50 large companies over $500,000 in the last two months alone.

THE BEST STATEMENT IS ___________

Approach 3: The Question Approach

1. Have you recently had problems with your generators?
2. Have you heard of Remington generators?
3. How would you like a generator that would increase efficiency by 25 percent?
4. Are your present generators as efficient as they should be?
5. Would you like a new generator?

THE BEST STATEMENT IS __________

Approach 4: The Reference Approach

1. Mr. Grunander, I was directed to you by Mr. Ott of Ashley Products. He recently purchased some of our electronic typewriters for his office. He suggested that you would also be interested in some that have increased the productivity of his support staff by 25 percent.
2. Mr. Grunander, Mr. Ott of Ashley Products suggested that I spend some time with you regarding my company's new electronic typewriters. I am sure you will find them as interesting as he did.
3. Mr. Grunander, many companies are currently using our new electronic typewriters to their satisfaction. I would like to explain how you can improve your productivity by up to 25 percent.
4. Mr. Grunander, I was recommended to you by Mr. Ott of Ashley Products. He has been extremely satisfied with our product and he suggested that you would be also.
5. Mr. Grunander, Mr. Ott across the street told me to come and see you. I have something exciting to show you and it will only take a few hours. Let me go to my car and bring in the rest of my merchandise.

THE BEST STATEMENT IS __________

Approach 5: The Introduction Approach

1. Hello, I'm Neil Wakefield. Glad to meet you.
2. How do you do? I'm from Thompson Electronics Corporation.
3. Hello, Mr. Smith! I'm Neil Wakefield representing Thompson Electronics.
4. Hello, Mr. Smith. I'm Neil Wakefield. I represent Thompson Electronics, a major firm in the Northwest. Can I speak to you for a minute?
5. Hey! Boy, I'm glad to see you. Let's chat for a while.

THE BEST STATEMENT IS __________

Exercise answers–best statements are: 1 - 4; 2 - 5; 3 - 3; 4 - 1; 5 - 4

TWELVE

THE PRESENTATION

Learning Objectives

When you finish studying the material in this chapter, you should be able to:

1. Identify the five types of sales presentations.
2. Explain the five buying decisions.
3. Describe how to turn a product feature into a product benefit.
4. Explain how to handle the issue of competition during a presentation.
5. Discuss several ways to establish credibility.
6. Identify the best types of visual aids to use during a presentation.
7. Explain how to utilize the five senses during a presentation.
8. Discuss the importance of using questions.
9. Explain the four Ss of increasing your average sale.
10. Describe the various promotional tools used in selling to the ultimate consumer and to the organizational buyer.

The Power of a Persuasive Presentation

One salesclerk in a candy store always had customers lined up waiting, while other salesclerks stood around with nothing to do. The owner of the store noted his popularity and asked for his secret. "It's easy," he said. "The others scoop up more than a pound of candy and then start taking away. I always scoop up less than a pound and then add to it."

THE PRESENTATION

The presentation is the core of the sale because this is when all of your product knowledge, information about why people buy, and preapproach information come together to make the sale. This is the moment you were working toward as you spent all those hard hours prospecting for customers. It is during this time, the presentation, that you will attempt to persuade the prospect that your product is the one that will best satisfy his/her need. The presentation includes all that the salesperson says and does during the sale. This is the main persuasive effort because you produce a **change of mind** in the customer that will end in a sale. This is often called the **meat and potatoes of the selling process** because it is the main course; that which provides the main substance of the sale. You can get your foot in the door with your ability to make positive first impressions, but if you can't tell your story with persuasion and sell your product, you will lose the sale.

TYPES OF SALES PRESENTATIONS

Before we discuss some of the important elements of the sales presentation, it is important for you to become aware of the different types of sales presentations used in the selling industry today. Professor Marvin Jolson surveyed hundreds of firms to determine the most used sales presentations and those presentations that are preferred by sales managers across the country. The following information presents the results of the survey and was taken from the article, **"Should the Sales Presentation be `Fresh' or `Canned'?"** that originally appeared in ***Business Horizons Magazine***. His original research results indicated that five presentations are presently being used. Additional research studies back up the findings of Dr. Jolson, however, most organized and unstructured presentations given today in a professional selling setting usually utilize some type of computer generated support system. The five most used presentations are:

- **Fully Automated**: Sound movies, slides, or film strips dominate this type of presentation. The salesperson's participation consists of setting up the projector, answering questions, and writing up the order. Many audio, visual, and multi-media systems are available.
- **Semi-automated**: The salesperson reads the presentation from a copy printed on flip charts, read-off binders, promotional broadsides, or brochures. The salesperson adds his/her comments when necessary.
- **Memorized**: The salesperson delivers a company-prepared message that has been memorized. Supplementary visual aids may or may not be used.
- **Organized**: The salesperson is allowed complete flexibility of wording; however, he/she does follow a company pattern, a checklist, or an outline. Visual aids are strongly encouraged.
- **Unstructured**: The salesperson is on his/her own to describe the product any way he/she sees fit. Generally, the presentation will vary from prospect to prospect.

Dr. Jolson's research also provides some additional information that is very important. The data below states the percentages in which each of the five above presentations are traditionally used in the selling industry. As you can see, the most used and recommended method is the **organized sales presentation**. It will be this type of presentation that will be emphasized throughout the remainder this chapter.

Usage of the Five Most Common Sales Presentations

	Percentage of Firms Using Each Presentation Type	Percentage of Firms Preferring Presentation Type
Fully Automated	9.3%	2.7%
Semi-Automated	33.3%	4.0%
Memorized	24.0%	9.3%
Organized	85.3%	44.0%
Unstructured	76.0%	40.0%

THE FIVE BUYING DECISIONS

Before preparing for any sales presentation, it is crucial that the salesperson understand that each buyer must make five decisions before walking out of the store with the product. There are five important questions or decisions that every customer must ask him/herself and answer before deciding to buy a product or service. "No" to any of the five buying decisions will defeat the sale for the salesperson. Also, all objections that will be raised during a sales presentation will fall under one of the five buying decisions. The five buying decisions are:

1. Do I really **need** the product?
2. Is this **product** the best solution to my need?
3. Is this the right **source** or **company**?
4. Is this the right **price**?
5. Is this the best **time** to buy?

Whatever you sell, put yourself in the prospect's position and realize that attention will have to be given to these five important questions in a satisfactory manner before the big commitment to buy is made. As a salesperson, you must help the customer come up with the right answers to these five questions. Think of how you react when you are a buyer. If the salesperson pressures you to make the fifth decision before you have answered the first four, you become disturbed, rushed, and a little irritated. Let's look at men's clothing and accessories. Let's suppose that you bought a suit recently. You started off seeking answers to questions like these:

- "I wonder if I really need a suit?"
  (Do I need the product?)

- "I wonder if I should get a tweed or a poly-wool?"
  (Is this product the best solution to my need?)

- "They don't seem to have much selection in my size; I wonder if the shop down the street has better choices?"
  (Is this the right source or company?)

- "Wow! Look at that price tag. I don't think I can afford that for a suit!"
  (Is this the right price?)

- "Maybe I ought to wait for the after-Christmas clearance sales!"
  (Is this the right time to buy?)

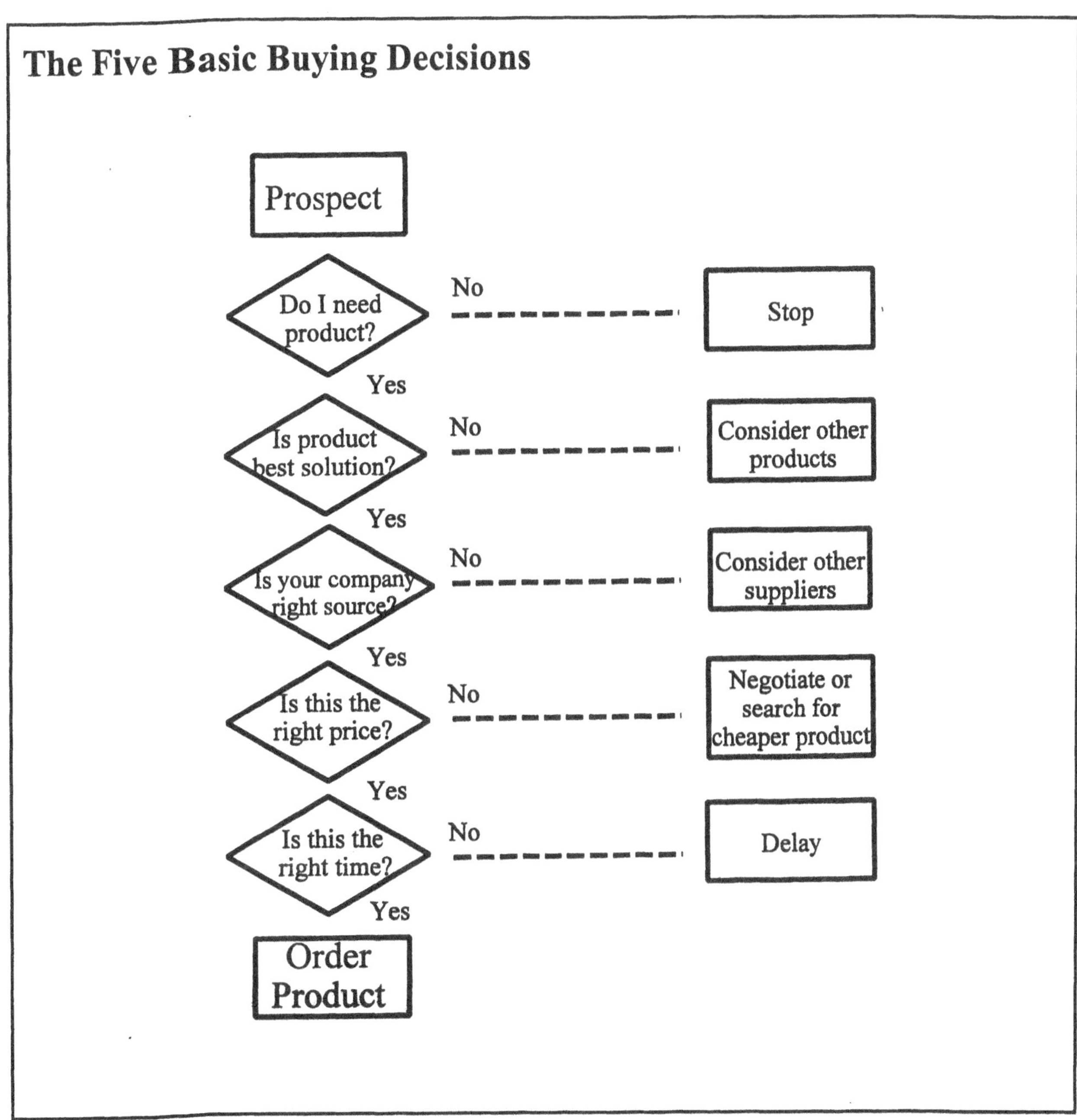

If you can recall a good clothing salesperson you bought from, the seller may have anticipated these five questions and helped you answer them in a way that would lead to closing the sale. The salesperson probably asked you for your color preference and size and then picked a suit and asked you to put on the coat "just to try it on to check for size." You couldn't object to trying it on for that purpose. With the proper size established, your decision process started into motion because of your active participation. The salesperson asked questions to get your preference concerning items like style, color, material, and price. He/she had you look at yourself in the mirror as he/she commented on the features and the benefits of two or three suits. The salesperson made sure making a choice was as easy as possible. The salesperson asked, "Which color do you like best?" That made you come to the part of the buying decision which we call the trial close. If everything had been answered in a positive manner up to this point, you said, "I'll take it!" which are the best three words a salesperson can hear. You may have stopped with a partial decision. The salesperson then asked you to try on the trousers; another trial close attempt by the salesperson. If you agreed, the sale was still moving towards being made as you became emotionally involved in the presentation. If you were reluctant, the salesperson reviewed the features and the benefits you would receive from the suit. The seller then justified the price with quality. If you were still reluctant, the seller might point out that by the time you make a decision, your selection would be vastly limited, and you would have to settle for much less than the beautiful suit you had selected today. Besides, you would also probably save about $25, because the salesperson would throw in a free tie with the suit purchase. If the salesperson helped you answer the five basic buying decisions positively, you bought. If not, you went to another store, or put off the decision.

Whatever your product or service is, think of your prospect as having to make these five important buying decisions. By asking some basic questions at the beginning of the presentation, you can quickly determine how far or close the buyer is toward the final purchase. Remember, the first four decisions must be made before the final one is made and these decisions are usually made in the sequence found in the previous illustration. Learn to recognize where the buyer is on the road towards the final purchase and become familiar with the five basic buying decisions.

TURNING FEATURES INTO BENEFITS

Besides learning about the importance of the five buying decisions, an additional powerful tool that a salesperson should use is the ability to turn product features into benefits for the buyer. A product **feature** is a **specific characteristic or quality of a product or service**. A buyer **benefit** is the **personal benefit the customer receives from using the product or service**. Every buyer asks one important question before finally deciding to buy a product. This question is, "What's in it for me?" Which is commonly called **WIIFM.**

The Ultimate Buying Question

WIIFM = What's In It For Me?

The customer doesn't really buy a tangible or physical product; the customer buys benefits–WIIFM. The salesperson must be creative and learn to turn features into benefits. The following examples found in the next illustration are what salespeople must do to be creative in turning features into buyer benefits.

Turning Features into Benefits

The average salesperson sells clothes;
The creative salesperson sells personal appearance.

The average salesperson sells life insurance;
The creative salesperson sells protection for loved ones.

The average salesperson sells household equipment;
The creative salesperson sells relief from drudgery.

The average salesperson sells books;
The creative salesperson sells the value of knowledge.

The average salesperson sells automobiles;
The creative salesperson sells the joy of the open road.

The average salesperson sells advertising;
The creative salesperson sells profit insurance.

A salesperson can't depend on the customer to translate the product feature into customer benefits. The salesperson must be creative and see the product in the eyes of the customer in terms of benefits because people buy benefits, not products. Below is an additional example to point out the difference between product features and buyer benefits. This example deals with automobile features.

We don't sell brakes;
We sell safer, surer stops. We sell security. We sell the ease of stopping.

We don't sell torsion bars;
We sell smooth, controlled rides. We sell easy handling, even over rough roads.

We don't sell insulation;
We sell quiet rides. We sell protection from heat and cold.

We don't sell power steering;
We sell ease of handling, the ability to park easily.

We don't sell air conditioning;
We sell driving and riding comfort. We sell clean traveling and filtered air.

Hopefully you are now getting the feeling of how to turn features into benefits. As you know, features alone have very little impact on the customer. Features become meaningful only when the customer can relate the feature to something that will be of personal benefit–**WIIFM**. To be successful and creative in changing features in such a manner that it is easy to understand, you can use three steps that will make the task easier. We call it "FAB."

FAB–A three step process for turning features into benefits

Step One: Feature–List the product feature.

Step Two: Advantage–Determine what the feature will do for the customer.

Step Three: Benefit–Explain how your customer can benefit from the product performance.

In other words, let's put the above three steps of FAB in a simple formula and apply the formula in and example dealing with jogging shoes.

Feature	+	**Advantage**	=	**Benefit**
(What the feature is)		(What the feature does)		(What the feature means to the buyer)

Feature	=	**Cushioned arch support.**
Advantage	=	**Provides foot support for running.**
Benefit	=	**You will have more personal comfort.**

Feature = Leather upper.
Advantage = Provides durable wear.
Benefit = Shoes will wear longer and save you money.

Feature = Reinforced toe.
Advantage = Protects toes.
Benefit = You will be less likely to injure your toes.

Feature = Cushioned insole.
Advantage = Helps prevent blisters.
Benefit = Your feet will be more comfortable and feel less tired.

An effective sales presentation begins by planning what you want to say and what you want to do. With this information, you should be able to prepare an effective sales presentation and appeal to strong buying motives by stressing buyer benefits. Before you give any presentation, sit down and identify at least five selling points or features. After you have done that, then you can translate the features into benefits using the three-step FAB approach introduced in this chapter. A successful realtor put the feature–benefit concept so simply by stating that **"features tell but benefits sell."** Look at the following example below and apply the three-step FAB process by filling in the blanks for the advantage and benefit steps of a portable hair dryer.

Assess Yourself–Applying the FAB Process to a Portable Hairdryer

Feature	Advantage	Benefit
Durable plastic		
6 foot heavy duty cord		
Three temperatures		
Automatic shut off		
2 year warranty		

HANDLING OF COMPETITION

Another important item brought up in a presentation is the issue of competition. When the buyer brings up the idea of competition and states that the same product you are selling can be purchased through a competitor at a lower price, handle it with class and sensitivity. Never put the competition down by degrading or accusing. Point out why your product is different and what additional items your product offers. The salesperson that spends his/her time handling competition by tearing it down and picking it apart is not a true professional. Whenever the issue of competition is brought up, you can do one of two things:

- Acknowledge the competition, praise it, and pass over it, going on with your presentation.
- Meet competition head on, armed with facts, and make accurate comparisons.

It is meeting competition head on with facts that will be covered and discussed in this chapter. Let's learn eight ways to put your competition to work for you.

Using Your Competition Effectively

It might be difficult to concede that competitors help you sell more, but this is actually true. In fact, if there were no competitors, there would be no need for salespeople. All a company would need is a big sign that states, "Here it is. Come and get it." While we might agree that fewer competitors would be acceptable, we can make the best of what we have and actually sell more because of them. Here are some helpful hints that will allow you to start using your competition to your advantage.

- <u>Know your competition</u>: The key to beating your competition to the sale is to learn all you can about the features of their products or services, which will make a difference in the major benefits to your common customers. This is comparable to an athletic team scouting a competitor before a game to learn its favorite and most successful plays. What they learn can help win the game. What a salesperson learns about his/her competition can help win the next sale. A retailing friend of ours would always spend some time during her lunch hour scanning the stores of her competitors. Also, she would keep a very close watch on the newspaper ads of her rivals in business.
- <u>Look for competitive weaknesses</u>: Before you can stress your own product or service superiority, you have to know where the competitor is vulnerable. You do this by learning about the competition and by concentrating on their weak points. You learn about competition much like your own customers do–by reading advertising, examining their products, attending trade shows, and talking with both satisfied and dissatisfied users.

- **Know your own weaknesses**: The same study of competitive weaknesses will bring out their strengths as well, and your own weaknesses by comparison. When you are aware of your own product and service weaknesses, you can set up strategies to compensate for them. You do this by stressing features and benefits that outweigh the competitor's advantages. Learn to accentuate the positive in your business.
- **Anticipate resistance**: As you study competition and compare it with your own product or service, anticipate the objections or resistance a prospect who is aware of your competition will raise. Be ready with a strategy and knowledge for minimizing or overcoming the objection. Remember our discussion earlier in this chapter about the five buying decisions? Good knowledge of this concept will come in handy in anticipating resistance.
- **Study your prospect's reaction**: Listen carefully to your prospect as he/she compares your product with that of a competitor. What impressed the buyer most? What differences seemed most important? From the prospect's reaction, you can reinforce those differences in your favor and downplay the advantages the competition seemed to have with the prospect.
- **Build your own enthusiasm**: A study of competition and your own product usually gives you greater respect for your own position in the market. As you learn more about your own selling advantages, you gain more enthusiasm, which shows up in your sales presentations and in talking about the competition. A thorough knowledge of your own product and the product offerings of the competition will create confidence, which is easily noticed by your potential buyers.
- **Learn from mistakes**: Experience is a great teacher as long as it is put to good use in making corrections, especially in selling. Your own mistakes help future sales. But, your competitors make mistakes too. Make an effort to uncover them, then use them to build your own sales plan.
- **Learn from successes**: Be alert for ideas that have worked well for your competitors. Test them if they seem appropriate for your selling situations and adapt them. No monopoly exits on ideas that work.

As you gain knowledge about your competition, you can learn to handle the objection of competition more easily when it is brought up in your presentation. Don't over worry about competition, but, don't ignore it either. Some sales people degrade competition, while others completely ignore it. I suggest that you acknowledge it and use it to your advantage. Make competition work for you, not against you.

ESTABLISHING CREDIBILITY

Credibility is crucial in building goodwill in the mind of customers. A good relationship with a potential buyer is based on trust. To gain this trust professional salespeople must have credibility and make their presentation and claims believable. Customers must be able to rely on and believe what salespeople say.

Much of the sales presentation deals in claims or promises of value that the prospect will receive from buying the product or service. Without proof the salesperson asks his/her prospect to believe that what he/she is saying is true. But today's prospects have learned that it is easy to promise anything. What they want is delivery and proof. Actions speak louder than words. The professional salesperson has to make promises now and then, but the salesperson knows that he/she must be prepared to back them up with evidence the prospect will believe. Here are seven kinds of proof you can use to back up your claims for the product or services you sell.

- **Guarantees and Warranties**: Perhaps the easiest tool to use to create credibility is the guarantee and warranty of the product from the company which created it. A **warranty** is usually written and covers the product performance or the workmanship. It will describe the maker's responsibility for the performance, the repair, or the replacement of defective parts. It basically covers the usage and performance of the product. A **guarantee** can be a written or verbal agreement that generally covers the satisfaction of the buyer when using the product or service. Most guarantees come with a comment like, "If you are dissatisfied for any reason, we will refund your money in full."
- **Success stories and case histories**: We all like to listen to stories and case histories, particularly how another person or firm handled a need or problem we have. Professional salespeople collect success stories and have case histories about their products or services, using them as testimonials. When you hear of one, get as much detail and as many specifics as you can. They make the story more believable to the prospect. There is comfort in numbers, and the risk is reduced when the prospect knows other people have been in the same situation.
- **News stories and articles**: If your product or service gets a favorable mention in the news, use the story or article for proof. News items can also be used as proof of other reasons why a prospect should buy, such as increasing property values if you sell real estate, shortages of materials related to your products, or an expert predicting a rising stock market if you sell mutual funds. For some reason, if it is written in a book, magazine, or newspaper, people are more apt to believe it–again, seeing is believing. A popular source to use is ***Consumer Reports***. This magazine contains tests of products manufactured throughout the world.
- **Visual proof**: When you cannot demonstrate a benefit live, the next best method of proof is a visual record. Still pictures or movies of the product in operation are helpful. Charts and diagrams can be used to prove a point, such as the results of a consumer survey or records of how a product is selling in other areas. Also, you can

prepare charts to show what an excellent repair record your company has or the maintenance that is required. One professional advises to "prove one point at a time." Avoid trying to cover several points with the same chart or graph.

- **Expert endorsements**: We tend to respect the opinions of authorities in their field when they testify to the quality or performance of the product a salesperson is recommending. Results from testing laboratories, a statement from the chief engineer of a well-known company, and leading professionals in your area who have used your product are all examples of proof that carry more weight than your own opinion as a salesperson.
- **Testimonials**: Satisfied customers are convincing evidence of your claims, especially those claims that cannot be demonstrated to the customer, like long wear, savings in operation, and long range benefits. Testimonials are more impressive when they are from people or firms with needs similar to those of the prospect. Some salespeople give prospects the phone numbers of present customers and encourage the prospects to call up other people and get their feedback instead of just relying on the salesperson's word. A salesperson should keep a good record of happy customers. To do this, a salesperson must follow-up constantly after sales are made.
- **The demonstration**: If your product can be demonstrated to the customer, it is an easy way to back up some of your personal claims. If your product is lighter than other products, the prospect can lift it to test the weight. The prospect can operate a machine to see how easily it works. The prospect can test drive the car, try out the sewing machine, use the typewriter, and lay on the bed. The prospect can actually experience the product by using it. The demonstration is a favorite tool to establish credibility. When people actually use the product, they become emotionally stimulated and begin to feel ownership of the product.

The demonstration involves showing what your product can do. You have heard the expression, "A picture is worth a thousand words." The demonstration allows you to jump up and down on a suit case to show its durability. It allows you to reach out and grab the prospect's attention. By involving the customer and giving the customer something to remember, you increase your chances of making the sale. You can awaken the customer's interest in a manner that no amount of verbal presentation can achieve.

VISUAL AIDS

One of the best ways to keep attention in a presentation is by using visual aids. Not only do visual aids gain and maintain attention, they also promote two-way conversation. The following includes many of the possibilities you can use as a visual aid.

- **You the salesperson**: You are the most important visual aid of the presentation. An enthusiastic and quality presentation given by the salesperson will create the perception in the mind of the customer that the product is also enthusiastic and of high quality. Customers will see the connection between the salesperson and the presentation. The salesperson should exhibit energy and confidence, this in turn will build credibility for the product he/she is selling. No other visual aid can or should replace you as the most important visual aid used during the presentation.
- **The product itself**: For the majority of demonstrations, the product itself is the best tool to use next to you, the salesperson. If the product is unique or eye catching, use it as the main visual aid of the presentation. When individuals see the product, observe it, examine it closely, see how it operates, see strong points, know what can be done with it, and what ought not to be done with it, they gain a strong impression.
- **Transparencies**: Transparencies used with an overhead projector can project images and concepts on the wall or screen. Many salespeople write on the overhead transparencies while they give their presentation. The use of transparencies is becoming more widely used in today's selling world.
- **Display boards**: Fastening a series of pictures or objects to a cork board or bulletin board is useful when selling at a trade show. Interesting demonstrations also involve using magnetic boards on which objects are attached and moved about freely to illustrate specific points.
- **Charts**: A variety of charts can be used for demonstration purposes. The most common type of chart is the flip chart. This is a series of illustrations in which salespeople can start with the first chart and describe the items on it. After the first chart has been explained, the salesperson moves through a series of additional charts. It is suggested that the salesperson use color and attractive visuals on the chart so that the attention of the prospect will be maintained.
- **Graphs**: Graphs are a particular type of illustration which often convey certain messages. The most commonly used graphs are line graphs, bar graphs, and pictographs. Graphs are an excellent tool to use to explain particular ideas and visualize specific selling points. Care should be used in constructing and interpreting graphs.
- **Posters**: Posters, very similar to charts, are large pictures or illustrations on soft paper or stiff board. They are usually made in a series and are shown one after the other. Posters are effective to use in situations where many people are being contacted at once–like at a trade show or exhibition.
- **Portfolios**: This sales tool is very popular for financial, insurance, and investment salespeople. It is a case that resembles a large book or binder. It may be made of plastic, paper, or of a more durable material like leather. The portfolio carries a series of visuals like charts, graphs, illustrations, testimonial letters, pictures, and any other visual aid that can strengthen the presentation. The portfolio is usually smaller than a flip chart and can easily be handled during a presentation.

- **Catalogs**: Catalogs are usually reference volumes and consist of illustrations of the many products being offered by the salesperson. A large catalog is an impressive means of demonstrating the size of your assortment and the volume of items you sell. It gives you readily available illustrations and descriptions of most items. It saves the salesperson the burden of carrying many products around.
- **Samples**: The use of samples is one of the best and most effective ways to demonstrate a product. For example, samples of food give the prospect an excellent idea of quality, taste, size, and color. The door-to-door salesperson finds samples one of the best ways to introduce a product. Marketing research shows that a prospect who has sampled the product is more likely to buy that product than if the appeals are directed only through advertising.
- **Audiovisual/Computer generated aids**: With the improvement and abundance of today's technology, audiovisual tools are becoming more popular in the sales presentation. Video tapes, slides, projector panels, tape recordings, and computer generated graphics are useful items to increase the number of senses being appealed to in a presentation. It is common place to see salespeople use computers systems that combine sight, sound and movement into a powerful, visual presentation.

Now that you have been exposed to several alternatives that can be incorporated into a presentation, consider the following hints in using visual aids but always remember the key point in the next illustration.

The Most Powerful Visual Aid

The salesperson is the most effective and persuasive visual aid used during the presentation.

- Be sure to practice using the visuals before the presentation.
- Keep control of the visual and don't allow the visual to remain in the hands of the buyer for a long period of time. This is a quick way to distract the attention of the buyer.
- Prepare in advance so that you may use the visual aid at the time that it will become the greatest strength.
- Keep your visuals in good condition. If the visual aids you are using show wear, they might create some credibility problems in the mind of the buyer.
- Remember that visual aids are to assist you in the selling job. They cannot do the selling job alone and should not become a crutch.

- Don't become so dependent on computer generated visuals or other electronic technologies that you become totally lost if some electrical problem suddenly occurs. Always be prepared to give or continue on the presentation if a problem with your technology-based visual occurs.

THE FIVE SENSES

People use the five senses of touching, smelling, tasting, seeing, and hearing to gather information about the things around them. A successful salesperson will attempt to appeal to as many of the five senses as possible during a presentation. The more senses you involve, the better the learning process will be. Look at the illustration that indicates the percentage of learning that comes from each of the five senses. Notice that using multiple senses appeals increase learning and retention.

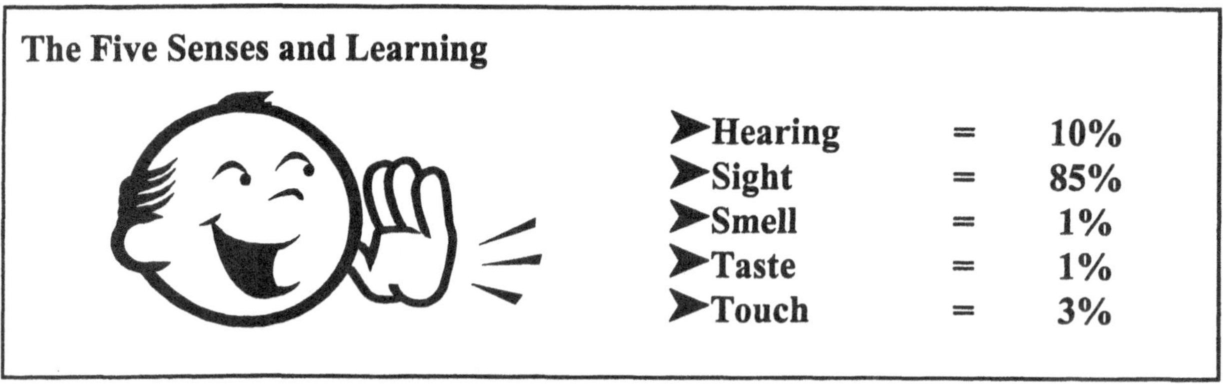

If you are selling a car, don't just talk about the car, get the buyer to sit behind the wheel and test drive it. If you are selling a computer system or software program, let the customer use it. If you are selling a smoke alarm, hold a match near it to set off the alarm buzzer. Creative salespeople of microwave ovens will place a cup of water in the oven and show how it will bring the cup of water to boil in less than one minute. In selling a suit, let the customer wrinkle the sleeve to show how well it keeps the press. Always be thinking of things you can do to involve more than just the sense of sight. By using more than one sense, you not only increase the learning process, but you also involve the customer by giving the customer a successful experience with the product.

QUESTIONING

The creative salesperson makes positive use of questions. Through the use of questions, you can gain customers' opinions and feelings, gather information about the customer, and find out if the customer is accepting what you are saying. Questions are a great tool because questions require responses, responses provide feedback, feedback provides information, and information is needed to make decisions. The use of questions in the sales presentation can increase the power of suggestion. You are able to ask questions and get the customer to agree with points that you emphasize during the presentation. The more you can get the customer to say **Yes** to minor questions, the better your chances are of getting the customer to say yes to the final big question to buy. Also, it is helpful to nod your head when you ask a question that desires a "yes" response in return. The following are some good questions to use in applying the power of suggestion in the questioning process.

Don't you agree?

You like that, don't you?

Isn't that true?

That's worthwhile, isn't it?

This product has what you want, doesn't it?

You can see the obvious benefits, can't you?

Questions are only effective if you use the right tone of voice and know when to modulate your voice. Use questions that encourage the customer to respond in a positive manner. The more you get the customer to say "yes," the better the feeling will be about your product and presentation. Always do what is necessary to establish and maintain a positive atmosphere. This is especially important during your use of question techniques.

THE FOUR "Ss" IN INCREASING YOUR AVERAGE SALE

The most used measure of success in selling is sales volume. There are many other considerations, of course, like customer goodwill and repeat sales, but when two salespeople are compared, the one who turns in the largest sales volume is usually considered more successful and valuable to the company.

Experience in talking to professional salespeople will tell you that increasing your sales can be done several ways. This goal must be prepared for before the presentation and applied during key parts of the presentation. We will be referring to four specific ideas that will be called the four "Ss"–**selling up, sell large quantities, suggestive selling,** and **stacking**.

Selling Up

Selling up consists of attempting to convince the customer to buy higher-priced and higher quality items than the customer originally intended to buy. Selling the higher-quality products will benefit the customer as well as the salesperson. By buying a higher-quality product, the customer will be saving money in the long run because the product will perform better, last longer, and have fewer breakdowns and problems. Suggest that the customer might prefer the better quality in such a way as, "You might prefer the wool suit instead of the polyester." Since everyone prefers higher quality, the customer will usually agree, and unless the price is particularly important, the customer will accept the better-quality merchandise.

Too many inexperienced salespeople assume that all customers want lower-priced merchandise–the bargains or good deals. But as a salesperson gains experience and wisdom, he/she learns to assume that the customer prefers good quality and begins to recommend it along with the benefits that will make the product well worth the price. Better-quality merchandise will lead to customer satisfaction. Experience will teach you that when a product fails to give full satisfaction, the customer tends to forget he/she paid less for it than a better-quality article and begins to give blame to the salesperson for not recommending a better product. No prospect should ever blame you for suggesting a higher-quality or higher-priced item if it will benefit the customer.

Sell Larger Quantities

Most people tend to buy only what they need for the moment. Some people learn that they can save money in the long run by buying a larger number of items at one time. The key to increasing the quantity sold is for the salesperson to be helpful with suggestions such as, "You'll save $30 if you take a dozen." You emphasize the satisfaction of saving money. Another example is, "You are ordering 75 units already. You can save an additional 15 percent if you order 100 units because you will be given a quantity discount." The majority of the buyers will appreciate your suggestion of buying larger quantities.

Suggestive Selling

One of the most successful tools in selling is **suggestive selling**. Suggestive selling is when the salesperson seeks to broaden the customer's original purchase with related items. Selling more than the customer intended to buy comes through suggesting related items, because your suggestion could save the customer much time and trouble later. Some examples of suggestion selling statements you may have heard are as follows:

"Would you want to look at a shirt and tie to go with your new suit?"

"Will you need any shoe polish and socks to go with your new shoes?"

"Would you like any candy or popcorn to go with your drink?"

"Let's look at some sheets and pillows for your new bed."

Suggestive selling is used after the buyer has already committed to buy a product. You will be surprised how the buyer will enlarge his/her purchase if you simply suggest additional related items.

Stacking

This technique is most popular in the retailing industry, but can be applied in all industries. **Stacking** shows courtesy and kindness on behalf of the salesperson. If a salesperson is busy with one customer while another customer walks into the office or store, the salesperson simply says, "I will be with you in a minute." As soon as the salesperson can break away from the present customer, the salesperson goes to assist the new customer. Stacking is simply recognizing unattended customers. It is showing decent courtesy that every person expects and deserves. The failure to "stack your customers" will result in lost sales and customers who will not return to your business.

PROMOTIONAL TOOLS

The purpose of the last area of this chapter is to expose you to terms, ideas, and concepts that are used daily in the selling industry in promoting products and services to the ultimate consumer and to channel members like wholesalers, retailers, and distributors. It is very important for a salesperson to realize that different strategies must be used when selling to a channel member instead of the consumer. When selling to the consumer, the salesperson will emphasize items like price, quality, and benefits. But, when a salesperson is selling to an industrial buyer like a wholesaler or retailer, the salesperson must also emphasize additional items like terms, discounts, allowances, profit, markup, and turnover. Most industrial buyers will agree that price is never the only item to consider when purchasing products that will be resold. An industrial buyer is concerned about profit margins and how fast the items will move in and out of the store. To aid you in developing an effective strategy, please become aware of the following promotional tools and use them in selling to the consumer and to industrial buyers that buy for organizations.

Terms

- **2/10 net 30**: This is basically a cash discount for buyers who pay within a specified period of time. This basically means that a 2 percent discount from the invoice price is offered to those paying within 10 days of the invoice date. The full amount is due at the end of 30 days if the discount is not taken. The percent discount and pay time periods can be altered to fit most individual situations. Most sellers working with small buyers are allowing 60, 90, and even 120 days to pay for products.

- **COD**: This means that the goods must be paid for when they are delivered. COD is simply "cash on delivery."

- **ROG**: This goes along with the 2/10 net 30 concept and means that the discount begins when the customer receives the goods instead of the date on the invoice. ROG means "receivement of goods."

Discounts

- **Cash discounts**: This is a reduction in the selling price when the buyer pays on the spot and no financing or terms are needed to complete the deal. Many sellerss will discount 5 to 10 percent if the buyer will pay at the time he/she buys the products.

- **Quantity discounts**: Quantity discounts are price reductions based on the amount purchased. They are generally granted to encourage large purchases. The more units you buy, the less the price is per individual unit.

- **Cumulative discounts**: These discounts are based on the total volume purchased over a long period of time. These discounts are advantageous to a seller because they tie customers more closely to the seller. They are really patronage discounts because the more total business a buyer gives a seller, the greater the discount.

- **Trade discounts**: Trade discounts are price reductions given to certain buying groups to compensate them for performing certain middleman marketing functions. Wholesalers will generally receive a larger discount than the retailer because they perform more marketing functions and buy in larger quantities than the retailer.

- **Seasonal discounts**: Manufacturers of goods that are in greater demand during certain seasons may offer discounts to middlemen during the off season. Sellers want to stimulate off-season sales in order to level out production. In the retail setting, a store may offer a product at a large discount after the demand has decreased. An example is discounting winter coats at the end of the winter season.

Transportation Policies

- **F.O.B. Plant**: F.O.B. or "freight on board" is a pricing term that is typically used with the name of a location. It means that the buyer pays for the freight charges of the goods when they leave the manufacturing plant until they reach the buyer's location. The legal title and responsibility for the goods passes to the buyer once the goods are turned over from the shipper to the buyer.

- **F.O.B. Destination**: This transportation policy has the seller paying for the freight or shipping charges until the products reach the destination. It also means that the seller takes title and the responsibility for the goods until the goods reach the destination point. The buyer likes this policy and it is a great incentive for the seller to use to encourage buyers to order goods from the seller.

- **Uniform Delivered Price**: This has been called a "Postage Stamp" policy because the same price is charged to all buyers, regardless of their location.

- **Zone Delivered Price**: An average freight charge to all buyers who fall into specific geographic regions or areas. The further away the buyer, the more it will cost to transport goods.

Stock

- **Close out**: Close outs are discounted items that are drastically reduced to move them out from the manufacturer. The items are new, but will no longer be produced by the company. This is a real incentive for a retailer as it allows the retailer to buy goods at cost or less and make a large mark-up when selling to the ultimate consumer.

- **Consignment**: Consignment is a "no risk" situation for the buyer. The seller agrees to buy back or take back those goods that the buyer can't sell during a specific period of time. What the retailer does not sell, he does not pay for.

- **Stock turnover**: Stock turnover is the number of times the average stock (inventory) is sold during a given period of time. It is most often used on an annual basis. A channel member would like a very high turnover. The more goods you move out, the more potential profit there is to be made.

Self-Discovery Experience–Organizing Major Selling Points

One of the first things you must do as you prepare for a sales presentation with a potential buyer is to list all the major selling points, or features, of your product. Let's suppose you are selling life insurance. You would sit down and list all the selling points you will emphasize during the presentation with your potential buyer. Look at the example below.

1. Provides for family security
2. History and background of the company
3. Testimonials
4. Price
5. Provides for spouse's security
6. Younger the consumer, the less expensive
7. Good investment

After you have listed between five and ten major selling points, you then look over your preapproach information and again arrange the selling points in the best sequence based on your buyer's wants and needs. Let's suppose you are selling to a young couple with one child who have recently purchased a small home. You would probably list the following selling points in order of importance to emphasize during your presentation with this young family like below.

1. Provides for spouse's security
2. Provides for family security
3. Price
4. Younger the consumer, the less expensive
5. Good investment
6. History and background of company
7. Testimonials

The main item you would emphasize with this family would be security. The other selling points will also be covered during the presentation of course, but the main emphasis would be on the security that life insurance will bring this young family. As you do your homework and get to know your prospect, you will effectively emphasize and draw attention to those items that will appeal to the strongest buying motive of your prospect.

On the next page are lists of products followed by some of the major selling points to be covered by the salesperson when delivering a sales presentation. Arrange the selling points in the best sequence by numbering them in the order of importance. Think of a prospect for each product situation.

Expensive Women's Makeup

_____ Price
_____ Long lasting
_____ Easy-to-open bottle
_____ Used by most celebrities
_____ Company reputation
_____ Salesperson's Reputation
_____ Ingredients
_____ Used by famous people

New Compact Automobile

_____ Type of motor
_____ Interior design
_____ Fuel consumption
_____ Options available
_____ Size of car
_____ Color of car
_____ Price
_____ Trunk space
_____ Maintenance requirements
_____ Service available
_____ Financing rate
_____ Dealer's reputation

House for a Family of Five

_____ Neighborhood characteristics
_____ Age of house
_____ Investment aspect
_____ Type of heating
_____ Mortgage loans available
_____ Shopping
_____ Quality of schools and their location
_____ Price
_____ Landscaping

Computer Equipment

_____ Company reputation
_____ Hard disk drive
_____ Price
_____ Warranty
_____ Speed of operation
_____ Service available
_____ Size of equipment and space savings
_____ Memory capacity
_____ Options available
_____ Brand name

Practical Application Exercise–Selling A Household Product

The purpose of this exercise is to allow you to incorporate some of the ideas that have been discussed concerning the presentation. You will be required to prepare and give **a ten-minute** presentation to a small group of buyers of your choice. The product you will sell must be a shopping good. The following are some examples of what you can use as the product for your presentation:

1. Hair dryer
2. Blender
3. Pop-corn popper
4. Waffle iron
5. Small toaster
6. Mix master
7. Radio
8. Tape recorder

As you prepare for this presentation, you will need to implement the following principles that have been discussed in class:

1. Must emphasize at least five major selling points.
2. Must stress product benefits in addition to product features.
3. Must involve showmanship by demonstrating the product, exhibiting enthusiasm, appealing to as many senses as possible, effectively using questions, and using visual aids.
4. Must demonstrate creativity and show individual imagination.

This ten-minute presentation must be well-planned, organized, and presented as it will be the first presentation in which you will be evaluated based on points by your fellow students. Below is the evaluation sheet that you will have your evaluators use in evaluating your performance.

	AREA	Poor	Fair	Good	Excellent
1.	**Did student identify five selling points?**	**0-1**	**2-3-4**	**5-6-7**	**8-9-10**
2.	**Were benefits stressed?**	**0-1**	**2-3-4**	**5-6-7**	**8-9-10**
3.	**Did student demonstrate showmanship?**	**0-2-4**	**6-8-10**	**12-14-16**	**18-19-20**
4.	**Was the presentation organized?**	**0-1**	**2-3-4**	**5-6-7**	**8-9-10**

THIRTEEN

HANDLING OBJECTIONS

Learning Objectives

When you finish studying the material in this chapter, you should be able to:

1. **Discuss the importance of attitude toward objections.**
2. **Identify the common reasons why people object.**
3. **Describe the five types of objections.**
4. **Identify several steps in overcoming the price objection.**
5. **Identify the ten golden rules of objections.**
6. **Discuss the six techniques in handling objections.**

Optimism–A key in overcoming obstacles and barriers.

An optimist is someone who goes after Moby Dick in a rowboat and takes the tartar sauce with him.

–Zig Ziglar

HANDLING OBJECTIONS

As we discuss the topic of handling objections, we will be looking at one of the most important elements in the sales process. Unless a salesperson can overcome objections, the sale will not be made and credibility will not be established. Objections are hurdles thrown in front of the salesperson that will need to be overcome. All salespeople will encounter objections during some phase of the sales process. The purpose of this chapter is to help you understand what objections really are and some techniques you can use to overcome them and turn objections into selling aids instead of selling obstacles.

ATTITUDE TOWARD OBJECTIONS

Let's assume that you are moving along in your presentation. You have determined the wants and needs of the customer. You have helped the customer select the best product and have spent time turning basic product features into customer benefits. You have carefully watched and listened to buying signals, and everything seems to be going your way. But now, the customer raises an objection. The customer seems to resist making a final decision to buy the product. It is at this time that many salespeople fail, because they stop selling since the customer appears to be no longer interested in the product. The most important thing for a salesperson to have at this moment is the proper attitude. A salesperson must realize that objections are part of the sales process. Objections should be welcomed with open arms, as they can become a powerful sales aid instead of a major obstacle. A salesperson should think of objections as if the prospect is seeking answers to honest questions so that he/she can decide whether the product will really fill an individual need or want. An objection is a question for which additional information is needed. People bring up objections because they need to feel that they are getting the best deal for their money and that they are making the right decision. Always have a positive attitude towards objections and expect objections at any time during the sales presentation. Experienced and successful salespeople also look at objections as closing opportunities. By giving objections, the customer is giving you a guidepost to his/her reactions and feelings. One successful investment salesperson with 20 years of experience puts it this way–"If my customer raises no objections, then my customer has no interest! I welcome any interaction from my customer." Learn how to let objections work for you instead of against you and remember the key points in the next illustration.

The Proper Attitude with Objections

- **Be positive.**
- **Expect objections to occur.**
- **Use objections as selling aids.**
- **Welcome objections with open arms.**

Whatever the reason is that causes the customer to object, the salesperson must not show a feeling of being bothered or annoyed. Even though the objection may be small or unimportant to you, it is important to the customer. At no time in handling objections should you show disinterest or an unconcerned attitude. By having the proper attitude in handling sales objections, you will find more success and will develop more self confidence.

WHY PEOPLE OBJECT

Every time a buyer gives you an objection, he/she is expressing feelings of insecurity that are common to all of us. We all try to avoid things that bring fear, punishment, pain, loss, uncertainty, and disapproval. People never enjoy the feeling of making a wrong buying decision. It is the salesperson's duty to help the prospect overcome these feelings. For a salesperson to help the prospect, the seller must first develop an understanding of why people object.

As mentioned earlier in this book, most people buy based on psychological reasons, and they also object to making a purchase for psychological reasons. In order to handle the objection, the salesperson must first learn the difference between an objection and an excuse. The most common forms of sales resistance are either objections or excuses. Real objections are concerns or hesitations the customer feels when deciding whether to purchase a new product. Real objections will tell you what is keeping the customer from buying. Once you have found out the real objection, you are then able to zero in on the reason and effectively overcome the objection. Excuses are a bit different. Customers give excuses to delay making a purchase or to avoid becoming involved in any pressure that may occur during a sale. A customer's excuses is seldom related to the merchandise being sold. They are generally insincere reasons. As you learn the difference between objections and excuses, you will become more successful in dealing with the feelings and the fears customers have in buying products.

TYPES OF OBJECTIONS

Many salespeople will tell you that you can learn to guess or anticipate most of the objections you will hear before ever talking with a potential buyer. Objections will differ for various products and services that are being sold. Therefore, as you attempt to determine the type of objections you will be faced with, consider the following five categories of common objections found in the next illustration. Do they look familiar? Remember the five basic buying decisions discussed in the previous chapter–all objections fall under those five decisions.

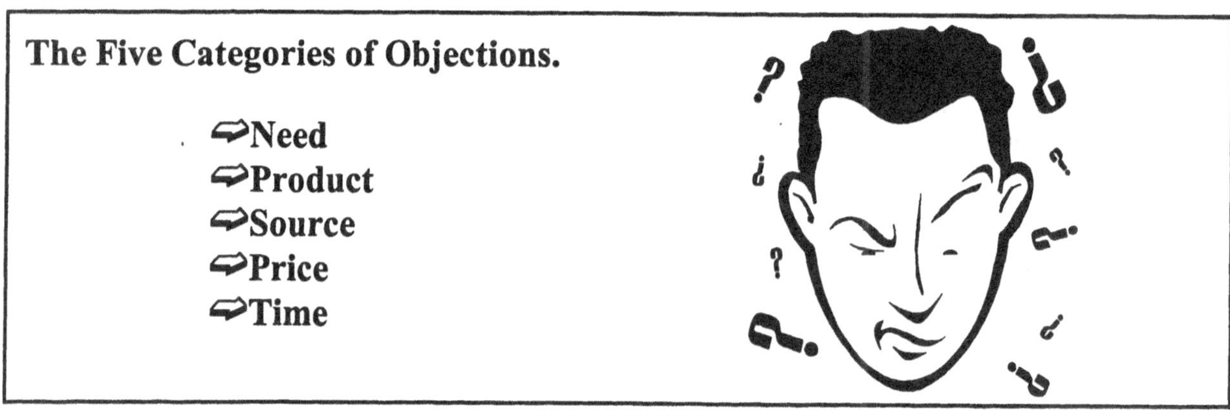

Need Objections

The first type of objection is the **need objection**. Some customers will not need the product you are showing. Other buyers may not be convinced that a need exists, so you must make them aware of the benefits of the product or service you are selling. Always take the approach of providing more information when this objection arises. Many buyers will realize that your product can benefit them after receiving additional information that explains the product or service. The most common remark given by the customer concerning the need objection is, "I am just looking." The ability to turn wants into needs can be a great tool in dealing with this objection.

One of the most common objections that will be raised by your customer is the objection dealing with the **product or service**. The customer may not like the style, model, color, quality, or some other feature of the product. Product knowledge on behalf of the salesperson is a "must" in overcoming this type of objection. Some customers will be concerned by the workmanship, material, or even the brand name. Whatever the product objection, be sure to answer it with confidence and with honesty. Some examples of this product objection are as follows:

✔"It looks cheap."

✔"I was looking for a lighter color."

✔"I don't like the feel of the material."

✔"It doesn't look like it will hold up over time."

✔"I usually buy another brand name."

Source Objections

The **source objection** deals with judging the credibility of the business or salesperson. Encourage the buyer to be interested in the company and the salesperson selling the product. The need to be convinced that your business has the service and that you are the right salesperson exists in the mind of most customers. Some common source objections deal with delivery, warranty, service, credit, and financing. Customers want a business that will be in business years down the road, so establishing credibility is very essential in overcoming this objection.

Some buyers get turned off with the personality of the salesperson. Many sales have been killed because of salespeople not knowing when to shut up or when to turn the sale over to another salesperson who can get along better with the buyer. One of my favorite sayings dealing with salespeople is found in the next illustration.

In one day Samson slew a thousand Philistines with the jawbone of an ass. Everyday, ten million sales are killed with the same weapon.

Everything should be done to adjust and adapt to the customer. The service and goodwill of a salesperson can help overcome the source objections. Be sure to maintain a good reputation and have a good collection of testimonial letters and referrals.

Price Objections

The **price objection** is the most common and volatile objection thrown at a salesperson. Some sellers feel that price may be the biggest obstacle they have to overcome in selling. Price is often a frustration for customers, because higher prices have become a daily occurrence in life. Most salespeople learn how to justify the price by pointing out the quality of the merchandise. Don't make up excuses for price; be ready to defend it by pointing out the difference between the initial price and the long-term cost of maintenance. If you really know your product and the products of your competitors, it won't be difficult to point out why the product is priced fairly. Price objections will occur more frequently than any other kind of objection and will usually cover up the buyer's real reason for being reluctant in buying your product. Some common price objections are as follows:

✔"I can't afford it."

✔"I don't have that kind of money right now."

✔"I am going to wait for prices to come down."

✔"Don't you have anything cheaper, or on sale?"

✔"I was looking for something a little less expensive."

✔"Your prices are high!"

Some people are honest in admitting that they do not have the money to buy your product, and good salespeople are able to work out convenient financing or installment payments. Some people will bring up the price objection because they want to bargain or negotiate with the salesperson for a better price.

Because salespeople will be faced with the price objection often, below are a number of steps to take in overcoming this objection.

■ **Identify the real reason for the objection**. Ask questions to get to the real reason for the price objection because the way you handle it depends on why the prospect feels as he/she does. The best question I have used is simply asking, "Would you mind telling me why you feel the price is too high?" By doing this, you transfer the responsibility to explain the price from you to the customer.

- **Be sure the customer is making correct comparisons**. If your questioning reveals that the customer is comparing your product with that of a competitive product, make sure the products are really comparable. If they are not comparable, then proceed to point out the benefits your product gives that are well worth the difference in price.
- **Combine price with benefits**. Many times the price objection is thrown at you without an opportunity to justify it with benefits. If this happens, acknowledge the objection but then proceed right on with the presentation of features and benefits that make the price seem more reasonable.
- **Minimize the difference**. Determine the difference in price between the product you recommend and a lower-priced one. Then, show that the difference is insignificant over the lifetime of the article when compared to the benefits during the same period. It is good to break the price down into smaller elements like months, weeks, or days to dramatize even less significance.
- **Emphasize the service**. Quality and value differences are important to point out, but often the salesperson forgets the services he/she provides that can be worth more than the price difference alone to the customer. Goodwill and customer service will bring back customers over and over again. If you have good service, be sure to emphasize it to your customer.

Time Objections

All customers will ask themselves, "When should I buy?" This is a problem that many buyers will not express and is found in the **time objection**. Because of debating in their mind when to buy, some buyers will give you excuses and stall in making the decision. Other people need more time before making the commitment, and some need to discuss the decision with a spouse or friend. Other customers are just fearful of making a wrong decision, so they take extra time to avoid making a mistake.

The salesperson has to look at the time objection in a positive manner. The seller should use this objection as an opportunity to give more information to the buyer. The salesperson talks about the product's high quality, features, dependability, warranty, or appearance. He can also discuss the store and mention the company's reputation. Some salespeople encourage people to buy because of a shortage in products or a price increase coming in the near future. Some common objections that deal with time are:

✔"I haven't made up my mind yet."

✔"I want to think it over."

✔"I would like to talk it over with my wife first."

✔"I think I'll wait until it goes on sale."

✔"I never buy the first product that I look at."

HINTS IN OVERCOMING OBJECTIONS

Before a discussion of specific methods and techniques that are used in overcoming objections, it is necessary to look at some general principles to remember in the process of handling objections. We will refer to these principles as **The Golden Rules in Overcoming Objections**. These general rules come from our professional experience and discussions with many successful professional salespeople. They are found in the next illustration.

The Ten Golden Rules In Overcoming Objections

1. **Always welcome objections with open arms.**
2. **Always listen to the objection.**
3. **Be relaxed and calm in handling objections.**
4. **Maintain good eye contact.**
5. **Repeat or restate the objection in question form.**
6. **Answer the objection.**
7. **Never argue.**
8. **Never fake an answer.**
9. **Treat all objections seriously.**
10. **Objections can be opportunities to close.**

EFFECTIVE TECHNIQUES IN HANDLING OBJECTIONS

There are several good techniques salespeople use to overcome objections. The following techniques will give you a variety of choices and allow you to adapt to each individual customer. Remember, some objections may require long answers while others can be answered in a statement or two. As long as the customer feels free to ask questions or raise objections, he/she is still interested in your product and involved in the presentation.

Indirect Denial

This method is often referred to as the **Yes, But Method**. This method is probably the most widely used method in answering objections. This method is very simple, but very effective. With this technique the salesperson acknowledges the objection and also protects the feelings of the customer. After agreeing with the customer, the salesperson then can proceed in explaining or justifying the objection. Keep in mind that most customers are emotionally involved in the objections they raise. This technique is good in calming their emotions. It allows you to discuss and justify your point-of-view without getting into an argument or trying to prove the customer wrong. This method can also be used when the customer has a misunderstanding about your product. An example of this method is as follows:

Customer: I've heard that the fuel injection system of the VW Jetta is a real source of trouble.

Salesperson: Yes, although it is a great fuel-saving feature, we did have some problems on our older models of years past. Our engineers corrected the defect, and you can see by the latest **Consumer Report** information I have that you needn't anticipate any more trouble with this model.

Again, this technique protects the customer's feelings in the first phrase, but allows you to take issue with the objection in the last part of your response. Another advantage of this approach is that it places both the seller and the buyer on the same side from the direct rebuttal approach. Another example of this method is given.

Customer: Your products are sure expensive.

Salesperson: Sure, our line is more expensive, but it is also the only hand-sewn line in its price range.

Counterquestions

Questions can be used not only to clarify objections but also to answer them. Often a simple "Why?" is effective in dealing with objections, because it draws forth additional thoughts from the buyer that are useful in helping the salesperson derive a clear picture of the buyer's concerns. In effect, the salesperson and the customer reverse roles, as the counterquestion forces the latter to justify his/her objection in the presentation.

Also this "why" question is effective in dealing with objections because it reveals the customer's true objection. The customer is forced to examine his/her own view, thus revealing the real reason why he/she is resistant to buying. As the transfer of responsibility is given to the buyer, the salesperson is given some time for thinking and formulating a new game plan. An example of this technique is as follows:

Customer: That is too much to pay for that product.

Salesperson: Why do you feel that way, sir?

Notice that the responsibility of clarification is on the buyer instead of the seller. This technique is helpful whenever the prospect gives you an ambiguous or judgmental statement.

Boomerang

This technique allows the salesperson to transform the customer's objection into a reason for buying. An example of this technique is as follows:

Customer: Yes, the 24-karat gold is beautiful, but the way prices are rising right now, there is no way we can afford it.

Salesperson: That is exactly why you should buy this now, because with prices going up all the time, you can't afford to pass it up.

This technique is very effective in countering price and expense objections. In using this method, be careful not to put your customer down because he/she will resent this. Be friendly and sincere and talk to your customer in a conversational manner. Another example of the boomerang method is below.

Customer: This house is too far from town.

Salesperson: This house will retain its value for years to come when houses nearer town will be incorporated into the city, be subject to higher taxes, and be in deteriorating neighborhoods. The Oakview Shopping Center, only a mile away, has an excellent assortment of stores with reasonable prices.

Direct Denial

This method is a head-on approach for handling objections. This method is used when the objection given is invalid or when the prospect leaves you no other alternative.

This technique is recommended only when the salesperson feels that the customer's objection is serious enough to warrant an immediate response. Because of the corrective nature this method has, an agreeable and informative tone of voice is necessary. An argumentative tone may give the appearance of high-pressure selling and thus create increased selling resistance. Also, the facts you use in overcoming this objection must be truthful, accurate, and reliable. Please look at the following two examples.

Customer: I hear that your company is on the verge of bankruptcy. I want to buy from a company that will be around in the future.

Salesperson: Oh no sir, someone has misinformed you. I can show you our latest financial statement. It proves that our firm is in excellent condition.

It is good to use empathy to help soften the customer's emotions. Use the direct-denial method only after you have prepared the customer for your response.

Customer: They sure are making products cheaper today. That product is made out of plastic instead of metal.

Salesperson: I understand your concern. However, the plastic is very strong and is just as safe as metal. In addition, this product is shockproof. We have found that the occasional user prefers this style. It is lightweight and also less expensive to manufacture, thus saving you additional money.

Counterbalance

There are certain situations in which the customer gives an objection that is valid, and you cannot truthfully deny it. Very few products exist in the world today that are perfect. In most situations you can overcome the objection by using the counterbalance technique, which is overbalancing the objection with benefits. You list the advantages and the disadvantages of the product on a T-account so that it looks like weighing the benefits of the product on a set of scales. Make sure that the advantages outweigh the disadvantages. An example of this method is as follows.

Customer: This processing unit is too noisy.

Salesperson: While it may make a little noise, you can remove it to clean it and you have greater flexibility through its interchangeable type elements. In addition, there are six other major advantages of this processing unit.

As you can see from the above example, the salesperson could not deny the objection of the customer, but several advantages are pointed out to counterbalance this objection. The technique is great to use in dealing with expensive products like investments, real estate, and specialty goods. Whatever the objection is, you can think of more benefits in order to give the product a more positive impression. Always remember that there is no perfect product. All products have some limitations and features to which the customer can legitimately object. This method allows the salesperson to simply make the prospect desire the product's advantages more than he/she dislikes the disadvantages. What many salespeople do is to visualize this method by listing each point with a possible picture or diagram explaining it.

Third-Party

Sometimes when the customer gives a strong objection, the salesperson may be wise not to try to counter it directly. Instead, the seller should try to neutralize the objection by mentioning other people who have used the product or service. The third-party method of handling objections uses the testimonial of another person. A testimonial is an example used by the salesperson of someone who has used the product or service and found it to be satisfactory. In this method, the salesperson can offer contrary evidence to the customer without possibly offending the customer. Here is an example of this technique.

Customer: We are only a small law firm; we don't need your type of tax service for the type of business we have.

Salesperson: Well, I can understand the thinking behind that, but Moore and Taylor across the street are about your same size, and they believe this tax service is the most valuable services they have ever purchased. Because they are small, they do not have the manpower to do the research we can provide. Feel free to call and discuss our service with them.

The Six Common Objection Techniques

✔**Indirect Denial Method**
–The "Yes, But"technique.
✔**Counterquestion Method**
–Asking the question "why" do you feel this way?"
✔**Boomerang Method**
–Transforming the objection into a reason for buying.
✔**Direct Denial Method**
–A head-on approach of politely disagreeing with the buyer on an objection that is false.
✔**Counterbalance Method**
–Using a balancing/T-account approach with an objection that is valid.
✔**Third-Party Approach**
–Using a testimonial of another buyer to neutralize the objection.

The previous illustration gives a good overview of the six objection techniques we have discussed in this chapter. It would be wise to become familiar and even comfortable with all six objection types as each will become a valuable tool in a specific selling situation because of the diversity of buyers that now exist in the marketplace.

Assess Yourself–Applying The Six Objection Techniques

Look at the following five objections listed below. For each of the five objections come up with a statement to overcome the objection. Also, identify which of the objection techniques discussed in this chapter your statement would fall under. The first one has already been done for you.

Objection	Statement	Objection Technique
Your tax preparation service seems costly.	**I have a list of several other clients that are your size and compete in your industry. I would encourage you to talk to them and see all the services we provide for the price we charge.**	**Third-Party Technique**
I just don't think that VCR brand is reliable.		
I am reluctant to buy from a new business with no established track record.		
I don't really understand high-tech computer systems.		
The business across the street is selling the same thing for $20 less.		

FOURTEEN

CLOSING THE SALE

Learning Objectives

1. Define closing the sale.
2. Explain how the law of averages affect closing the sale.
3. Identify the four reasons why salespeople fail to close the sale.
4. Discuss the closing clock as it relates to closing the sale.
5. Describe the fourteen different closing techniques.

Creativity In Closing The Sale.

A young couple paid a visit to Donald Wright's music store looking for the right piano for their new home. Mr. Wright directed them to a particular piano. After he explained in great detail the sound box construction, stringing scale, pin blocks, etc., the couple seemed satisfied with the piano's quality, but they were still undecided about its styling. As they were about to leave to look at more pianos elsewhere, Mr. Wright suggested that they take a couple of benches home to compare with the styling of their other home furniture. They did, and came back later that same day to buy the piano. Since then, Mr. Wright has used this particular technique numerous times and with great success.

CLOSING THE SALE

We must always keep in mind that the ultimate goal of a salesperson is to sell products and services. The ultimate compliment of a good sales presentation is for the customer to buy the product. The closing stage is a natural step in the selling process. It is not a time in which the seller and buyer enter a power struggle like two mountain sheep locking horns. It is a time in which the buyer and seller benefit from each other. The closing moment of a sale should be planned for and expected. Sales managers train their salespeople that to be successful in selling you must be able to ask for the order, or close the sale. Your success as a salesperson not only depends on your product and your ability to be persuasive, but also is totally dependent on your knowledge of closing techniques and how to use them. If you do not ask for the order, you are not a salesperson; you merely become a conversationalist who is providing the customer with information.

THE LAW OF AVERAGES

When you begin to develop some good closing techniques, you must consider the concept of the **law of averages**. The law of averages states that **if you make a given number of sales presentations, you are going to make a given number of sales**. This law governs the success of all individuals in selling. Selling experts point out that their sales are in direct proportion to the number of good contacts a salesperson makes. This law goes a step further with its relationship to the salesperson's attempt to close the sale. If you sat down with any professional salesperson and had him or her analyze past sales presentations that resulted in sales, chances are good that his/her buyers were closely associated with the number of selling attempts it took to close the sale. In a recent survey of 100 professional salespeople, each one averaging $100,000 or more in income, it was discovered that they make their sale on the average of the **fifth closing attempt**. If you do not use a variety of different closing techniques and fail to close often, and with every customer, you will be cheating yourself out of a higher standard of living.

The Law of Averages

If you make a given number of sales presentations, you are going to make a given number of sales.

A salesperson must keep asking for the order throughout the sales presentation. Consider the following statistics of those salespersons who ask for the order:

***44 percent give up after one "NO."**
***22 percent give up after two "NOs."**
***14 percent give up after three "NOs."**
***12 percent give up after four "NOs."**

If you add up all the above percentages, you will get 92 percent of all salespeople giving up without asking for the order the fifth time. This leaves only 8 percent who will ask for the order more than four times. Also, sixty percent of all customers say "no" four times before saying "yes." Author and sales trainer Hank Trisler puts it this way:

> **"Here's the real key to selling. You ask, you get. The more you ask, the more you get. If you don't ask you don't get. You can go to all the seminars that come to your town, read all the books, listen to all the tapes. If you don't learn to ask, you're going to go broke."**

Let us put it this way: If your goal is to win the local country club golf tournament this year, it wouldn't make sense to practice every week and then attempt to play the tournament with nothing but a driver and a putter. Yet, this is what many salespeople do every day of their lives. The reason is that they do not spend the time learning and practicing a variety of effective closing techniques. This chapter will expose you to several basic closing techniques that are successfully applied in the selling industry. Before we discuss the closing techniques, it is important to become aware of some obstacles that prevent salespeople from closing the sale.

OBSTACLES TO CLOSING THE SALE

The closing stage of the sales process is one of the most difficult experiences salespeople go through–especially new and inexperienced salespeople. When you think about it, the closing is simply "asking the customer to buy." In fact, customers expect to be asked by salespeople to buy the product or service being demonstrated. If buyers expect to be asked by the seller, then why do so many salespeople have such difficulty in asking the buyer to buy? Four major reasons will surface in answering the previous question. The four reasons that become obstacles are fear, guilt, no need, and forgetfulness.

The Four Reasons Why Salespeople Fail to Close the Sale

- **Fear of rejection**
- **Guilt**
- **No need**
- **Forgetfulness**

Fear of Rejection

Research studies have shown that the number one reason why salespeople fail to close a sale is because of fear–fear of rejection and being turned down. To avoid this fear, salespeople simply don't ask for the order. We all have fear of having our ego and self-esteem deflated. So, the tendency is not to ask for the order but rather plan another sales call, then ask for the order at a later time. Customers know that the main purpose of your profession is to sell products. In order to sell products you must ask people to buy. For this reason, customers expect you to ask; they may not look forward to it or encourage it, but they expect it. Chances are that if you do not ask the customer to buy, the customer will not ask you for the product. As you gain experience, you will realize that the step of closing should come as naturally as the other six steps of selling that have been discussed in this book. The law of averages will play in your favor only if you learn to ask each customer to buy your product and attempt to overcome the fear by attempting to close the sale.

Guilt

The second reason why salespeople fail to close the sale is because of guilt. Some people have guilty feelings or feel uncomfortable in their profession as they ask people for things. Many of us have been taught not to ask for things because we will become dependent and have to return the favor in the near future. Some salespeople feel as if they are intruders begging for a living instead of people helping other people to solve serious problems. This guilt feeling usually exists in the heart of those sellers who do not understand the product they are selling or the benefits their products can bring potential buyers. Our society and economy as a whole relies heavily on the selling profession. Salespeople help speed the acceptance of new products that can better the lives of people. When guilt enters as a barrier to the closing of the sale, salespeople need to do some soul searching and analyze their profession.

No Need

Many salespeople fail to close sales because they feel no need to do so. They think the prospect will automatically buy at the end of the presentation. Even though it does happened, you must learn to ask customers to buy since the majority of customers won't ask for the order. The last twenty years of selling in the United States has seen a 180 degree shift from what has been called the "hard sale" to a concept called the **"soft sale."** The soft sale is simply giving the buyer more room and time, and less pressure and initial help from the salesperson. Well, this soft sale approach has gone to the extreme in some cases to the point that customers are finding it hard to get any person in a retail type store to assist them, the theory being that if customers want help or assistance, they will ask for it.

Forgetfulness

On occasion, some salespeople get so bogged down and involved in their presentation that the thought of trying to close the sale slips their mind. They become confused and lose control of the sale, and the closing opportunities walk out the door. Salespeople that have this problem will be found checking back on a lot of call backs and will have poor closing records on initial sales presentations. The problem of failing to close on the initial presentation is that the emotional involvement and level of the buyer will wear off as one, two, and three days pass by. Success of closing increases as closing attempts are made during the first sales presentation with the customer.

CLOSING TECHNIQUES

On the following pages in this chapter are basic closing techniques used in the selling industry today. Some of the techniques are very simple, while others require more skill and persuasion. Learn these techniques and start using them everyday. Only through practical application will you find the best group of techniques that will work for you.

The Trial Close

The trial closing technique is probably the most effective one to use. By using this technique called the **trial close,** you can get a feel during the presentation of how close the prospect is to making the major decision to buy. This closing technique is to be used at any time during the presentation and usually precedes one of the other major closing techniques. In fact, this technique is a good introduction to the other techniques. Because there is not one specific closing time during the presentation, you must make continual efforts to get the buyer's order at the time that will be easiest to make the buying decision. A good rule of thumb is for a salesperson to close often and early--the trial close allows you to do this.

Every presentation has a **closing clock,** ticking away from the moment the sales presentation begins. This closing clock consists of several opportunities to close the sale. Trial closes are the tools you can use to gain signals from the buyer that will indicate how close the customer is to making a buying decision. A trial close is an attempt to find out if the prospect is ready to buy without actually insisting on a final decision. An example of a trial close is to ask the customer if he/she is interested in the color or some other minor point about the product. You might say, "Do you like the brown or the blue chair best?" If the prospect shows real interest even on this minor point, an order clinching close attempt could be your next step. You will find out as you use this technique that the trial close will usually lead you into using one of the other closing techniques. This is why the technique is called a trial close; you can use it several times and fail until you become aware of the best opportunity to capitalize on. It takes some of the pressure off of you by letting you ask the buyer to make a minor decision instead of the one major decision. Below are some examples of some verbal and nonverbal signs that may indicate a good time to use a trial close.

- The customer asks questions on price, delivery, or warranty.
- The customer's voice or tone changes.
- The customer looks at the product favorably.
- The customer reaches out to touch or handle the product.
- The customer attempts to look at a checkbook or wallet.
- The customer makes a positive statement about some product feature.
- The customer nods his head repeatedly or leans forward in the chair.

The Closing Clock

Several opportunities to close the sale are found during every presentation.

The Basic Close

Other names for this close are the "order blank" and the "assumptive close." This technique is very simple. You simply use a direct approach and ask for the order. The word **ask** is the most important word in closing sales. You must ask for the order in most cases to receive an order. You simply ask the potential buyer a question, the answer to which you fill out on an order form or application. You don't ask the customer, "Do you want to buy?" You assume the buyer wants to buy and say something like, "What is your correct full name, sir?" or "Where do you want the product delivered?"

Do you realize that as long as the customer doesn't stop you, he/she has purchased the product? You assume that the customer has bought, and you merely fill out the application until the customer stops you–if the customer stops you. After you have filled out the entire order form, you hand the customer a pen and ask him to please "O.K. it." Refrain from using the phrase "Will you sign it?" Most of us have been warned to always look at anything in detail before signing it.

One item you need to understand is the closing question. **A closing question is any question you ask in which the answer confirms the fact that your customer has bought.** Only two things will happen at the point in which you ask a closing question using the basic close: (1) The customer goes along with you, or (2) The customer gives you a reason for not going along. As a salesperson you will learn to capitalize on either one.

Ben Franklin Close

This closing technique is one of my favorites. It is especially effective for the customer who is very logical or rational. This technique simply allows you to summarize the advantages and the disadvantages that are set up on a type of a T-Account. This simple close is used best with a customer that has a hard time making up his/her mind until he/she has had a chance to think it over and weigh the benefits.

Let me explain why this close is called the Ben Franklin close. As you know, Americans have long considered Benjamin Franklin as one of our wisest men. Whenever Ben Franklin found himself in a situation of buying a product or making an important decision, he would want to make sure he was doing the right thing. If the decision was a wrong one, he wanted to make sure he avoided it. He would take a sheet of plain white paper and draw a line down the middle and on the left side he would write "yes" and on the right side he would write "no." He would then put all the reasons favoring the decision and all the reasons against it. When you do this with a prospect, give him/her all the help in the world to find reasons favoring the decision to buy. Even go to the extent to suggest a few. If you do it right, you should come up with at least 10 reasons favoring the decision to buy the product. When you get to the "no" side of the paper, shut up. It will be hard to achieve more than three reasons against the decision. You now can simply point out that if the paper represented a set of scales, the reasons favoring the decision clearly outweigh the reasons against the decision. At this time you proceed to write up the order.

The Lost Sale Close

One concept that every salesperson must learn is that you won't sell 100 percent of the people 100 percent of the time. Some people are just not ready to buy at the time you are selling. The **Lost Sale Close** is used when you have lost the sale–when everything else you have tried has failed. This means you don't practice this technique every day because this technique, if not handled right, will really hurt you. This closing technique requires tact, sincerity, and a lot of sensitivity.

When you have lost the sale, you can end the presentation by saying something like this, "Pardon me, sir; but before I leave, what didn't the product have that you were looking for?" This is a simple question that can be used for an evaluation. If the customer brings up something you forgot to mention, you are back into the ball game. If the customer mentions something that you can't provide, then you may want to look into it for future presentations. Whatever the response of the customer, the lost sale close provides you with an excellent opportunity to gain helpful information that can be used in future sales.

I'll Think It Over Close

If you have never heard of this objection, "I want to think it over!" then you haven't spent much time as a buyer. This excuse is one of the most common reasons for putting off the buying decision. You can learn as a salesperson to capitalize on this expression and turn it into one of the most effective closes used today.

When a customer tells you, "I'll think it over," you say to him, "That's fine, sir. Obviously you wouldn't take time to think it over unless you were really interested. I'm sure you are not telling me this just to get rid of me. So, I may assume that you are going to give this very careful consideration. You are very serious about purchasing this product. For this reason I can see why you would want more time to think about it." Your customer will say something like this, "Yes, I'm going to give this more time." You then say, "Just to clarify my thinking, what specific thing do you want to think over?" If he/she doesn't give you anything, then start suggesting items. "Is it ...? Is it ...?" Eventually he/she will probably say, "Yeah, that's it." You can then attempt to start clarifying or providing more information that may encourage the customer to buy.

The Turnover Close

A technique that is very successful for inexperienced salespeople and those salespeople who may have a personality conflict with the buyer is the **turnover close**. This is used when you turn over the sales presentation to another salesperson who has a better chance of making the sale. The junior or new salesperson may say something like this; "Mr. Taylor is a bit more familiar with this line of goods than I am." You then smoothly turn the sale over to the other salesperson. It is important that you do this before the customer begins to walk out the door. If you don't do it until the end of the sale, the situation could turn out to be very awkward. It may be wise after the other salesperson has committed the buyer to buy to turn the sale back over to the original salesperson.

The Continued Affirmation Close

This close is also called the "stimulus-response" or "yes-building" close. This closing technique involves using a series of leading questions that make it easier for the customer to say **yes** when asked for the order. Be sure that your approach in using this technique is rapid, enthusiastic, logical, and includes some major issues from the buyer's point-of-view. Many successful salespeople will agree that psychology plays an important role in this technique. A series of "yes" answers leads to a final easy "yes" answer that brings the sale to a close.

You will notice from the following examples that each "yes" answer paves the way for further commitment. Below is a manufacturer's representative attempting to sell a buyer on a line of products.

> The ads will appear in some well-known magazines beginning the first of February. They are attractive and informative ads, aren't they?
>
> These ads should help create additional store traffic for you and tie in beautifully with your local advertising, shouldn't they?
>
> You will notice that the percentage of markup is higher than our competitors. You can use the extra markup, can't you?
>
> These products, with the help of some point-of-purchase displays that we will provide for you, will make an attractive display, won't they?
>
> Some important factors for you are high turnover and a fair profit, isn't that true?
>
> If I can show you how these products will bring in a large profit from a small investment, you would be interested, wouldn't you?

Here is a second example of what a typical car salesperson may say in applying the **continued affirmation close.**

That is a pretty color of blue, isn't it?

Sit behind the wheel. Isn't there a lot of room behind there?

Our financing rate of 5 percent is lower than other car dealers in the area, isn't that true?

Our six year, 70,000 mile warranty is one of the best in the marketplace, isn't it?

Let's go take care of the financing so that you can drive away in this beautiful car tonight.

Special Deal Close

This closing technique is very effective when you have failed to close the sale after several closing attempts. The reason why this closing technique is called a **special deal** is because you offer the customer something extra for buying the product now. For example, some inducements that are commonly used are premiums, discounts, trade-in allowances, promotional tools, longer pay periods for credit, free accessories and free delivery. You are giving the customer a "special offer" if the product is bought now.

This technique should not be used on the first closing attempt, only after the customer is reluctant to make the buying decision today. We suggest that you avoid getting into the habit of using this close everyday as some salespeople have. The reason is that a danger exists in using this technique because you create the impression that the first or second offer is not the best offer, and some customers may feel that if they put off the purchase a little longer, they may then be able to get a better bargain. The most common inducement used in this closing technique is to encourage people to buy by cutting the original price. Below are some examples of the special deal close.

If you buy ten of these items, I'll throw in another single item free.

We'll give you a free car wash with every purchase of 10 gallons or more.

Buy today, and I'll save you an extra 10 percent.

If you buy this 21-inch console color T.V. set today, you will receive a portable black and white set free.

If you order new carpeting within the next three days, you will receive a better grade of padding at no extra charge.

The Standing-Room Only Close

As we discussed above, one of the biggest barriers to buying is the customer's option to put off the decision until later. The **standing-room only close** not only gives strong reason for buying now, but also supports the prospect's decision by indicating that if everybody else is buying it, it must be a good product. It makes the decision to buy a little less risky. This close is especially good for products that are unique, one-of-a-kind, or in high demand. Some examples of this close are as follows:

We only have one product left, and it will take us months to order another one. If you like it, you might as well buy it.

Another couple was in earlier looking at this beautiful home, and they said that they were coming back this afternoon to let me know what they have decided. I told them I couldn't hold it unless I had earnest money. It is an excellent buy, so I'd advise you to take it now. It may not be here tomorrow.

You'd better buy this set of tires today while they are on sale, because prices will be going up 20 percent tomorrow.

Like the special deal close, this close should also be held in reserve until late in the sales presentation because it can also weaken your presentation. This close is tailor-made for those customers who become a challenge when asked to make a commitment. If this technique is not used in an ethical manner, it could really hurt the credibility of the salesperson.

The Success Story or Testimonial Close

You can often restate closing points most convincingly in the form of a story about a prospect who was in a similar situation. We all like to profit or learn from the mistakes or successes of others. The technique capitalizes on using experiences of other people and in many cases is more effective than your personal experiences or opinions. You want to get across the point that your prospect would be unwise to delay his/her decision to purchase. By pointing out the benefits received or the loss suffered by another person who was in a similar situation, your prospects may realize that they should buy today. It is very effective if you can use names, dates, and other specific details so the situation will be as realistic to the buyer as possible. Some professional salespeople have gone to the extent of having previous customers write up their story in their own words and use this as a helpful tool in the presentation. We call these testimonial letters. Testimonials may encourage the customer to follow the example and buy. An example of this method would be as follows. "Tony Anderson thought the same as you do about small cars but bought one because of the gas mileage. Because his car was more maneuverable, he was able to avoid a head-on collision last month. He says that he will always buy small cars from now on."

The Alternative of Choice Close

This technique gives customers a limited choice and will lead them into making the final decision to buy. One way of getting the buyer to make the major decision is by having him make minor decisions like color, style, features, financing, or a choice between two products you offer–we covered this in describing the trial close. People generally have found that it is easier to make a minor decision than a major one. Also, the minor decisions will literally carry the big and final decision. Risk is always involved in making a major purchase decision so a salesperson should avoid creating a situation for the buyer to say "yes" or "no." Instead of asking the buyer if he wants to buy a suit, you ask "Which color of suit do you prefer, the blue suit or the brown one?" By getting a decision between two alternatives, you help the prospect make a choice between two or three products that your company offers. Always give the customer a choice between your products, not a choice between buying and not buying. This technique has been called the **Yes,Yes** technique because the buyer is asked to respond with a "yes" answer to two alternatives that you provide. Instead of asking the buyer, "Do you want to buy the car?" which the buyer will respond by saying yes or no, you ask the buyer "Which car do you prefer, the Toyota Camry or the Avalon?" Some additional examples of this closing are as follows:

Would you prefer to have the chair delivered today or the first part of next week?

Would you rather finance the stereo system or pay for it in cash?

Do you prefer the wingtips or the slip-on shoes?

The "BIQ" Close

This technique is very effective because it summarizes key points of the presentation, provides a powerful suggestion, and ends up in a closing question. It is traditional used toward the end of the presentation as you prepare to summarize your key points. The technique uses the following format:

Based on (one or more of the following):

-Successes of others.
-Benefits other customers have achieved.
-Concerns you (the prospect) have expressed.

I'd like to suggest (the action you want to take):

Question, (such as one of the following):
-Would that be okay?
-Would that be fair?
-Would that be all right with you?

An example of this technique would be as follows. "Based on your concern for buying a car with low maintenance and repair costs, I'd suggest you buy a Toyota Camry, one of the top ten rated cares each year by ***J.D. Powers and Associates***. Would that be okay?

The Trap Close

This closing technique I have saved until the last because it is one of the hardest to master and the most persuasive to use. However, when it is used by a masterful sales professional, it is a beautiful tool to use. Only experienced salespeople who really know their product should make this technique a habit. The reason why is that it can backfire and make you look like a pressuring fool. The **trap close** is when you close a sale on a final objection by making your sale contingent on a specific point–a point that you know you can satisfy and provide.

The trap close is used by making your sale completely dependent on one point. This is used when you know you can satisfy or prove the claim you are about to state to the buyer. This technique is very useful with objections that you know are false. For example, your buyer may be very concerned about delivery, you can simply say, "If I can promise you delivery in two days, then do we have a deal?" The buyer may think, "Now how can he do that, delivery in two days!" If the buyer thinks this, and if you can deliver in two days, you have the setting of using the trap close.

Trap closes are used frequently in handling price objections. You can take advantage of this objection by saying something like, "If I can get you these units for the price you indicated, then may I have your order?" Be sure you can back up what you are saying; if so, the trap close is an effective tool to use.

Puppy Dog Close

This last technique encourages the buyer to borrow the product for a designated time period and keep the product in his/her possession for a while before a commitment is made. Most parents can recall the experience of going to the supermarket and seeing a person out front with a box of puppies to give away or sell. The seller of the puppies knows that if the puppy gets into the home, even for one day, the odds of making it a permanent placement dramatically increases. The child pleads with the parent to have a puppy and after an emotional appeal the child wins. The child becomes instantly attached to the puppy and promises the parent that he/she will do whatever it takes to take care of the puppy. As most parents know, this lasts only a few weeks at best. However, the emotional attachment and possession of the product are great selling strategies and salespeople use this technique in very much the same way. Allowing the customer to use the product with no money down and with no initial commitment reduces the perceived risk. This was the closing technique used in the opening story of the piano salesperson found after the chapter objectives. The salesperson know that if he could get the piano benches in the home, the customer would feel more comfortable with the piano purchase possibility. This technique has also been called **on approval.**" You allow the buyer to have the product "on approval" and let the buyer use the product for a short time period. Having the physical possession of the product creates the feeling of ownership and creates a strong emotional attachment. This closing technique is successful with products like water purifiers, art, mail-order products, credit cards, exercise equipment, and high technology products.

The Puppy Dog Close

An on-approval close that encourages the buyer to borrow the product before a final decision is made–or a "Try it out free to see if you like it!"approach.

The closing of a sale can be compared to the final act of a dramatic production. Just as a play or show builds up to a climax, so does a good sales presentation. An appropriate background has been developed, characters introduced, information presented, questions answered, and now the play reaches the conclusion. If all has gone well in the dramatic production, the curtain will fall and the audience will leave with a satisfied feeling. If all has gone well in the sales presentation, the buyer will be satisfied and will leave with your product. A salesperson must expect the buyer to buy–always assume the positive. Assume as you are giving the presentation that the buyer is going to buy until he/she indicates otherwise. Look forward to and identify buying signals given off by the buyer that will let you know that now may be the time to ask for the order. Remember, closing is simply asking for the order as pointed out in this last illustration.

The key is to ask!

Closing the sale is simply <u>asking</u> for the order.

Assess Yourself–Applying The Alternative of Choice Close

Look over the following closing statements and rewrite each statement using the alternative of choice close. Remember that you are turning a yes/no question into a yes/yes question. The first statement has been done for you.

Do you want us to deliver the appliance to your home?	**What would you prefer? We can deliver the appliance to you by this evening or would tomorrow morning be fine?**
Do you want the Toyota Siena Van?	
How will you pay for the computer system?	
Would you like to schedule an appointment to review your taxes?	

FIFTEEN

SERVICING THE SALE

Learning Objectives

When you finish studying the material in this chapter, you should be able to:

1. Define servicing the sale.
2. Explain why every existing customer is a potential source of more sales.
3. Discuss what is meant by the "An Appreciating Asset" concept.
4. Discuss how much follow-up a salesperson should do after a sale.
5. Identify several ways to keep customers for life.
6. Describe how to develop a personal customer service program.
7. Explain how complaining customers become gold mines.
8. Identify the benefits of servicing the sale.
9. Discuss the four common threads for long-term success.

Stay close to your customers!

When sales at the Harley-Davidson Company, the legendary American motorcycle manufacturer, suddenly began to plummet several years ago, senior management had to turn things around–fast. Harley-Davidson's executives hit the streets to seek out their customers. They attended rallies and conventions to see just how Harley-Davidson enthusiasts customized and modified their motorcycles. They even went on a cross-country road trip atop Harley-Davidson motorcycles to find out just how well they stood up to life on the road. It worked! With the wealth of information that was gathered, Harley-Davidson was able to make major improvements on their current models as well as design some new ones, and sales climbed back up as a result. In addition, the company boosted its customer loyalty rate to an incredible 90 percent, all because people at Harley-Davidson put themselves in touch with their customers, listening closely to what they had to say, and took action.

–Taken from *Bits & Pieces for Salespeople*

SERVICING THE SALE

In the book ***Thriving on Chaos***, a best selling business book of the 1980s, the author Tom Peters discusses many strategies that bring success in the present management revolution taking place in America. In the chapter titled, **Provide Superior Service/Emphasize the Intangibles,** he relates the following experience between a customer and the retail chain of Nordstrom:

> "So you want to buy a suit? Well, one of our seminar participants did. He is an executive for a large national retailer, headquartered in Portland, Oregon. His two daughters and his wife are Nordstrom fans. They constantly bubble about it and pester him to shop there. He was frankly fed up with all the talk. Moreover, despite their comments to the contrary, he secretly suspected that Nordstrom charged an arm and a leg.
>
> But he did need a suit badly. And a major sale was going on. At worst, he figured, he didn't have too much to lose, especially with the sale. Reluctantly, he went to Nordstrom.
>
> The service in the store was good, he had to admit. And he did find a fine suit on sale, although he also picked up a second suit–at full price. Nordstrom promises same-day alterations. He noted, however, that there was a little asterisk next to the promise–next-day alteration was promised during sales. He chortled at this small chink in the armor.
>
> He came back at 5:45 P.M. the next day to pick up his suits. It was fifteen minutes before closing. He needed the suits for a trip that night. To his surprise, though he'd only been there once, his salesperson greeted him by name! The fellow trotted upstairs to pick

> up the suits. Five minutes had passed by and the salesperson reappeared–without the goods. They hadn't been finished..
>
> Though he needed the suits, our friend admits to secret glee. Without the suits, he took off for a Monday appointment in Seattle, after which he proceeded to Dallas for the big meeting of the trip.
>
> He checked into his hotel and went up to his room. A message light informed him that a package had arrived for him. A bellhop fetched it–Federal Express, mailing fee $98. Yes, it was from Nordstrom. In it were two suits. On top of them were three $25 silk ties (which he hadn't ordered) thrown in gratis! There was also a note of apology from the salesperson, who had called his home and learned his travel arrangements from one of his daughters. With a smile of resignation, he admits that he's now a believer."

Nordstrom's secret? A superior level of service. Customer service is the focal point of discussion for this last chapter. Your future in selling will be heavily dependent on the relationship you establish and maintain with your customer. As a salesperson you will never stop selling. The completion of one sale is just a stepping stone to more sales. Until a customer is happy and satisfied in using your product or service, the sale is incomplete. Joe Girard, well-known author and named the world's greatest salesperson 12 times, says, "For me a good sale is one where the customer goes out with what he came in for, at a good enough price so that he tells his friends, his relatives, and his co-workers to buy a car from Joe Girard." Some salespeople become so self-oriented that they forget to be customer-oriented. They forget that they are totally dependent on the customer. As shown in the Nordstrom example, the customer is the life-blood of their company and every salesperson knows it. This chapter will discuss the importance of maintaining a positive and healthy relationship after the sale.

POTENTIAL SOURCE FOR MORE SALES

One of the most important principles that every salesperson must understand is the difference between **generating** customers and **retaining** customers. Generating customers is what prospecting and advertising accomplishes. It is the process of acquiring new customers. Retaining customers is the process of keeping your present customers happy so that they will come back again and buy. The Better Business Bureau of Greater Salt Lake says that it costs five times as much to get a new customer as it does to keep one. Do you see why servicing the sale is such a good investment? As you service the sale, you will learn that every customer is a potential source for more sales. This is more apparent with industrial products because the salesperson calls on the same customers regularly. But, even in other types of selling such as books, cars, appliances, insurance, and real estate, the customer is a valuable asset and the most important resource for more sales.

An Appreciating Asset

A local supermarket manager once told me that when a customer walks into his store, he sees $720,000 stamped on the customer's forehead. I asked what he meant and he explained his idea of every customer being **AN APPRECIATED ASSET**. He explained an interesting formula. Let's say that a typical family of four purchases $150 of groceries from a store each week. You multiply the $150 by the four weeks in a month and end up with $600. Over a twelve-month period, this adds up to $7,200. Over a ten-year period, the total becomes $72,000. Also, as we consider the customer's powerful word-of-mouth advertising, we can see that a specific customer can influence at least one single person each year. Ten people over a ten year period multiplied by $72,000 becomes $720,000. Can you see why every customer is an appreciating asset? If a salesperson looks at every customer in this way, the seller will likely take a new view of service. No matter what you sell, you can work out a formula to determine the appreciating value of the customer as an asset. Simply do the following formula found in the next figure:

A Simple Formula for Determining a Customer's Value

$ _____ x 4 weeks = $ _____
$ _____ x 12 months = $ _____
$ _____ x 10 years = $ _____
$ _____ x 10 people = $ _____

As every salesperson considers the future dollar potential that a single customer can produce, extra mile efforts in servicing the needs of individual customers should be made daily practice. The dollar amounts are only the tip of the iceberg. The repeat customer is also any company's principal vehicle for powerful word-of-mouth advertising. Research points out that happy customers will tell on the average of three people. A typical dissatisfied customer will tell ten people. Unhappy customers, multiplied over and over, make the "appreciating asset" concept quite powerful.

The key to repeat sales is an enthusiastic customer, not just a "satisfied one." Ask a satisfied customer how he likes a salesperson, and he will respond like this: "Oh, he's okay."

But, the customer who is enthusiastic about the product and the salesperson will respond, "He's the greatest. You can't go wrong with that salesperson. Let me tell you what he did for me." Most customers like to play the role of Paul Revere. If they have poor or unsatisfactory service, they will warn their friends, family, and associates just as Paul Revere warned the people of his day that the "British are coming!" The customer will say, "Don't buy products from that company." On the other hand, if the customer is happy, he will tell his friends of the great service. If you deliver what the customer wants without any problems, the customer will become an asset for you instead of a liability. When you deliver more than the customer expected and go the extra mile, this develops a customer who is enthusiastic and turned on. This will encourage more business with the same person and with those whom the person can influence to buy from you.

Today's successful salespeople learn to do several things that give the customer "more" than he/she expected. The customer then becomes excited and enthusiastic about the product which, in turn, produces the climate for repeat sales and new sales. The goal of every sale should be to develop a positive relationship for you and your company. As a local automotive repair manager puts it, "I like the challenge of taking organizational relationships and turn them into long-term professional friendships." When you start to get repeat business, you will have evidence that shows success in servicing and following up on the sale. The goal that every salesperson should establish is to look at each individual customer in terms of potential sales and value instead of the present purchase. This perceptual change will be called the ability to **"Triple A Protect"** the customer. The symbol that you will see in the next illustration is the national logo for the ***American Automobile Association***. Whenever you see this symbol on the back of a car, on the sign of a hotel, or in front of a restaurant, you know that there is some association with this national company. Motorists have peace of mind and security knowing that "Triple A" will be there in case of a transportation breakdown. By looking at customers as assets that appreciate and gain value over time, you will be more likely to provide the care and excellent service to satisfy their needs and take care of their problems. **Triple A Protection** is simply a change in attitude and perception to look at customers as valuable assets that deserve nurturing. Hopefully, you will always remember this concept as you see the well-known symbol found in the next illustration.

Providing "Triple A Protection" to all Customers

DETERMINING THE AMOUNT OF FOLLOW-UP

Remember that the basic purpose of the eight steps of selling is to generate and increase sales. Servicing the sale is an investment, so you'd better learn which customers make the best investment for future sales. Basically, the time spent on servicing and follow-up should be based upon two considerations:

- **The size of the order.**
- **The importance of the sale.**

A good rule of thumb to follow is to spend more time as the size of the order increases. If the customer gives you a large order, you'd better spend the needed time to make sure he or she is happy with your service, delivery, and the product. This does not mean that customers who give you a smaller order do not need attention. If you are working with a customer who can give you more future business, you should take the extra care with the first order, even if it is a small order. If a small order could produce bigger sales down the road, spend more time and adequately service the customer. A good rule of thumb to follow is to have your average service be comparable to your competitors best service–with this principle put into practice, you will never have to worry about losing customers to your competition.

One important element must be considered in any customer service program developed by a salesperson. The individual customer perceives service in his or her own terms. Some customers can be satisfied with a minimal level of service, while others demand extra mile service on every purchase. A salesperson should always keep a high standard of service so that everyone stays happy. A certain amount of servicing should be included in every sale that a salesperson is involved in.

UNDERSTANDING CUSTOMER BEHAVIOR

It has been said that you never get a second chance to make a good first impression. The most crucial contact of all is the first one that the customer makes with your business, because if you lose the customer here, the customer is likely lost forever. This reminds me of a past experience with a local ice cream parlor. One summer afternoon around 3:00 p.m., I walked into the ice cream shop with my two young daughters. As we walked up to the appropriate counter, I noticed that we were the only people in the shop. Behind the counter was a young female employee. Being so occupied with talking to her boyfriend on the phone, she refused to immediately acknowledge us. Growing impatient, I made a couple of "clearing the throat sounds" to grab her attention. Finally, the young lady looked up and said, "You got a number?"

"I got a what?" I asked, trying to control my emotions and anger. "You got a number? You gotta have a number." I replied, "Lady, my daughters and I are the only customers in the store! I don't need a number. Can't you see how ridiculous this is?" But she failed to see the absurdity and insisted that we take a number before being waited upon. By now, it was obvious that she was more interested in following procedures than helping the customer. I slowly went to the take-a-number machine, pulled number 37 and walked back to the young lady behind the counter. With that, she promptly went to her number counter and yelled out "Number 37!" I said to her, "Thanks for acknowledging us. We have now got your number and will never forget it!" With that last statement, my daughters and I quickly left the shop and drove down the road to one of her competitors and purchased our ice cream.

It is imperative that those having initial contact with customers do their utmost to help the customer and make him/her feel appreciated rather than treating the customer as an interruption. A local body shop repair company has up on their wall the following poster that displays this idea very well.

What is a Customer?

A Customer is the most important person ever in this office...in person or by mail.

A Customer is not dependent on us... we are dependent on him.

A Customer is not an interruption of our work ... he is the purpose of it. We are not doing a favor by serving him ... he is doing us a favor by giving us the opportunity to do so.

A Customer is not someone to argue or match wits with. Nobody ever won an argument with a customer.

A Customer is a person who brings us his wants. It is our job to handle them profitably to him and ourselves.

Today in the world of selling, customers seem to exchange their hard-earned money for only two things:

- **Good feelings**
- **Solutions to problems**

The success and failure of a salesperson depends on how many people are rewarded with those two things. Former IBM Vice-President Francis "Buck" Rodgers said, "The secret is to understand the customer's problems and provide solutions so as to help the customer be profitable and feel good about the transaction." If the customer buys solutions to problems and good feelings, then it is the seller's duty to provide these two things to the buyer. Tom Hopkins, a well-known national sales trainer states that the buyer always **buys first emotionally**, and then second **justifies it with logic**. Most people don't buy what they need, they buy what they want. Customers are more willing to buy when they are feeling good toward you and the product. If you create negative feelings, the customer will probably go away. People are more willing to spend money when they are feeling good. It takes a personal touch to keep customers coming back.

In the book, ***How to Win Customers and Keep Them For Life***, the author Dr. Michael LeBoeuf suggests six powerful keys for all salespeople to refer to in providing the "right touch" to the buyer. This book is one of the best for learning excellent customer service strategies and is highly recommend it for reading. This right touch addresses the "good feelings" all customers need to receive when interacting with customers in selling situations. Dr. LeBoeuf's six keys are as follows:

- **Put yourself in the glad emotional state**. Remember, people buy when they feel glad and feelings are contagious. Be the carrier and not the catcher. People like to do business when and where they feel good.
- **Never tell customers your problems**. Ninety percent of them don't care and the rest will actually be glad that you are as miserable as they are. Telling people your problems makes them sad and sad people only buy at funeral homes. If you want to run customers off, just keep telling them bad news.
- **Remember that customers buy for their reasons, not ours**. To quote Bernard Shaw, "It is unwise to do unto others as you would have them do unto you. Their tastes may not be the same." Every customer has a different emotional makeup and different problems that need to be solved. You win and keep customers by giving them what they want and not what you think they should want.
- **Act as if you are the only personal contact that the customer has with the company and behave as if the entire company's image depends on you**. That is what IBMs encourages its employees to do, and its record for outstanding customer

service speaks for itself. When you are dealing with a customer, you are the company to that customer, and his/her decision to become or remain a customer depends on you.

- **Use both logic and emotion to win and keep customers**. While the overwhelming majority of buying decisions are made emotionally, never underestimate the importance of logic. Emotion causes customers to buy, but logic keeps them sold and coming back.
- **Use the problem-solving approach to move customers from mad, sad, or scared to glad**. According to psychologists, a person is capable of experiencing only four basic emotions. They are **glad, sad, mad**, and **scared**. Those are the only feelings we ever have, and at any given time we are in one of those four emotional states. Whenever a customer has a problem calmly ask him, "What is the situation now?" and "What would you like it to be?" Once you know the answers to these two questions, you can decide how to solve his/her problem. Even if you can't solve the problem, letting him/her express it and taking the time to listen will make him/her feel better. If you pay attention to the customer, he/she will come back. If you pay attention only to the goods, he/she will not come back.

DEVELOPING A PERSONAL CUSTOMER SERVICE PROGRAM

Depending on your selling situation, the industry, the product, and the competition, the following are examples to consider in putting together a customer service program. Each of the items are important in developing long-term relationships with the customer.

- **Develop a personal file**: After the initial sale is made, develop a personal file on the customer and obtain as much information as possible. Below are some examples of the information you should try to acquire.
  - ✔The customer's name and address.
  - ✔Name of spouse and children.
  - ✔List of customer's hobbies and interests.
  - ✔Dates of important events like marriage, birth date, and children's birth dates.
  - ✔Organizations and club memberships.
  - ✔List of the exact product purchased with the purchase date.
- **Feedback system**: After the sale has been completed, solicit feedback from the buyer and have the buyer identify what he liked or disliked about the product and the presentation. Most organizations have a survey card which is given to the buyer at the end of the sale or sent in the mail a week later. Not only should you gain feedback after the sale, but obtain feedback months down the road.

- **Thank you letter**: Write a thank you letter after the sale and send it to the buyer. Let the buyer know how much you appreciate his/her business. If you want to be very personable, send them a thank you card written in your own handwriting.
- **Follow-up on details**: If the product involves delivery, installation, or any other activity after the sale, follow-up and make sure all these things are taken care of.
- **Be responsive by handling complaints and problems promptly**: Don't ignore any complaint or problem, no matter how small it is. They tend to grow into bigger problems with neglect. Make it a personal policy to react to every problem within 24 hours after the buyer makes you aware of the problem. Do more than the customer expects in satisfying the problem.
- **Be a friend**: Do things for your customers as you would a friend. Send the customer a birthday card, a small present on his anniversary, and paper clippings from the newspaper that deal with members of the customer's family.
- **Installation**: Many of today's products require some amount of installation after the sale. Except in rare instances, installation will be handled by people other than the salesperson. Get to know these people and develop good working friendships with them. If a product is to be installed on a specific date or time, follow-up on it for the buyer. Make the buyer aware of any problems that may exist.
- **Delivery**: The role of delivery in customer service will differ according to the type of selling. In selling situations where customers take the product with them, many firms develop checklists. For example, the next figure shows a checklist used by a local automobile dealership. Notice that the checklist begins as soon as the customer signs the contract. It is suggested that you develop a personal checklist that is tailor-made to your product. Go over it each time a sale is made and use it as a follow-up to keep the customer happy. You may come up with items that will shorten or lengthen the list, but it serves as a reminder that closing the sale is just the beginning in maintaining a lasting relationship.
- **Educate**: A very common practice for most salespeople is to spend time with the buyer and teach him or her how to use and take care of the product that has been purchased. Spend time and educate the buyer on the proper use of the product. This will save you time with buyers that have a tendency not to follow operating instructions.
- **Send prospects to your customers**: If your customers are also in business, send them prospects or supply leads just as you hope they will do for you. It is just natural to respond kindly to a person who has been friendly or has done us a favor.
- **Have on-going focus groups**: Invite selected customers to come in and discuss what they like and dislike in an open forum. Try to make this a monthly habit.
- **Be reliable**: Without question, excellent performance with consistency is what customers want. They want service, products, and salespeople they can count on. Customers want the salesperson to do what he/she says he/she will do, do it when he/she says he/she will do it, and do it right the first time on the deadline given.

A Checklist for Creating Happy Customers

- ✔Go over car prep, checklist.
- ✔Cover owner's manual and service requirements.
- ✔Cover warranty and conditions.
- ✔Introduce customer to the service manager and service facilities.
- ✔Demonstrate all controls on the car.
- ✔Show how to check fluids, air, and so forth.
- ✔Review payment schedule.
- ✔Make appointment for check up in future.
- ✔Recheck title, license, insurance and other paperwork.
- ✔Set a specific time and date for follow-up phone call.
- ✔Obtain prospect name and other important personal data.
- ✔Thank and compliment the customer on his/her choice.

COMPLAINING CUSTOMERS ARE GOLD MINES

It was discussed that you should always handle complaints and problems promptly. Customers that have problems and verbalize complaints are gold mines of future business or a blueprint for disaster. Success is totally dependent on how you handle the situation. A salesperson must learn quickly to recognize if the anger is against the seller, product, or the company. This knowledge will allow him/her to better understand the root of the customer's problem. Some specific guidelines that are helpful in handling major problems and complaints that emerge after the initial sale are the following:

- Take every complaint seriously.
- Always welcome complaints.
- Get the company's top management involved in supporting, listening to, and resolving complaints.
- Set up a system to document and follow-up on complaints.
- Always listen to the customer with understanding.
- Find out exactly what the customer wants.
- Always follow-up with a phone call to ensure satisfaction.

- Set deadlines and goals in satisfying complaints.
- If the customer doesn't like your solution, ask him/her what he would consider a **fair settlement**.
- Never embarrass the customer or make him/her lose face.

The bottom line to remember when dealing with customers who have problems, difficulties, and need adjustments is to realize that it is the customer who writes the check for the company. Never forget that complaining customers can be great gold mines.

Complaining Customers are Gold Mines

BENEFITS OF SERVICING THE SALE

When you take time to treat your customers as you want to be treated, you are involved in what we call **Goodwill**. Goodwill is so important that many companies put it on their balance sheets as an asset. It is the value they feel they have earned over the years by providing customers with quality goods and services. The two key words are **earned** and **years**. Goodwill is earned in ways that go beyond just keeping customers satisfied. Goodwill must be earned through careful customer cultivation. It is important to sell the right product in the right amounts, to make sure the customer knows how to use and care for the product, and to give all the service and time necessary to maintain a high level of satisfaction. If you do this, the following benefits will come your way.

- You will gain repeat business.
- You will gain new prospect leads.
- You will create friendship, trust, and confidence with the customer.
- Your orders will increase in size.
- You will increase overall sales and the net profit for you and the company.

LONG-TERM SUCCESS

Every year, trade publications like ***Sales and Marketing Management***, and ***Personal Selling Power***, select top salespeople in the United States. There are some clearly identifiable common threads that run through these salespeople's stories about their success. The first is **putting their customer's needs above their own**. This may sound as if they are at their customer's beck and call, but while they do view their role as doing whatever needs to be done to keep the customer happy, their relationship is such that customers usually do not make unreasonable requests at unusual hours.

The second common thread is **their ability to help customers define their needs**. Successful salespeople are looked to for advice and counsel in solving problems. The third area is their **long-term outlook when servicing customers**. They are able to identify what efforts will have the best payoff one to five years into the future, rather than just meeting this current month's sales quota. They see a closed sale as just one additional step in the building process leading to higher sales further down the road. The fourth common thread of successful salespeople is the knowledge that **most customers need a consistent level of performance over a long time period from their salespeople**. Not just isolated instances of service, but service on a high level day after day, year after year basis. If you can incorporate these four ideas into your daily selling activities, plant them in your heart and mind, customer service will bring increased sales and long-term relationships with your customers.

Characteristics of Top Salespeople

- ➩**They put their customer's needs above their own.**
- ➩**They have the ability to help customers define their needs.**
- ➩**They have a long-term outlook when servicing customers.**
- ➩**The have the knowledge that most customers need a consistent level of performance over a long time period from their salespeople.**

In closing, excellent customer service is like the Chinese Bamboo Tree found in the next illustration. The Chinese Bamboo Tree shows no sign of growth for five years. You can water and fertilize the tree every year, but you will not see any growth. During the fifth year, the tree will grow approximately 90 feet in a six-week period. The years of watering and fertilizing are like good customer service. After awhile, you will eventually see repeat business and referred business. Don't become discouraged providing day by day service to your customers. In one way or another, tremendous results will come your way.

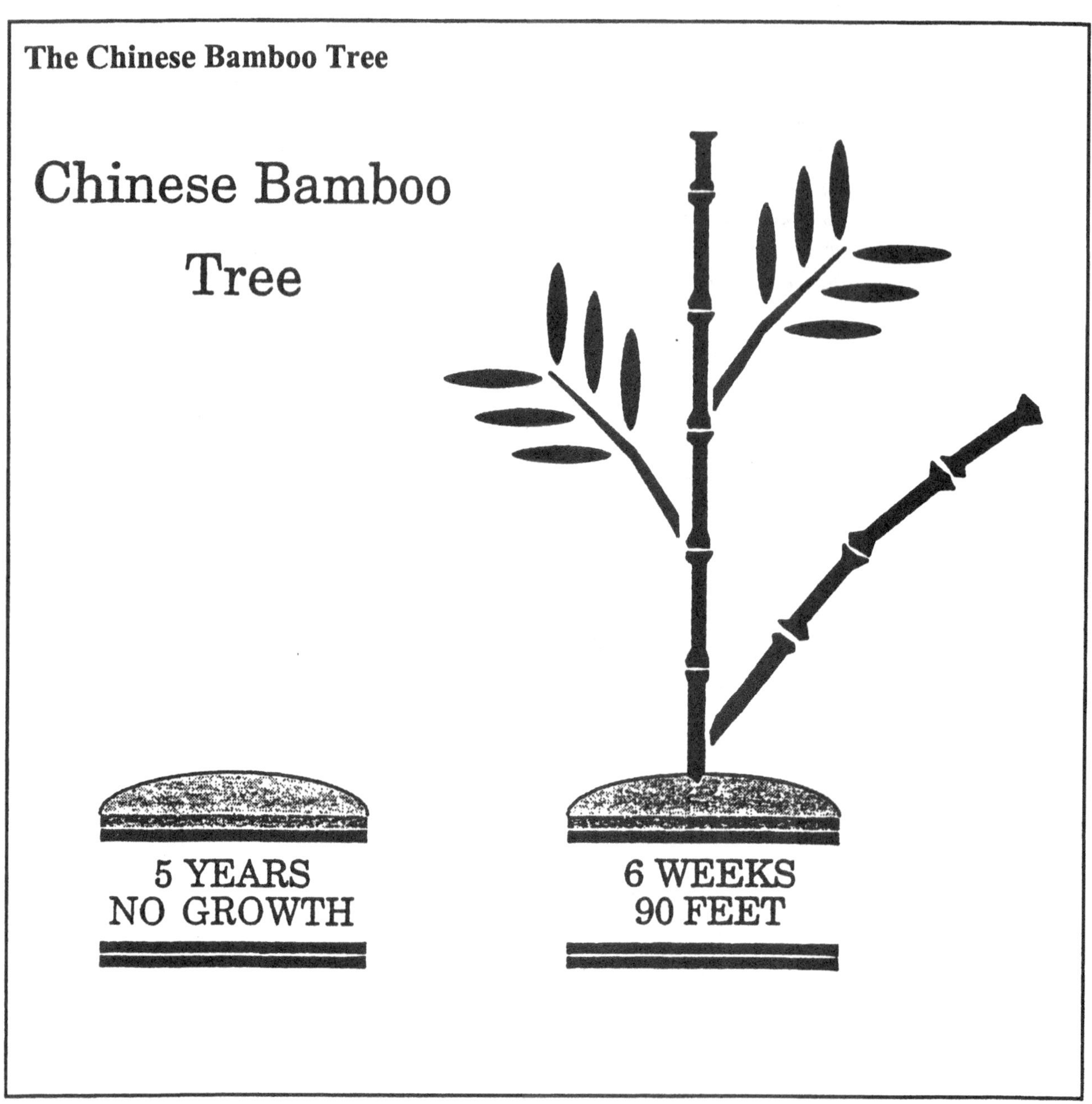

The Chinese Bamboo Tree

THE CUSTOMER WHO NEVER CAME BACK

I'm the nice customer. You know me. I'm the one who never complains no matter what kind of service I get.

I'll go into a restaurant, and I'll sit while the waitress gossips with her boyfriend, never bothering to see if my hamburger is ready. Sometimes a party who came in after I did gets my order. But, I don't say a word in complaint when the girl tells me, "Oh, I'm sorry. I'll order another hamburger for you." I just wait.

It's the same when I go to the service station for gasoline or to have my car serviced. I don't throw my weight around. I try to be thoughtful of the other person. If the service station attendant isn't courteous and doesn't offer to clean my windshield, check under the hood, and sweep out the floorboard, I don't make a scene. I'm as polite as can be. I don't believe in rudeness.

The other day I bought a toaster that burned out two weeks after I had it. I certainly hated to take it back, but I thought maybe they would know where to send it and, that I could pay for having it repaired. But I didn't get a chance to tell them this. They were so busy telling me that I had burned it out on purpose, and I couldn't think of anything to do but leave. I smiled and said, "Thank you and goodbye."

I never kick, I never nag, I never criticize, and I wouldn't dream of making a scene as I have seen people do in public places. I think that's uncalled for. No, I'm the nice customer, and I'll tell you who else I am. **I'M THE CUSTOMER WHO NEVER COMES BACK!**

That is my answer for getting pushed around too much. That is why I take whatever is handed out, because I know I'm not coming back. It's true that this doesn't relieve my feelings as quickly as telling what I think at the time. However, in the long run it's far more deadly than "blowing my top."

In fact, a nice customer like myself, multiplied by others of my kind, can just about ruin a business if we're pushed around. And there are lot of nice people in the world just like me. When we get rude treatment, we go down the street to another store and eat our hamburgers and buy our goods where they are smart enough to hire help who appreciates nice customers.

I don't care what business you're in. Maybe you live in a different town. Maybe I've never heard of you. But, if you are going for broke or your business is bad, maybe there are enough people like me who do know you. Who am I? **I'M THE CUSTOMER WHO NEVER CAME BACK.**

Practical Application Exercise–Selling a Service

In recent years the number of consumer dollars spent on services in our society has steadily increased. Consumers feel the need for assistance from a knowledgeable salesperson when making purchasing decisions concerning intangible goods like services. The selling of services requires effective visual aids and a more powerful persuasive presentation by the salesperson. This presentation will require you to prepare a **ten-minute presentation** selling a service to a group of buyers. Because your buyers can't touch or feel the product you will be selling, you must be creative and persuasive in the presentation and with your visual aids.

In preparing this presentation on selling a service, choose one of the following services to sell:

1. Banking service
2. Vacation package or travel service
3. Transportation or moving service
4. Advertising
5. Investments or real estate
6. Burial insurance or plot
7. Spa membership or physical fitness program
8. Weight loss program
9. Hair styling service
10. Car repair service
11. House or carpet cleaning service
12. Life insurance

This presentation will be worth 50 points and will be evaluated by your buyers using the form below. Your score is be based on the overall average score from all your evaluators.

Service Evaluation Form

Area		Poor	Good	Excellent
1.	Was the **approach** warm and positive?	0-1-2-3	4-5-6-7	8-9-10
2.	Were good **visual aids** used?	0-2-4	6-8-10-12	13-14-15
3.	Was the **presentation** well-prepared and organized?	0-2-4	6-8-10-12	13-14-15
4.	Did the student **close the sale** and ask for the order?	0-1-2-3	4-5-6-7	8-9-10

PREPARING FOR THE FINAL SALES PRESENTATION

As you know, you are given several opportunities to give mini presentations during the semester. The purpose of these mini presentations has been to give you confidence in front of a group. Another reason is to prepare you for the major presentation that will be given in front of a group of your choice. This major presentation will be weighed heavily and become a major part of your final grade. This final sales presentation will be evaluated by those observing your presentation.

SELECTING A PRODUCT FOR THE FINAL SALES PRESENTATION

The hardest part of the final presentation is to select a product. Many students have a tendency to select a product for their final sales presentation that does not allow them to show off their selling skills. I suggest that you select a product that fulfills all of the requirements of the following checklist:

_____ Can be demonstrated easily.

_____ Has between 5-10 selling points.

_____ Adequate product knowledge can be attained.

_____ High interest or background is found.

_____ Can be strengthened through visual aids.

_____ Can be brought to class and easily set up.

_____ Is legally, morally, and ethically appropriate.

Keeping the checklist points in mind will help you select a product that will be to your advantage in making your final sales presentation a successful and rewarding experience. It is very important that you select your product now. When you decide on the product, start preparing for your final presentation by becoming acquainted with the following guidelines and specifications found on the next page that will be strictly followed in class.

Your instructor will explain the following five options for your final presentation:

1. In-class to the full class.
2. In-class to a small group of five.
3. Out-of-class to five customers.
4. Out-of-class to five friends.
5. Video taped and have five individuals review.

FINAL PRESENTATION GUIDELINES

1. The student will assume the role of a sales agent, representative, or distributor making a presentation to a buyer. The buyer must be either the ultimate consumer if the product is over $50 in value or an organizational buyer if the product is under $50 in value.

2. The student will have one minute to set the stage before his or her presentation. The student will give the class some background information so the role play presentation can be as realistic as possible.

3. The student will have a choice of choosing the product that he or she will sell. The student must have prior approval of the instructor and follow the suggested guidelines on picking a product for the final sales presentation.

4. The student is responsible to furnish his or her own materials including the merchandise, pictures, visual aids, video equipment, order book, pen or pencil, and any audio aids that are needed. It is also recommended that the student complete the **Final Sales Presentation Position Paper** and give this to the group of buyers to read before his/her final presentation so they can educate themselves on the role they should play.

5. During the presentation, the buyers are encouraged to participate–in fact, interaction is highly recommended.

6. The student will have **five to fifteen minutes** to complete the presentation. The student will be given a formal warning at twelve minutes into the presentation so that adequate time can be given to close the sale. The presentation must take at least five minutes. If the student goes over time, he or she will be cut off by the instructor.

7. Have fun during this presentation. This final presentation is the capstone experience for the entire semester. It is an opportunity for you to apply everything we have discussed concerning the selling process. **"Act as if"** this experience is enjoyable and let your enthusiasm be exhibited.

FINAL SALES PRESENTATION POSITION PAPER

The purpose of the position paper is to provide the buyer and the instructor with information dealing with your final sales presentation. Remember, this final sales presentation makes up a large portion of your final grade and is the capstone experience for the class. To make sure you communicate the necessary information to everyone involved, please fill out this paper with the required information.

PRESENTATION DATE ______________________

NAME OF SELLER __________________________

NAMES OF BUYERS _________________________

PRODUCT BEING SOLD ______________________

BRIEF DESCRIPTION OF PRODUCT:

BUYER INFORMATION:

Name:

Position or title:

Description of store and products sold:

Stage for selling situation:

Customer's or company's present needs and situation:

COMPETITORS:

COMMON QUESTIONS AND OBJECTIONS TO PRODUCT OR SERVICE:

EVALUATION OF THE FINAL SALES PRESENTATION

As you know, one of the most important ways to improve one's future performance is by evaluating one's past performance. By looking at what an individual has done in the past, one can improve his/her performance in the future. As the last assignment in this class, I am asking you to do just that--review the evaluation sheets on your final sales presentation. Class members evaluated your final sales presentation, and these peers of yours can provide you with valuable information that will assist you in preparing yourself for success in the world of selling. Look back over your class members' evaluation sheets and provide me with a **two-to-three page typed report** that contains the following information:

1. Your general reaction to the scores you received on your final sales presentation.

2. Do you generally agree with the evaluations you received? If you do, why? If you don't, Why?

3. Identify the three major strengths that were indicated by your evaluation sheets. Why do you believe these three areas were rated so high?

4. Identify the three major weaknesses, if any, that were identified by your evaluation sheets. Why do you believe these three areas were rated so low?

5. If you had to do the presentation again, what would you change or do differently? Why?

6. Examine the whole course and identify what you liked or disliked about the class. What are some suggestions and recommendations that you feel should be considered in the future?

use reference approach for full credit

NAME ____________________

DATE ____________________

PRODUCT ____________________

SALES PRESENTATION EVALUATION SHEET

		POOR	FAIR	GOOD	EXCELLENT
1.	**APPROACH:** Opening statement; positive first impression; developed proper selling atmosphere.	0-1-2	3-4-5	6-7-8	9-10
2.	**PRESENTATION**: Benefits shown; showmanship; product knowledge; organization; customer involvement.	0-1-2-3	4-6-8	10-12-14	16-18-20
3.	**VISUAL AIDS**: Product and other visual/audio tools; logical order; appealing to five senses.	0-1-2	3-4-5	6-7-8	9-10
4.	**APPEARANCE/POISE/ CONFIDENCE**:	0-1-2	3-4-5	6-7-8	9-10
5.	**VOICE**: Tone, volume, enthusiasm, modulation.	0-1	2-3	4	5
6.	**HANDLING OBJECTIONS**: Understood and answered all questions and objections; responded calmly under pressure.	0-2-4	6-7-8	10-11-12	13-14-15
7.	**CLOSE**: Summary, recognized closing signals, asked for the order with an appropriate technique.	0-2-4	6-7-8	10-11-12	13-14-15
8.	**CUSTOMER RELATIONS**: Sincere interest and caring attitude towards customer.	0-2-4	6-7-8	10-11-12	13-14-15

Total Points _____/100 Pts.

GENERAL COMMENTS:

INDEX